THE COMPLETE COMPANY POLICIES

This book is about a much neglected but essential element of the success of any business: company policy. This is a comprehensive guide to determining what policies your company needs, and how to draft and approve the relevant documents and implement them throughout the organization.

From anti-bribery laws to data privacy and health and safety, your business is faced with a range of legal and regulatory obligations that must be identified and documented properly. These obligations must be addressed for internal and external stakeholders. The task of identifying and documenting effective policies is an essential step in establishing good corporate governance and ultimately a culture of compliance. These policies in turn provide a solid foundation for the reputation and commercial success of the organization, and form an essential "bridge" between the company's strategy and the various procedures needed to carry it out. With many useful templates and practical examples, this book will help you to ensure the accuracy and completeness of your policy documents. It covers all areas of your business, including financial reporting, anti-money laundering, anti-fraud, conflicts of interest, data privacy and security, remote working, social media, whistleblowing, and more.

This book will be useful to company directors, company secretaries and senior managers, and their advisers, including consultants, auditors, and solicitors. It will be particularly relevant to any business that needs to create new policies or review their existing policies in light of current regulations and standards.

Ian Long is a company lawyer and policy expert with many years' experience in the international corporate sector, including Aon Centre for Innovation & Analytics, AIB Bank, Bank of Ireland Group, Pepper Asset Servicing, Groupon Inc., and Novartis International. He has written and lectured extensively on corporate policies and ESG/sustainability. He is currently in practice as Risk Management Lawyer at Beauchamps, one of Ireland's leading law firms.

"The Complete Company Policies adds to the compendium of corporate governance knowledge, and provides proven, practical samples and templates. It also provides sound guidance to the boards and senior executives of companies where environmental, social, governance and data stewardship are rightly seen as strategic imperatives."

Deirdre Smith, CDir, M.Inst.D, BA BAI (Eng), Chartered Director of Green Point Consultancy, Dublin

"This is a welcome guide to the much-neglected subject of corporate policies. The book will be extremely useful in putting together a set of coherent policies for the business. I would recommend The Complete Company Policies to enable your business to show what it's trying to do and why."

David W Duffy, FCA, Co- Founder and CEO of The Corporate Governance Institute

THE COMPLETE COMPANY POLICIES

Documents and Guidance

Ian Long

LONDON AND NEW YORK

Cover image: © Getty Images / onurdongel

First published 2024
by Routledge
4 Park Square, Milton Park, Abingdon, Oxon OX14 4RN

and by Routledge
605 Third Avenue, New York, NY 10158

Routledge is an imprint of the Taylor & Francis Group, an informa business

© 2024 Ian Long

The right of Ian Long to be identified as author of this work has been asserted in accordance with sections 77 and 78 of the Copyright, Designs and Patents Act 1988.

All rights reserved. No part of this book may be reprinted or reproduced or utilised in any form or by any electronic, mechanical, or other means, now known or hereafter invented, including photocopying and recording, or in any information storage or retrieval system, without permission in writing from the publishers.

Trademark notice: Product or corporate names may be trademarks or registered trademarks, and are used only for identification and explanation without intent to infringe.

British Library Cataloguing-in-Publication Data
A catalogue record for this book is available from the British Library

Library of Congress Cataloging-in-Publication Data
Names: Long, Ian, author.
Title: The complete company policies : documents and guidance / Ian Long.
Description: Abingdon, Oxon ; New York, NY : Routledge, 2024. | Includes bibliographical references and index.
Identifiers: LCCN 2023041094 (print) | LCCN 2023041095 (ebook) | ISBN 9781032194011 (hardback) | ISBN 9781032194042 (paperback) | ISBN 9781003258995 (ebook)
Subjects: LCSH: Management. | Administrative procedure. | Corporate governance.
Classification: LCC HD31.2 .L66 2024 (print) | LCC HD31.2 (ebook) | DDC 658—dc23/eng/20230906
LC record available at https://lccn.loc.gov/2023041094
LC ebook record available at https://lccn.loc.gov/2023041095

ISBN: 978-1-032-19401-1 (hbk)
ISBN: 978-1-032-19404-2 (pbk)
ISBN: 978-1-003-25899-5 (ebk)

DOI: 10.4324/9781003258995

Typeset in Joanna
by Apex CoVantage, LLC

CONTENTS

PART I
General 1

1 Company policies 3
2 Strategy and policies 11
3 Corporate governance 21
4 Policy formation and implementation 30

PART II
Corporate conduct 39

5 Data protection and data security 41
6 Corporate social responsibility 65
7 Health and safety 75
8 Fair employment 83
9 Environment and sustainability 95

PART III
Individual conduct   113

10 Anti-bribery and corruption   115

11 Conduct and conflicts of interest   125

12 Social media   133

13 Remote working   143

14 Speak up/Whistleblowing   153

PART IV
Finance   175

15 Anti-fraud   177

16 Anti-money laundering   186

17 Insider trading   196

18 Accounting and audit   204

    Sources of additional information   218

Appendices   227
    Appendix 1 United Nations Guiding Principles on Business and Human Rights 2011   229
    Appendix 2 COP 27 at Sharm el-Sheikh Implementation Plan 2022   233
    Appendix 3 EU Whistleblowing Directive – DIRECTIVE (EU) 2019/1937 OF THE EUROPEAN PARLIAMENT AND OF THE COUNCIL of 23 October 2019 on the protection of persons who report breaches of Union law   243
    Appendix 4 COVID-19: Back to the workplace – Adapting workplaces and protecting workers; EU guidance for a safe return to the workplace – (European Agency for Safety & Health at Work)   260
    Index   272

PART I

GENERAL

1

COMPANY POLICIES

Introduction

This is not just a book about business. Nor is it a book about rules and regulations. So what is it about? It's about a much-neglected but essential element of the success of any business: policy. In other words, the company's policy on the many and various activities that affect its performance, and could make the difference between success and failure. In particular, we're concerned here about putting the right policies in place to support the company's strategy and to provide a sound basis for

- business processes and procedures
- good corporate governance and
- a culture of compliance

to enable the organization to achieve its financial and non-financial objectives.

The book aims to highlight the importance of company policies in addressing the business and regulatory issues that face all sorts of companies in a competitive and increasingly regulated world. Cash may be king but policy is at least a senior member of the royal family. In addition to the day-to-day pressures of cash flow and winning new business, a plethora of rules and regulations dictate what the company can and cannot do. From anti-bribery laws to data privacy and health and safety, the company is faced with a set of legal and regulatory obligations that must be identified, documented, and addressed for the information of internal and external stakeholders. These obligations will form the basis of appropriate policy documents aimed at ensuring compliance.

The book will act as a handbook for decision-makers to help them determine what policies are required, to produce the relevant text, and to ensure accuracy and completeness. This in turn will help the organization to achieve specific objectives as set out in its strategy and formal policy documents. The tasks of identifying and documenting effective company policies are essential steps in the process of establishing good corporate governance and ultimately a culture of compliance. These will provide a solid foundation for the reputation and commercial success of the organization.

The approach in this book is to survey the most important subject matters of company policy, describe the latest developments and set out a suggested policy document to capture the relevant commitments. Accordingly, each chapter will introduce a specific subject matter and discuss the issues to be considered in terms of policy.

Mission and strategy

The CEO and the board of directors know what business they're in, or they should. This may be reflected in something like a *mission statement*. Below are some famous ones:

- **Starbucks** – To inspire and nurture the human spirit – one person, one cup, and one neighbourhood at a time.
- **Amazon** – Our mission is to continually raise the bar of the customer experience by using the internet and technology to help consumers find, discover, and buy anything, and empower businesses and content creators to maximize their success.

- **Nike** – Our mission is what drives us to do everything possible to expand human potential. We do that by creating ground-breaking sport innovations, by making our products more sustainably, by building a creative and diverse global team and by making a positive impact in communities where we live and work.

So having decided what business they're in, the company's decision-makers will draw up a mission statement and a strategy to execute it. That might sound complex and difficult but it's the easy part. The hard part is to put in place a suite of robust and relevant *policies* to define what the strategy looks like in specific parts of the business and to meet specific requirements, both commercial and regulatory. These policies form an essential "bridge" between the company's strategy and the procedures and processes required to carry it out. Decision-makers don't need a book to tell them what their business is, or maybe even what strategy to adopt, but they certainly need guidance and direction as to an effective set of policies to steer the business in the right direction. Many large and medium-sized companies, from the Starbucks, Amazons, and Nikes of this world to professional services firms, to family-owned businesses, struggle with devising and implementing policies that are relevant to their business. And not just relevant at a point in time. These policies must be reviewed and updated regularly to keep pace with business and regulatory changes. Company directors and managers know their business but may not be experts in setting clear and effective policies across a range of business functions. They need a book like this.

The board meeting

In an ideal world, board meetings are where questions of policy should be discussed and decided. Good corporate governance requires the directors to approve policy documents. Below is an imagined account of a board meeting where a question of policy arose by accident. (Any resemblance to actual events is unintentional.) Ideally, all policy matters should feature on the meeting's agenda but that's not what happens here:

> It was the last board meeting before Christmas and the directors wanted a short and snappy affair. There were spouses and partners

to be placated. And children to be catered for or faced down, as the case may be.

The CEO gave a summary of the last quarter. The meeting then turned to financial matters and the Finance Director listed certain items of expenditure to be reported at the next AGM in February.

"Why are we reporting some of these items if we don't have to?", asked the Chairman.

"It's policy", said the Finance Director.

"What policy is that?"

"Eh, our policy on financial reporting to shareholders."

"Where is that written down? Can I see it?" asked the Chairman, getting a little impatient.

"Well, we don't have anything in writing but we've always done it this way," replied the Finance Director.

There was silence around the table. The Chairman looked up and looked down again. He made a note to himself to ask the Company Secretary how many of their policies were written down and how many were on the basis that the company had always "done it that way". The Finance Director made a note to himself to ask his deputy the same thing.

The meeting rattled through the remaining items on the agenda and everyone went off to enjoy Christmas. The company's policy on financial reporting could wait until next year.

"It's policy"

In a highly competitive and increasingly regulated environment, it may not be enough any longer to operate on the basis that "it's policy". Why was the policy adopted? Where is it written down and is it correct and up-to-date? And what do we mean by a *policy* anyway? There are many and various definitions and before we examine the process of policy formation, the business must set out its approach or *strategy*. In deciding to adopt a corporate policy and then implement it throughout the organization, the company must be clear about what it's trying to achieve. The objective here is to understand and document the company's strategy or commitment to every relevant activity. This will be communicated as appropriate to employees, clients, customers, suppliers, and other third parties such as a regulator.

So before we proceed to examine the area of policy, we should be clear about our understanding of the strategy that underlies it. Business strategy may be understood as a course of action or set of decisions to help the company achieve specific objectives. In other words, the strategy is a master plan to secure a competitive position for the company, carry on operations, and meet the needs of customers so as to achieve the company's objectives. This is about setting priorities and determining actions to achieve them.

But we're not primarily concerned in this book with strategy. We're concerned with identifying and documenting the set of policies that are needed to execute it. We're also concerned with implementing these policies and monitoring compliance with them so as to ensure they're implemented throughout the organization. Our initial focus, however, will be the policy document that needs to carry a heavy load over a period of time to an audience that may need some persuasion. Buy-in is not a given.

In a general sense, a policy is a system of principles or rules to guide company decisions so as to achieve certain defined outcomes. These principles or rules may or may not apply to all operations across the organization and may or may not be documented (normally they would be.) In this sense a policy lays out an approach or a commitment to carry out business in a particular way under specific headings or in accordance with specific principles or rules.

However, we will adopt a more focused definition for the purposes of this book. We will regard a company policy as a *written statement of intent that applies to one or more specified functions of the organization and is implemented by guidelines, standards, or procedures that are also written down.* In this sense, policies play a central role in what is referred to as good corporate governance, that is, all the processes or procedures that govern the internal operations of the company.

The relevant policies are usually adopted by a specific body within the organization, for example the board of directors or an executive committee or similar body.

Specific policies

And so what specific policies does the company need? To a great extent this depends on the size and complexity of the organization, the nature of the business, the business sector, and whether the company operates in a regulated industry such as financial services or pharmaceuticals, or an unregulated industry such as online sales and marketing. This is because many company policies address legal or regulatory issues that affect some industries more than others. As a basic requirement, the company should have a Code of Conduct or Code of Ethics to lay down fundamental principles of behaviour but it may also need to put in place a range of other policies according to the factors set out above.

This book examines the origins and implementation of specific policies required by the company. Although one size doesn't fit all, there are enough common areas of concern to industry that allow the treatment of an otherwise disparate subject in a single text. For example, every company must have a documented approach to its financial accounts and reporting. Likewise there must be a policy on data protection if the company handles personal data, which it probably does. It will handle personal data relating to directors, employees, customers, and suppliers. Ultimately the nature of the business will decide. In addition, we will consider some policy samples and templates that provide a simple practical approach to drafting and completing any policy to be adopted for the benefit of the company.

Not all policies carry the same weight or can be given the same priority. Data protection and data security are vital to a technology company, and so these policies will dictate the company's approach to all of its operations. A professional services firm on the other hand will be guided by its conflicts of interest policy as to screening of new clients, which is essential to its business.

Classification

We will next consider how to classify the various policies we have identified as necessary. We can do this in a number of ways. Company policies may be classified according to their source, that is a specific business need or a regulatory requirement, or how they apply to different functions, for example, Finance, HR, and Engineering. Or how they affect different levels in the organisation, from the board of directors to the sales and marketing team. In this book, however, we will adopt a classification based on their content and in particular:

- individual conduct of employees
- corporate conduct, i.e., the company or organization itself and
- financial obligations

Individual conduct

These are policies that provide for the conduct of individuals who are employed by the company, whether as full-time permanent employees or on a temporary, as-needs basis such as consultants or contractors. These policies may also provide for corporate conduct but they are aimed mainly at individual employees. The focus here is on individual rather than corporate behaviour.

Individual policies include the following:

- Code of conduct/ethics
- Conflicts of interest
- Social media
- Remote working
- Speak Up/Whistleblowing

Corporate conduct

In this category are policies that aim to regulate the conduct of the company itself. As a legal entity, the company has legal obligations as well as a range of corporate responsibilities to its employees, suppliers, and customers. It will want to be seen as a good corporate citizen and to behave responsibly in its relations with public authorities and society in general.

These policies include:

- Data privacy and security
- Corporate social responsibility
- Health and safety
- Environment
- Fair employment
- Anti-bribery and corruption

Finance

Financial policies are a separate category primarily concerned with accounting and reporting of financial results for the company. Typically they will provide a set of principles or rules about money and how the company accounts for, and reports on, money matters. Specific policies may provide for ways and means to prevent fraud and money laundering.

- Financial accounting/reporting
- Audit
- Anti-fraud
- Anti-money laundering
- Insider trading

Finally, we will discuss the process of ensuring that policies are reviewed and updated if necessary. There should be a scheduled review at agreed intervals to ensure that policy documents take account of business and regulatory developments as they happen. For example, data privacy laws have changed in recent years all over the world, for example, the General Data Protection Regulation 2018 (GDPR) in Europe and the California Consumer Privacy Act of 2019 (CCPA) in the US. The review process will require the involvement, if possible, of those employees who were responsible for the creation of the policy. Of course, some of them may have moved on to other roles or may have left the organization.

Any updates to the policy document must reflect the rest of the document in terms of both content and style. Consistency is as important as accuracy.

2

STRATEGY AND POLICIES

Introduction

As we discussed in the Introduction, the company's decision-makers will agree on a *strategy* to achieve the financial and non-financial objectives of the company. This will set out at a high level the approach of the company to fulfilling its purpose and the reason why it exists. The strategy may be reflected in a *mission statement* or something similar. This is a short statement, almost a slogan, of why the company exists, what kind of product or service it provides, and its market. It may include the company's values or commitments, its competitive advantage, or its intended future state – the vision.

> We define mission as the reason for existence. Your mission is the motivating force behind what you do. Your mission is your purpose. A worthwhile mission is one that serves others. Your vision, however, is the picture of your success in the future. It is the picture of success five to ten years out. Imagine it's ten years from now, and you have

succeeded in delivering your mission, what would that success look like? How would you describe it? Mission and vision each have an important yet distinct role to play.[1]

In this chapter, we discuss the relationship between the company's strategy, whether expressed in a mission statement or not, and the policies designed.

A mission is not simply a description of the company but an expression of its hopes and intentions. The purpose is to communicate the company's purpose and direction to its employees, customers and other stakeholders. Here are a few examples:

Tesco: Serving shoppers a little better every day
Lloyd's Bank: Our purpose at Lloyds Banking Group is to Help Britain Prosper
EY: Building a better working world
Tesla: To accelerate the world's transition to sustainable energy
TED: Spread ideas
LinkedIn: To connect the world's professionals to make them more productive and successful
Amazon: To be Earth's most customer-centric company, where customers can find and discover anything they might want to buy online, and endeavours to offer its customers the lowest possible prices.

Definition of strategy

Whether or not it's expressed in a mission statement, a strategy may be defined simply as a high-level, long-term plan for the company to get to where it wants to be. It will include the objectives, the products or services the company plans to provide, and the market for these products or services to sell at a profit. The strategy outlines the actions and decisions the company plans to take to achieve its objectives. By setting out what the company needs to do, it can guide the decision-making process for hiring staff and allocating resources to the best effect. The strategy will also help different functions to work together successfully.

It's essential to test all relevant assumptions to make sure the company's strategy is robust and effective. Assumptions are not necessarily correct. This will also ensure that all decisions may be presented on the basis of clear evidence. The strategy must align with the company's objectives, the nature of its business, and the sector in which it operates or plans to operate. As an example, Google aims to provide the best internet experience to its users. This is known to users as Google Search. All the company's products and services are carefully aligned with its main objective.

Instead of focussing on more and customers for the company's products or services, the strategy may be simply to sell more of the same to its existing customers. It is generally easier to retain a customer than to attract a new one. This is the strategy adopted by many banks and online retailers. If a bank customer has a current account, he or she may be sold a personal loan or even a mortgage. Amazon sells books, music, computer devices and a wide range of other products to its customers. Alternatively, a large company might decide to grow through merger or acquisition with a competitor instead of growing its own business, particularly in an emerging market. It may be easier and more profitable to buy or merge with another company.

A business strategy is a powerful tool for the company not only to achieve its objectives but also to guide many of its actions and decisions. A robust and effective strategy will also help to ensure good investment decisions, such as expenditure, and prioritization of key projects and other activities for maximum profit. Finally, the strategy will provide the basis for policies that set out the company's approach to specific aspects of its operations, such as data privacy or health and safety. These policies will in turn be implemented by relevant processes and procedures.

Together, the strategy and company policies combine the *ends* (objectives) for which the company is striving and the *means* (policies, processes and procedures) by which it seeks to get there.

Developing a strategy

According to a leading US academic, Michael Porter of Harvard University, three key principles underlie any business strategy:[2]

1   Creating a unique and valuable position in the market;
2   Making trade-offs by choosing "what not to do" (versus "what to do"); and
3   Creating "fit" by aligning the company's activities with each other to support the agreed strategy.

Applying these principles, the company will follow certain steps in developing a business strategy:

- *Realistic, long-term objectives*: What products or services will the company provide? What is the market for them? What actions and decisions are needed to get the products or services to market successfully?
- *Opportunity*: What opportunities may exist in the future and how will they come about? Does the company have all the information it needs? What are the risks and challenges to be expected and how does the company plan to mitigate against them?
- *Innovation*: Are the company's products or services unique and clearly differentiated from the competition? Business-to-consumer (B2C) businesses can differentiate their products or services by superior technology, features, or design. For example, Apple launched the iPod as a truly innovative product even if it was more expensive than similar products on the market.
- *Competition*: Is the market for the company's products or services not served already or served with little or no competition? Can the company capture market share, build a brand, and position itself in the marketplace so as to make it hard for any new entrants?
- *Economies of scale*: Can the company keep prices down while keeping innovation? For example, Tesco aims to sell goods at a lower price than convenience stores or local grocery shops, increasing its sales through a large customer base and so generating higher profits.
- *Time to market*: Has the company considered "build versus buy"? It may be cheaper to buy some or all of the products or services that are already available or outsource them to a third-party provider. This may save the cost of production and getting the products to market.
- *Reviews*: The company must review and update its strategy to ensure that it remains valid at all times and will meet the agreed objectives.
- *Risks and failures*: Has the company identified any relevant risks to achieving the objectives of the strategy? Are there any insights to be gained from failures in the past?
- *Stakeholders*: The company should keep employees, as key internal stakeholders, fully informed of the planned strategy so they will know of all relevant initiatives to be carried out. Likewise, external stakeholders such as investors, partners, suppliers, and customers should also be

kept informed. In particular, they will need to know how the strategy may affect company forecasts for revenues and shareholder value.

Strategic management

Having developed a strategy as outlined above, how should the company manage it? How does the company formulate and implement its objectives, taking into account the resources available to it and the business environment in which it operates? Strategic management provides direction to the business, develops the required policies and plans, and allocates the necessary resources. Strategic management has been described as comprising two major processes: formulation and implementation of strategy.[3]

Formulation

This process requires the company to analyse the business environment in which it operates. The analysis will include:

- external environment – political, economic, social, technological and legal;
- industry environment – competition, bargaining power of customers and suppliers, alternative sources of its products and services; and
- internal environment – the company's strengths and weaknesses.

Based on this analysis, the company needs to make a series of strategic decisions about how it will compete and succeed, as set out above in the steps to developing a strategy. The end result will be a set of clear objectives and actions.

Implementation

The next process in strategic management is *implementation*, which involves decisions regarding how the company's resources – people, processes, systems – will be directed towards the objectives. Successful implementation will lead to a defined structure of available resources, leadership, communications, and performance measurement to see how it's all working (or not).

Elements of the strategy

After following the process and steps set out above, the development of a successful business strategy will ensure that it includes certain key elements. They include:

- *Vision*: A vision for the direction of the business will provide a sound basis for clear instructions in the business strategy as to what needs to be done and who will do it.
- *Core values*: The business strategy determines what should and should not be done, according to the company's values, e.g. integrity.
- *SWOT analysis*: A SWOT analysis (strengths, weaknesses, opportunities, and threats) enables the company to take advantage of its strengths and opportunities and to mitigate against its weaknesses and internal and external threats.
- *Tactics*: These are the operational details of the company's activities, including policies, processes, and procedures.
- *Resource allocation plan*: A business strategy should include where the resources will be found to execute the plan, how the resources will be allocated, and who will do it.
- *Measurement*: Finally, the strategy should measure the company's performance to show whether it has achieved or failed to achieve the specified objectives.

Company policies

If strategy is all about ends or objectives, company policies are the means to achieve them. Identifying and documenting effective policies are an essential step in the process of implementing the strategy, establishing good corporate governance, and ultimately a culture of compliance. These in turn provide a solid foundation for the reputation and commercial success of the organization. The challenge is to develop a set of robust and relevant policies to define what the company's strategy looks like in specific situations and to meet specific requirements, whether business or regulatory. These policies form an essential "bridge" between the strategy and the procedures and processes needed to carry it out.

In a general sense, a policy is a system of principles or rules to guide company decisions so as to achieve certain defined outcomes. These principles or rules may or may not apply to all operations across the organization and may or may not be documented. In this sense, a policy lays out an approach or a commitment to carry out business in a particular way or in accordance with specific principles or values. "Policy" may also refer to the process of making important decisions, including choices between alternative projects or spending priorities. Policies can be understood as political, managerial, financial, and administrative mechanisms to achieve specific objectives.

However, we will adopt a more specific definition for the purposes of this book. We will regard a company policy as a written statement of intent that applies to one or more specified functions of the organization and is implemented by guidelines, standards, or procedures that are also written down. In this sense, policies play a central role in good *corporate governance*, that is, all the processes or procedures that govern the internal operations of the company. These policies are usually adopted by a specific body within the organization, for example, the board of directors or an executive committee or similar body.

A policy in this sense can help the organization to adopt a clear and consistent approach to decision-making, both subjective and objective. *Subjective* decisions require an assessment of the relative merits of a number of factors, such as work-life balance or fair treatment of employees. By contrast, *objective* decisions often apply to operational matters such as data security or gender balance: these can be tested by reference to objective criteria. Whatever kinds of decisions are involved, a company policy aims to determine actions in order to achieve specified business outcomes. Policies may or may not reflect legal or regulatory obligations (while always complying with any that apply) but they are more than mere instruments of compliance.

Policy content

Although the content will vary according to the purpose of a specific policy, typically it will follow a structure that has become standard and may therefore be familiar to anyone responsible for the first draft. A comprehensive policy document will comprise the following elements and usually in the following order:

- *Objective or purpose*: Why is the policy being adopted? What does the company hope to achieve?

- *Scope and applicability*: What does the policy apply to? Just as important, what does it not apply to? Who is affected and how?
- *Roles and responsibilities*: Who is responsible for what in making sure that the policy is implemented?
- *Commitments*: What specific laws, regulations, or best practices apply to those operations within scope of the policy? What is the company committing to do in order to comply?
- *Enforcement/escalation*: What are the consequences of non-compliance?
- *Review*: When will the policy be reviewed and how will this be done?
- *Definitions of key words*

We will discuss further the contents and format of a robust company policy in Chapter 4.

Policy framework

Just like the strategy itself, company policies don't exist in a vacuum. They are derived from the company's purpose and values, in short why the company exists. As we've seen, a *mission statement* is often the place where this is all set out, in a (hopefully) succinct few words of inspiration. Equally, the policies that are adopted on foot of the company's mission statement may in turn provide a basis for guidelines, standards, and operating procedures needed to implement them. Together, these form a policy *framework* to ensure that the company makes the right decisions about the right things. Not every decision requires a formal and documented policy, guideline or standard, or even a procedure, but the big decisions are more likely to be sound if they follow an approach that has proven itself in the past. This approach may be set out in formal policy documents. The decision about where to source paper clips may not affect the company's survival but will be easier to make if the company follows a defined process to identify a provider with a demonstrable track record in office stationery.

And policies are adopted for all sorts of reasons, business and regulatory. The company may wish to be seen as a good corporate citizen by promoting best practice in areas such as corporate social responsibility or environmental protection. Government or a regulator may expect to see a formal company policy on an important requirement, for example, data privacy. It may be that a policy is needed for legal reasons, for example, procurement, to set out the company's terms and conditions for doing business with suppliers. Whatever the reason, the board and management of a company will be persuaded to devote time and effort to a policy document with a clear business or regulatory purpose.

Corporate governance

Company policies play a vital role in the *corporate governance* of an organization, that is the collection of rules and regulations adopted to control its activities and that determine the rights and duties of all stakeholders, internal and external. The internal stakeholders are the directors, managers, employees, and shareholders. The external stakeholders include customers, creditors, suppliers, and regulators. Good corporate governance is necessary to manage and, if possible, avoid conflicts of interest that may arise between the various stakeholders, in particular directors and shareholders. It also helps to ensure accountability of all concerned so that the company makes the right decisions for the right reasons, and is seen to do so.

We will discuss corporate governance in detail in Chapter 3.

Culture of compliance

In addition to playing a central role in compliance with legal and regulatory requirements, and in corporate governance, company policies are vital to creating a *culture* of compliance. It starts with an organization that is true to its mission and core values, where directors and senior managers lead the way by expressing their commitment to compliance and encourage open communication and honest feedback. What does culture mean for this purpose?

> Creating a culture of compliance means embedding good behaviors at all levels of your organization. It means helping people to make better decisions in following your business's rules, regulations and policies.[4]

Culture is a mindset shared by everyone in the organization that goes beyond ticking boxes. It's about doing the right thing over and above the technical requirements. Training and awareness are essential to fostering a compliance culture, and relevant policies may provide the basis for training materials to be used for this purpose.

The objective is an attitude of respect and responsibility for the company's reputation. Everyone from the CEO to the receptionist takes care to protect and enhance the standing of the company among its customers, suppliers, and the wider community. There's a collective commitment to the values and purpose of the company as these are set out in its *mission statement* or a specific company policy such as the code of conduct for all employees. This commitment is embedded in everything the company does. At the level of the individual, a culture of compliance sets the bar for personal behaviour while on duty. Compliance is a minimum, not a maximum. But culture aims higher. It has often been said that "culture eats compliance for breakfast". If compliance is about ticking boxes, culture is about ticking them for the right reasons and then ticking others that go beyond compliance towards good corporate citizenship.

References

1 Riaz Khadem and Linda Khadem, "There's a Difference Between Your Company's Vision and Its Mission", *Entrepreneur*, 11 October 2018, www.entrepreneur.com/leadership/theres-a-difference-between-your-companys-vision-and-its/321515.
2 Michael E. Porter, "What is a Strategy?", *Harvard Business Review*, November–December 1996, https://maaw.info/ArticleSummaries/ArtSumPorter96.htm.
3 James Brian Quinn, Henry Mintzberg, Robert M James, and Sumantra Ghosal, "The Strategy Process: Concepts, Contexts, and Cases", Prentice Hall, 1995, www.abebooks.co.uk/book-search/author/quinn-james-brian-mintzberg-henry/.
4 Kezia Farnham, Diligent Corporation, "How to Create a Culture of Compliance: 7 Crucial Building Blocks", 14 October 2021, www.diligent.com/resources/blog/culture-of-compliance.

3

CORPORATE GOVERNANCE

Introduction

Corporate governance does not exist in a vacuum. The rules of engagement within a company are not there to decorate the company secretary's office. They are there to ensure transparency and accountability, or should be. Ultimately corporate governance is derived from the need to identify who is responsible for what. And the entire set of company policies goes to identifying who that is and what they're responsible for in specific functions of the organization.

Corporate governance is an enormous subject. It's beyond the scope of this book to examine the theory and practice of corporate governance as it affects a company's strategy and operations. Hundreds of theses and tomes have been written on a subject that lends itself to heavy academic discussion. We will confine ourselves in this chapter to the relationship between corporate governance and policy identification and implementation.

DOI: 10.4324/9781003258995-4

The concept of corporate governance can be seen from a number of different perspectives that change its meaning and scope. These perspectives include the following:[1]

- *Law and regulation:* From this point of view, corporate governance asks what the legal obligations of the company are and what are the consequences of not complying with them.
- *Accounting and reporting*: The company must report on its financial position to its shareholders and others. To do this, it needs people and systems to perform the relevant tasks, and these must be subject to some form of governance.
- *Finance*: Internal control and risk management are needed to meet the requirements of the providers of finance to the company such as bankers and investors. In this perspective, auditing is linked to accounting and reporting.
- *Economics*: The company is an economic construct designed to maximize revenue and minimize cost. The role of corporate governance is to oversee the processes involved so as to achieve the greatest possible value for shareholders.
- *Organization design*: The board of directors and the other company structures form part of a design that brings into play a hierarchy between them, with a set of dynamics that govern how they work with each other in the company's operations.
- *Management and leadership*: Corporate governance decides how the company is managed and led. The board sits at the top and guides and directs operations.
- *Marketing*: Corporate governance plays a central role in the "net present value" of all existing and future customer relationships, to the extent this constitutes the real value of the company.
- *Strategy*: Setting the company's strategy ultimately results in a form of corporate governance that decides how resources are allocated and monitored as to their use and effectiveness. After all, this is why board members are called *directors*.
- *Ethics*: Outside the boundaries of law and regulation, the board is concerned with the question of what the right thing is to do in terms of ethical or moral principles.

Definition

So how do we define what corporate governance is for our purposes? In a narrow technical sense it's about the various mechanisms within the organization to guide its operations and report on performance. But in the modern world of social media, any commercial for-profit organization is at the centre of online as well as real-world society and so must comply with new obligations such as those imposed by corporate social responsibility and ethics.

Corporate social responsibility, or CSR, is a form of business self-regulation that aims to contribute to the good of society by various charitable or philanthropic activities. In corporate terms, CSR is regarded as a strategic initiative that contributes to the company's reputation or the reputation of one of its brands.[2] CSR goes beyond compliance with strict regulatory requirements and engages in activities that further some social good such as environmental protection or equality. Companies may engage in CSR for strategic or ethical purposes. The financial and non-financial benefits that accrue to the company are the results of positive public relations and high ethical standards. The adoption of CSR will encourage the company to make a positive impact on the environment and internal and external stakeholders including customers, employees, investors, and society in general. ISO 26000 is the recognized international standard for CSR. It was released by the International Standards Organization in November 2010 and its goal is to contribute to global sustainable development by encouraging businesses and other organizations to practice social responsibility.[3] In addition to the emerging world of CSR, the new agenda for corporate governance features obligations arising from ethics as opposed to law and regulation. Business ethics is the study of ethical principles and moral or ethical problems that arise in a business environment.

The scope of CSR has greatly increased during the outbreak of the coronavirus disease, COVID-19, which was declared a pandemic by the World Health Organization in March 2020. We will consider CSR further in Chapter 6.

Company policies play a vital role in the corporate governance of an organization, that is the collection of rules and regulations adopted to control its activities and that determine the rights and duties of all stakeholders in the organization, internal and external. The internal stakeholders are the directors, managers, employees, and shareholders. The external stakeholders include customers, creditors, auditors, and regulators. Good corporate governance is necessary to manage and, if possible, avoid conflicts of interest that may arise between the various stakeholders, in particular directors and shareholders. It also helps to ensure accountability of all concerned such that the company makes the right decisions for the right reasons and is seen to do so.

> Accountability must come from within, and that requires an effective governance system that is itself accountable. All three major players in corporate governance, the board, the shareholders, and the management, must be able to act and must be motivated and informed enough to act correctly. There is no one perfect corporate governance model, just as there is no one perfect financial structure. The ultimate aim of a corporate governance structure must be that it is continually re-evaluated so that the governance structure itself can adapt to changing times and needs.[4]

Pillars of governance

What are often referred to as the six pillars of good corporate governance are: accountability, fairness, transparency, assurance, leadership, and stakeholder management. All are critical to the success of a company and to solid relationships with its stakeholders – directors, employees, customers, shareholders, and regulators.

- *Accountability*: Accountability is about the ownership of company strategy and the tasks needed to achieve to achieve company objectives. This also means owing reward and risk in clear context of a predetermined value proposition. When the idea of accountability is approached with this positive outlook, people will be more open to it as a means to improve their performance. This applies from the staff all the way up to top leadership embracing risk management within defined formal appetite for risk. This also includes fostering a culture of compliance to create real and perceived beliefs that the entity is operating within internal and external boundaries.
- *Fairness*: Fairness means treating all stakeholders fairly and reasonably and providing suitable redress for any violation. This needs effective

communication to ensure protection of the company's human and capital resources.
- *Transparency:* Transparency means having "nothing to hide" so that the company's processes and transactions are open and observable to outsiders as necessary. The company will make necessary disclosures to inform all concerned about its decisions. This is an essential element. Transparency is a critical component of good corporate governance because it ensures that the company's actions can be monitored at any time.
- *Independent assurance:* In the journey to transparency, it is vital that non-executive directors and overseers gain confidence that the company's executives are leading the company towards pre-defined objectives as set out in the strategy. Independent assurance aims to provide independent and professional opinions that reduce the risk of bad decisions based on bad information. This amounts to verification by a third party that test results are accurate and provide a fair and equitable basis for acceptance and that quality control is accurate.
- *Leadership:* The company's leaders define the values and principles that frame not only what the company is trying to achieve but also how it goes about that objective. Leaders are responsible for key strategic issues and for proving direction to establish the right culture to drive the performance of the business. Without clear direction and policies, the organization will struggle to achieve its long-term goals.
- *Stakeholder engagement:* Key stakeholders must be identified and managed to ensure they successfully interact with the business. Stakeholder engagement, including investor relations in the case of a listed company, should be included in the company's strategic plan.

Environment, social and governance (ESG)

Any discussion of corporate governance has to include the principles of environment, social, and governance, or ESG for short. These principles form the basis of European and international legislation. ESG comprises the "rules of engagement" for corporations in dealing with: the environment, for example, climate change and sustainability; social matters, for example, employment rights and human rights; and governance, for example. corporate governance as discussed in this chapter. Companies and organizations of all sizes must address the impact of these new requirements as a matter of urgency. More and more legislation around the world is forcing them to do so. Compliance with ESG requirements is no longer a "nice to have" but a "must have".

We will consider the key elements of ESG in detail in Chapter 9.

Roles and responsibilities

Company directors did not always take their responsibilities seriously, or at least non-executive directors. They often fitted board meetings in between golf and dinner at their private club. Lord Boothby, a former Conservative Member of Parliament in the UK, described his experience with board service:

> No effort of any kind is called for. You go to a meeting once a month, in a car supplied by the company. You look grave and sage. If you have five of them, it is total heaven, like having a permanent hot bath.[5]

All of this was swept away by much-needed reforms in the late 20th century. To understand corporate governance as it operates today, we should start with the people who are ultimately responsible, that is the company's board of directors. Shareholders elect the directors to take responsibility, and in some cases a large shareholder will insist on a representative on the board and make it a condition of their continued investment in the company. (In Germany employees have the right to elect half the seats on the boards of major companies.) The directors have oversight of the company's operations. They are responsible to the shareholders at an annual general meeting. One of the objectives of corporate governance is to ensure that oversight and responsibility are effective and seen to be so.

So corporate governance includes all the processes and procedures that set out and are designed to pursue the company's objectives in the context of the social, regulatory, and business environment. These include monitoring the actions, policies, practices, and decisions of the company and its stakeholders. In many ways corporate governance can be seen as an attempt to align the interests of the various stakeholders in the company. Interest in the subject, particularly from the point of view of accountability, greatly increased following the high-profile collapses of a number of large corporations in 2001 and 2002 such as Enron Corp. and MCI (formerly WorldCom) due to accounting fraud in many cases, and again after the international financial crisis in 2008 triggered by the collapse of the US investment firm Lehman Brothers. Corporate scandals of various kinds engaged the interest of the public and led to the enactment of the Sarbanes–Oxley Act in the US in 2002. Corporate failures in Australia such as HIH and One.Tel led to the Corporate Law Economic Reform Program (Audit Reform & Corporate Disclosure) Act 2004, also called CLERP 9, that aimed to improve standards of corporate governance in that country. Similar corporate failures in other countries led to the regulators taking a keen interest, for example the Parmalat scandal in Italy where a multinational food company concealed the extent of its debts, leading to financial loss for thousands of investors in the company

Governance models

In the UK the priority is to protect the interests of shareholders. The Cadbury Code introduced in 1992 provides for, among other things, the separation of the roles of CEO and Chairman and the independence of non-executive directors. For these and other reasons the UK became a model of good corporate governance around the world, despite the scandals of Polly Peck in 1990, and the Robert Maxwell group of companies the following year. (Polly Peck was a small textile company that expanded rapidly in the 1980s and then collapsed in 1990 with debts of £1.3 billion. The CEO Asil Nadir fled to Northern Cyprus in 1993. In December, 1991 the Daily Mirror revealed that its proprietor Robert Maxwell had stolen more than €500 million from the pension fund of Mirror Group Newspapers and other companies that he controlled. His body was later discovered in the Atlantic Ocean after he fell or jumped off his yacht.)

The committee that was set up in response to these scandals led to the code of conduct named after Sir Adrian Cadbury of chocolate fame. The Cadbury Code of 1992 is a voluntary code of conduct for the boards of directors of listed companies. This was a modest "revolution" in corporate governance that applies to larger companies.

In later years and in particular the financial crisis of 2007 to 2009, the Cadbury Code was complemented by further codes of conduct. These included the UK Corporate Governance Code in 2020 (formerly known as the Combined Code) that sets out standards of good practice for listed companies on board composition and development, remuneration, shareholder relations, accountability, and audit. The Code is published by the Financial Reporting Council.

Germany has a system of corporate governance that is quite different from those in the English-speaking, common law world, including the US. There is a dual board structure, that is a board of management that runs the day-to-day operations and reports to a supervisory board half of whose members represent the employees. A company manager may not sit on the supervisory board. Many other European countries have adopted a similar system of governance.

Corporate governance in the US is very different. In many cases, depending on the State involved, the company's management and board of directors have a wide discretion in making decisions without fear of action by the shareholders. In addition, companies are often allowed to appoint the same individual as Chief Executive Officer (CEO) and Chairman, for example Bill Gates of Microsoft Corporation occupied both positions for more than 20 years. However, the US system is highly legalistic and relies heavily on rules laid down by the Securities and Exchange Commission rather than gentlemen's agreement like the Cadbury Code in the UK. The greatest change in the history of corporate governance came about as a result of US legislation and not codes of conduct. This was the Sarbanes–Oxley Act of 2002 that, among other things, required the company's CEO and chief financial offer to certify personally the financial statements. These senior executives must take individual responsibility for the accuracy and completeness of corporate financial reports. The Act defines the interaction of external auditors and internal corporate audit committees and sets out specific limits on the conduct of corporate officers and provide for penalties for non-compliance.

G20/OECD Principles of Corporate Governance

The G20/OECD Principles of Corporate Governance 2015 are available online in the OECD iLibrary, at www.oecd-ilibrary.org/governance/g20-oecd-principles-of-corporate-governance-2015_9789264236882-en

G20, or Group of Twenty, is an intergovernmental forum comprising 19 countries and the European Union. OECD is the Organisation for Economic

Co-operation and Development, an intergovernmental organisation with 38 member countries.

References

1 Donal Nordberg, "Governance Principles and Issues", Sage, 2010, https://uk.sagepub.com/en-gb/eur/corporate-governance/book232619.
2 Zachary S. Johnson, "Good Guys Can Finish First: How Brand Reputation Affects Extension Evaluations", Society for Consumer Psychology, 2019, https://myscp.onlinelibrary.wiley.com/doi/abs/10.1002/jcpy.1109.
3 International Standards Organization, "ISO 26000 Social Responsibility", 2010, www.iso.org/iso-26000-social-responsibility.html.
4 Robert A.G. Monks and Neil Minow, "Corporate Governance", John Wiley & Sons, July 2011, www.wiley.com/en-ie/Corporate+Governance%2C+5th+Edition-p-9780470972595.
5 Law Teacher, "Position of a Non Executive Director", 24 June 2019, www.lawteacher.net/free-law-essays/business-law/position-of-a-non-executive-director-business-law-essay.php#ftn4.

4

POLICY FORMATION AND IMPLEMENTATION

Introduction

We discussed in Chapter 2 the development of company *strategy*, that is defining the company's approach to fulfilling its purpose and the reason why it exists. We also discussed the role of company *policies* to support the strategy. In this chapter, we consider how the company should go about formulating the policies needed to implement the strategy and provide a basis for relevant processes and procedures. "Formulation" here means identifying and producing policies the company needs to ensure that its strategy achieves its financial and non-financial objectives. We also discuss the deployment or implementation of policies, without which a policy document remains just that, words on a page.

Policies matter for all sorts of reasons. They define and communicate objectives, how they are to be achieved, company expectations, and attitudes to risk, and they guide corporate and individual conduct so as to promote a culture of compliance. They establish governance and accountability, that is, who does what and how to measure it.

The typical company policy is a neglected child in the world of corporate governance. The board and senior management team will often lavish attention on the strategy and the mission statement, and leave the underlying policies to their own devices, so to speak. Strategy is sexy, policy is dull. Strategy is poetry, policy is very definitely prose. It becomes everyone's job and therefore no-one's job to identify and produce the policy documents. As a result, company policies are often poorly drafted or inaccurate, or worse, completely absent. Even if they exist, there may be no defined process to identify what policies are required and to review and update them as necessary. In some cases, it may not even be possible to locate the company's policy documents.

And without effective implementation throughout the company, the best-written policy document is dead. It may make interesting reading but it remains worthless as a real contribution to the business. Only when the policy is deployed or implemented as a living, breathing organism does it add real value and help the company to succeed in its mission. In this chapter, we consider the steps that are needed to do turn a document into a vital business tool.

Policy writing

The essentials of good policy writing are the same as those for any form of writing in a business context. Like any other business document, a company policy is a purposeful piece of writing that conveys relevant information in a clear and concise manner. We should devote as much time and attention to writing an effective policy as we did to the company's strategy and mission statement.

So having decided that we need a specific policy, how do we go about writing it? The first decision to be made is: who is going to write it? Someone should own the policy and will take charge of the entire process of writing, editing, re-writing, and periodic review. This individual may or may not also be the document author. Ideally, the author should be an expert who is familiar with the subject matter and the organization. If not the author, the policy owner will delegate the writing to an appropriate subject matter expert, and give authority to administrators to ensure effective management of the policy through to implementation. This will include communication and training.

An effective policy document will have some or all of these characteristics:

- Standard format for ease of use, e.g. a template
- Simple language and easy to understand
- Clear link to company's objectives as set out in the strategy
- Clear scope and application, i.e. who and what it applies to
- Specific requirements for compliance
- Defined roles and responsibilities
- Sound basis for processes and procedures
- Explicit requirements for review and update

Of course, as we have seen, the content must be reviewed and updated regularly. Laws and regulations have a nasty habit of changing, as do customs and practices in different industries. And the policy must change to take account of them. There should be a timetable that sets out how often these reviews should take place, perhaps annually or at most every two years.

In addition to setting out the company's approach to a specific subject matter, a policy document doubles as a legal statement of the basis for the company's actions in that area. This will include the principles and values of the company and any relevant laws and regulations. The document should also set out the rights and obligations of the company and its employees in complying with all these requirements.

We should be clear that a policy is very different from a *procedure* and they perform different functions. A policy sets out what the company expects of itself and its employees, while a procedure describes how the various requirements of the policy should be implemented. So the policy says *what* should be done, and the procedure describes *how* it should be done.

Policy template

Below is a template to use as the basis for any policy document:

POLICY TEMPLATE

1 Purpose of the policy

   What is this policy meant to accomplish?

2   Scope of the policy

Indicate the policy's target individuals and their official positions, including anyone who is affected by the policy directly or indirectly.

3   Policy statement

State the company's principles and standards for actions. Make subheadings out of the key points. Provide information under those subheadings in the form of numbered paragraphs.

4   Procedures

These are detailed steps to help achieve the goals laid out in the policy statement, including rules and regulations to be obeyed.

5   Policy administration duties

   5.1   Administrators for policy compliance. Indicate individuals who are in charge of policy compliance. Include their official positions and specify their duties.
   5.2   Administrators for policy implementation. Indicate who is in charge of implementing the policy. Include their official positions and specify their duties.
   5.3   Administrators for policy review. Indicate policy review experts who are in charge of reviewing the policy. Include their official positions and specify their duties.

6   Approval authority

List everyone who bears the responsibility of giving final approval to the policy, whether it is new or reviewed.

7   Management of policy records

Indicate how the policy record will be properly stored to enable easy access to it throughout the company.

8   Resources

Link to related policy documents or documents that are referred to in the policy.

9   Definitions

Define specific terms that might be easily misunderstood or hard to understand.

10. Adoption date

    The date when the policy is officially adopted and comes into effect.

11. Review date

    Indicate if the policy has been reviewed and the date it occurred. If it is a new policy, set a date for review.

12. Contact for feedback

    Provide an email address or online forum for feedback. Use an official email address accessible to everyone handling feedback on the policy, not an individual's inbox.

13. Appendix

    Include informational materials that will further help the reader to understand the policy. List all appropriate documents, charts, diagrams, web pages, and other resources.

Policy management

It is essential to establish a policy management system to ensure that company policies are properly formulated and implemented. The system will manage the policy *lifecycle* from identification, production, update and review, communication, and implementation. The benefits to the company are as follows:

- Incorporation of necessary changes due to regulatory or business requirements
- Consistency and completeness of policy documents
- Clear accountability for compliance with policy obligations
- Accurate and up-to-date records of access for training purposes
- Sound basis for version control and clear audit trails

We can define the typical stages of a robust management system.

A. Identification

What policies do we need? Can we identify specific requirements based on our strategy, the nature of our business, and the competitive and regulatory environment in which we operate? Ideally, a policy document should address business obligations (internal), regulatory obligations (external), and risks and liabilities. A policy is needed for data privacy and security but not the office cleaning arrangements.

B. Develop and update

Whether creating a new policy or reviewing and updating an existing one, the company is engaged in a continuing process of policy development in response to changing internal and external obligations. Therefore directors or senior managers need to confirm the policy is needed and, if so, to update it as required and track compliance with it.

These stages A and B together may be referred to as *policy formulation*. This is similar to that required for the company's strategy, as we discussed in Chapter 2. In order to identify what policies it needs, the company must analyse the business environment in which it operates and so determine the actions required to succeed in that environment. These will be reflected in policies that are clear and consistent, and must be reviewed on a periodic basis and updated as necessary.

C. Communicate

For a policy to be effective, it must be read and understood. Obviously, all relevant personnel must have easy access to the policy document in a safe and secure repository. The policy may not apply to everyone, and so it should be targeted at a specific audience who needs to know. The company's accounting policy is directly relevant to the finance people but not to Human Resources or Customer Services.

All staff may agree to comply with the new policy but they may not know how to do so. They will need appropriate training to make them aware of what the policy means and to make sure they understand what they need to do to comply with it. They may have signed to confirm this but a signature is not enough to ensure proper understanding.

An interesting case in Australia in 2016 shows the importance of training and awareness. In the case of *Con P v. Hillsbus Co Pty Ltd*,[1] a bus passenger complained that the driver had been looking at his phone and touching it while he was driving. In addition to rules that prohibited the use of mobile phones, the bus company's policy also prohibited employees from using "a mobile phone or other similar device" while they operated or worked on a bus. Arising from the complaint, the bus driver was sacked because he had acted in breach of the company's policy.

In his challenge to the dismissal, the bus driver explained that the device was an old mobile phone he was using to listen to music. The phone did not have a SIM card and could not be used to make or receive calls. He argued that the device was not a working mobile phone. The Fair Employment Commission decided the dismissal was valid because the bus driver had been using a mobile phone and so was in breach of the policy. The Commission noted that employees were provided with copies of their contract of employment but not any updates or changes as they were made over time. However, in this case the bus driver was aware of the ban on mobile phones.

The Commission took into account the lack of information from Hillsbus about how the policy was to apply to music devices. There was no definition of what was a "similar device" and drivers were able to use a small transistor radio or other devices that could play music. In the circumstances the Commission decided that the dismissal was harsh, unjust, and unreasonable. It ordered the bus driver should be reinstated to his job with compensation for any loss.

D. Implement

As well as communication, the policy must be implemented or enforced. This will require a set of controls to ensure compliance and safeguard the company against identified risks. These controls should be monitored to make sure they remain effective. Any violation of the policy should be recorded.

The policy must be distributed to all company employees and/or contactors who are affected. This may be done by email (with an attachment or a link) or by hard copy. Employees should know where to look for their policy documents and not be overwhelmed by a minefield of folders on a shared drive. Ideally, they should be able to find any document with no more than three clicks. All employees or contractors should be asked to sign to confirm they have read and understood the policy.

E. Maintain

In the final stage the policy is reviewed periodically for continued relevance and accuracy. Version control is essential for this purpose. The management system will ensure that steps are taken at the appropriate time for review, updating, or retirement of the document, as the case may be. The policy may be out-of-date or no longer needed.

Ideally, the policy document should set out a schedule for regular reviews or at least a maximum period within which a review should take place. Relevant laws and regulations will change over time, as will industry practice.

These stages C, D, and E together may be referred to as *policy implementation*. Having formulated the policy document, it must be implemented throughout the organization and maintained on an ongoing basis. Otherwise it will quickly become out-of-date.

Reference

1 *Cabcharge T/A Hillsbus Co Pty Ltd*, 2016, Fair Work Commission, Australia, [2016] FWC 1901.

PART II

CORPORATE CONDUCT

This Part discusses policies that aim to regulate the conduct of the company itself. As a legal entity, the company has legal obligations as well as a range of corporate responsibilities to its employees, suppliers, and clients/customers.

5

DATA PROTECTION AND DATA SECURITY

Introduction

Data protection and data security are related but separate subjects. They both define the commitment of any company that processes a significant amount of computer data, or digital information, to protecting and securing the rights of their customers and employees and their data. (This is data or information, called *personal data*, that identifies or could identify an individual.) This commitment effectively applies to every company that does business of any kind with customers who are individuals. Data *protection* concerns the relationship between data, technology, privacy, and the relevant legal issues, including the fundamental rights of individuals as to the obtaining, use and disclosure of their personal data. Data *security* seeks to enforce these rights and protect data from attack by third parties, including the actions of unauthorized users.

DOI: 10.4324/9781003258995-7

Data protection

Although a relatively new subject, data protection goes back a surprisingly long way. Back to 1995 to be exact. This was the year of a European Union (formerly European Communities) Directive on the "protection of individuals with regard to the processing of personal data and on the free movement of such data".[1] Driven by an aspiration to Europe-wide privacy for individuals, the Member States of the former EC agreed on a single measure that would govern the processing of personal data. The 1995 Directive imposed new requirements and granted extensive rights of data protection to European citizens.

Data protection is essentially that area of the law that governs what may and may not be done with personal information, or data. This information may be in electronic form, for example stored on a computer hard drive, or manual, for example paper-based form. Although the law applies to all electronically processed personal data, it applies only to some types of paper-based records. These are records kept in a structured way, for example in an index or some other structured form. The General Data Protection Regulation (GDPR) of the EU came into force in May 2018 and updated the 1995 Directive to take account of new technology in the previous 20 years and more.[2] GDPR imposed a new regime on companies and organizations of all kinds that hold personal data relating to their clients, customers, employees, and third parties: in other words, almost every organization that does business with individual customers or provides a service to them. Among other things, GDPR made it a legal requirement for companies and organizations of a certain size that store or use personal information to appoint a Data Protection Officer.

In the UK, the Data Protection Act 2018 was introduced at the same time as GDPR to provide for data protection in a similar way after the UK's departure from the EU.[3] GDPR became a model for many other laws across the world, including legislation in Turkey, Chile, Japan, Brazil, South Korea, Argentina, and Kenya. In the US the California Consumer Privacy Act[4] (CCPA) adopted on 28 June 2018, has many similarities with GDPR. At time of writing, other states in the US are in the process of adopting similar laws. CCPA was intended to enhance privacy rights and consumer protection for residents of California, US. It became effective on 1 January, 2020.

In order to understand the scope of data protection, we should consider four basic terms that are used in this chapter.

- Personal data – information that identifies a living individual, e.g. a person's name, address, email address, shareholding, directorships, CCTV image, photograph on a website, etc.
- Processing – any activity that can be carried out concerning personal data, e.g. obtaining, storing, printing, filing, copying, or transferring this data to a third part.
- Controller – any organization that controls the processing of personal data, e.g. retailers, banks, insurance companies, stockbrokers, law firms, and government departments. In fact virtually all organizations, including limited companies, are controllers for this purpose.
- Data subject – the individual person who is the subject of any relevant personal data.

Data protection, also called data privacy, is a complex subject as it tries to balance the legitimate processing of data for business purposes while protecting the privacy of the individual. For example, the UK Data Protection Act 2018 and the equivalent legislation in other countries ensure that personal data is accessible to those whom it concerns, and provides redress if there are errors. This is to ensure that individuals are treated fairly, for example in the case of credit checking for loans. Similar to legislation in other countries, the 2018 Act provides that only personal data can only be processed for legitimate and lawful purposes. The Act also introduces some new offences, including obtaining or disclosing personal data without consent, or retaining the data without consent. Selling, or offering to sell, personal data obtained or disclosed in these circumstances is also an offence.

The 2018 Act supplements the EU's GDPR which came into effect on 25 May 2018 and applies throughout the European Union. Since Brexit, it no longer applies to the UK.

GDPR is an EU regulation on data privacy that governs data processing in Europe and the transfer of personal data to countries outside the EU. The regulation aims to increase individuals' control over their personal data and at the same time to simplify the regulatory environment for cross-border trade. This is a delicate balancing act. GDPR contains provisions for the processing of data relating to individuals, or *data subjects*, and applies to any company (the *controller*) that processes the personal data in the EU.

GDPR is technically a *regulation* and not a *directive*, which means among other things it is directly binding and applicable in every Member State of the EU but some its provisions may be adapted to meet the needs of individual countries. Since the GDPR became law in 2018, companies face significant fines of up to €20 million or 4% of their annual revenue – whichever is the greater – if they fail to company. The GDPR has forced many companies to examine their data privacy risks and take appropriate steps to mitigate the risk of unauthorized disclosure of data relating to customers, suppliers, and employees. One of these steps is to put in place a robust data protection policy for the guidance of all those in the company who handle personal data in the course of their work. A sample data protection policy is set out at the end of this chapter.

Rights and principles

GDPR

GDPR provides that personal data relating to EU citizens must be:

(a) *processed lawfully, fairly and in a transparent manner in relation to the data subject* ("lawfulness, fairness and transparency");
(b) *collected for specified, explicit, and legitimate purposes and not further processed in a manner that is incompatible with those purposes* ("purpose limitation");
(c) *adequate, relevant, and limited to what is necessary in relation to the purposes for which they are processed* ("data minimisation");
(d) *Accurate and, where necessary, kept up to date; every reasonable step must be taken to ensure that personal data that are inaccurate, having regard to the purposes for which they are processed, are erased or rectified without delay* ("accuracy");
(e) *kept in a form which permits identification of data subjects for no longer than is necessary for the purposes for which the personal data are processed* ("storage limitation"); and
(f) *processed in a manner that ensures appropriate security of the personal data, including protection against unauthorised or unlawful processing and against accidental loss, destruction, or damage, using appropriate technical or organisational measures* ("integrity and confidentiality").

(Article 5[5])

An individual's personal data may not be processed unless there is at least one legal basis to do so. These include:

(a) *If the data subject has given consent to the processing of his or her personal data;*
(b) *To fulfil contractual obligations with a data subject, or for tasks at the request of a data subject who is in the process of entering into a contract;*
(c) *To comply with a data controller's legal obligations;*
(d) *To protect the vital interests of a data subject or another individual;*
(e) *To perform a task in the public interest or in official authority;*
(f) *For the legitimate interests of a data controller or a third party, unless these interests are overridden by interests of the data subject or her or his rights.*

(Article 6[6])

Will compensation be awarded in the event of breach? In one of the few cases to come before the courts, the UK Supreme Court rules out damages for loss of control of personal data. In the case of *Lloyd v. Google LLC*[7] the court decided that damages are not available for breach of the Data Protection Act 1998 (the UK equivalent of GDPR) in this respect. Even if damages for loss of control had been available, the case could not be brought as a "class action", that is, an action by a class or group of people, because it would have been necessary to assess the extent of the unlawful data processing in each individual case.

Although compensation may or may not be awarded in a particular case, companies that handle large amounts of personal data should be aware that a regulator has wide powers to impose fines for breach of data protection obligations. For example, in August 2021 WhatsApp was subject to a fine of €225 million by the Data Protection Commissioner in Ireland due to failure to comply with GDPR requirements. These included failure to provide information to WhatsApp users as to the use of their personal data.

CCPA

CCPA is the nearest US equivalent of GDPR and provides for similar rights and principles as regards personal information relating to residents, or *consumers*, of California. They are entitled to know what personal information is collected about them and whether this information has been sold or otherwise disclosed, and to whom. They can object to the sale, and access the relevant information at any time. Finally, similar to GDPR they can ask the company to delete any personal information about them. However, unlike GDPR it only applies to any company that collects personal information and does business in California, and complies with at least one of the following requirements[8]:

- Gross revenues in excess of $25 million;
- The company buys, receives, or sells the personal information of 50,000 or more individuals or households; or
- The company earns more than half of its annual revenue from selling individuals' personal information.

Cookies and marketing

A specific EU regulation will complement the GDPR rules on data processing by providing specific rules for electronic communications such as marketing. This is the ePrivacy Regulation which was first proposed in 2018 and is still in draft form pending agreement by the various EU institutions.[9] The new Regulation aims to simplify the rules regarding cookies and will mean that EU websites will not need to show consent pop-ups anymore in order to place cookies on a user's device when he or she visits a website. (Cookies are small pieces of computer code that identify a visitor to that site.) When the Regulation comes into effect any data that is processed by these means must be done anonymously so that it will not identify any individual user. Therefore no user consent will be needed. However, even though there will be fewer restrictions on the collection of this data, the new Regulation sets out rules about how the data must be stored, protected, and deleted if necessary. Companies should note that, unlike GDPR, the ePrivacy Regulation will apply not only to processing of personal data but also to business-to-business (B2B) marketing. The new requirements are aimed specifically at website owners and software providers, for example, Meta (formerly Facebook), Google, and Zoom – basically the entire online industry.

With this new Regulation, the European Union wants to strengthen the privacy of citizens in online communication and further regulate data protection in the EU. Basically, it's concerned with restoring people's trust in digital communication channels. The proposed ePrivacy Regulation is intended to ensure that privacy and data protection will no longer be restricted by national borders in the future (at least within the EU).

One major change will affect the use of cookies. Rejecting cookies that are not necessary will become simpler for web users and, for example, may be regulated via browser settings. Website operators may only use cookies if users explicitly agree to it or they are "technically necessary cookies" that enable the proper functioning of a website (e.g., login cookies). Even if the user doesn't agree, all content should still be displayed to them in the future. Instead of an opt-out, a double opt-in would be required.

To implement this, browser manufacturers could also be put under obligation. Web browsers in the future should offer users the possibility to regulate tracking of their behaviour. Is anybody allowed to read my cookie data? And if yes, are these only direct providers and what about third parties? Data protection settings should be as strict as possible directly following installation. In general, tracking services should only be allowed without permission by the user if they serve a purely statistical purpose.

The ePrivacy Regulation will apply to machine-to-machine communication. This is the EU's response to the challenges of the Internet of Things. The proposal is that devices can only transfer personal data if the user has agreed to it. This could apply to GPS data for smartphones, for example. In general, it should apply that users must be informed about which data is being collected from them and for what purpose. Therefore, it shouldn't be possible to hide an agreement in the small print or link it to another service. For example, if user data needs to be transferred for online shopping, this is permitted. However, it will not be permitted to use this data for advertising purposes at the same time: a specific agreement would be needed to do this.

The new Regulation will also regulate telephone marketing more strictly. The proposal is that telephone calls for solicitation purposes should only be allowed if the caller reveals their telephone number or if they use an integrated code to indicate that it's an advertising call.

When will the ePrivacy Regulation come into force? In February 2021, the EU Council of Ministers agreed on a common draft of the Regulation, and the EU Commission and Parliament are still negotiating with each other and with the Council. Although it will take some time for the ePrivacy Regulation to become legally effective – it will come into force almost two years (20 months) after final approval by the Commission and the Parliament – there has been an important change in cookie tracking since December, 2021. On that date, Germany's new Telecommunications Telemedia Data Protection Act (TTDSG) implemented some aspects of the ePrivacy Regulation in that country.

European Data Act

In June, 2023 the European Commission announced that an agreement had been reached between the European Parliament and the Council of Ministers to implement new legislation called the European Data Act.[10] The Act aims to boost the EU's data economy by unlocking the vast amount of data held on millions of machines and devices and fostering a competitive and reliable European "cloud" market. It aims to ensure that the benefits of the digital revolution are shared by everyone.

The European Data Act includes:

- Measures that enable users of connected devices to access the data generated by these devices and by services related to these devices; users will be able to share this data with third parties.
- Measures to protect companies from unfair contractual terms that are imposed unilaterally by the other party; these measures aim to safeguard EU companies from unfair agreements, foster fair negotiations, and enable companies to participate more confidently in the digital marketplace.
- Mechanisms for public sector bodies to access and use data held by the private sector in cases of emergency such as floods and wildfires, or when implementing a legal mandate where the required data is not readily available through other means.
- New rules that grant customers the freedom to switch between various cloud data-processing service providers; these rules aim to promote competition and choice in the market while preventing vendor lock-in.
- Measures to promote the development of interoperability standards for data sharing and data processing, in line with the EU's Standardisation Strategy.

Data security

Whereas data protection, as we have seen, concerns data, technology, and privacy in the context of legal rights, data security seeks to enforce these rights and protect data from attack by third parties, including the actions of unauthorized users.

Various international standards apply to data security in the context of what they refer to as "information security". The best-known standards are provided by the International Standards Organization (ISO) and the International Electrotechnical Commission (IEC).[11] These set out requirements for an information security management system (ISMS), although there are more than a dozen standards in the ISO/IEC 27000 "family". Use of these or similar standards will enable companies of all kinds to manage the security of their assets such as financial information, intellectual property, employee details, or information entrusted by third parties.

Like other ISO standards, certification of compliance with ISO/IEC 27001 is possible but not obligatory. Some organizations choose to implement the standard in order to show compliance with the best practice it contains while others may decide to opt for certification to reassure their customers and clients. However, ISO does not perform the certification. This is done by independent certification bodies. Certification can be a useful tool to enhance the company's reputation by demonstrating that its products or services will meet customer expectations. In some industries, certification is a legal or contractual requirement.

At a minimum, all information stored in computer systems, that is data, must be "owned" so that everyone is clear as to who is responsible to protect and control access to that data. Information security, also known as "infosec", seeks to protect this information by mitigating the various risks to its availability and use. This includes preventing or reducing the risk of unauthorized access to data, or the unlawful use or disclosure of that data. The ultimate objective is to protect the confidentiality, integrity, and availability of data while ensuring the effective implementation of policy.

A specific industry standard applies to credit card and debit card payments. The Payment Card Industry Data Security Standard (PCI DSS) is an international information security standard for organizations that handle cardholder information for the major credit and debit cards. The PCI DSS Standard is mandated by the card brands themselves, for example

MasterCard, Visa, but is administered by the Payment Card Industry Security Standards Council. The standard aims to increase controls over cardholder data in order to reduce credit card fraud.

So data security is concerned to prevent attacks on computer systems. We can define an attack as any attempt to disable, destroy, or steal information through unauthorized access. A *cyberattack* is any action against computer networks or personal computer devices such as a laptop or smartphone. The attacker may be employed by a sovereign state, individual, group, or organization. Cyberattacks can range from installing *spyware*, that is, malicious software that acts to gather information about an individual or company, to attempting to destroy the computer infrastructure of an entire country.

Of course, breaches of data security can occur even in the absence of a deliberate attack. A *data breach* is the intentional or unintentional release of private or confidential information to an unauthorized third party. This may involve financial information such as credit card and debit card details, bank details, or other information such as an individual's personal health or a company's intellectual property. Needless to say, a data breach can cost the company dearly between direct costs, for example remediation, investigation, and indirect costs, for example reputational damage.

A sample data security policy is set out at the end of this chapter.

In September 2021 it was reported that the personal data of more than one million South African citizens may have been exposed after a cyberattack at a debt recovery firm. The firm, Debt-IN Consultants, confirmed the attack and that the relevant data included customer names and contact details, employment and salary information, and debt-related information including payments made. The firm said the data breach only came to light when it was discovered that confidential consumer data and voice recordings of calls with customers had been posted on hidden internet sites.[12]

Data protection laws in many countries require notification of a data breach to the authorities and to any people affected. A company whose data has been subject to a data breach must inform customers and take steps to provide redress as appropriate. For example, the GDPR provides that the company must inform the data regulator and any individuals affected as soon as possible.[13] (In September 2021 the UK government revealed plans to remove "administrative burdens" to ensure more flexible, risk-based "privacy management". In addition to changing the rules on accountability, the

Department for Digital, Culture, Media, and Sport proposed to tackle over-reporting of personal data breaches by increasing the threshold for notifying the Information Commissioner's Office of such incidents[14])

In January, 2023 the European Union implemented the Network and Information Security Directive,[15] known as NIS2. The new Directive will improve the existing cyber security status across EU in different ways by:

- creating the necessary cyber crisis management structure;
- increasing the level of harmonization regarding security requirements and reporting obligations;
- encouraging Members States to introduce new areas of interest such as supply chain, vulnerability management, internet and cyber security strategies; and
- helping Member States to address common cyber security issues.

The new Directive has three parts:

1 National capabilities: EU Member States must have certain national cybersecurity capabilities, e.g. cyber policies and procedures.
2 Cross-border collaboration: Collaboration between EU Member States.
3 National supervision of critical sectors: EU Member States have to supervise the cyber security of critical market operators in their country, e.g. energy, transport, water, health, digital infrastructure, and finance sector.

The Member States have 20 months from publication in the *Official Journal of the European Union* to incorporate the new Directive into their national legal systems. This means the Directive will come into force in mid-2025.

Information management

As we've seen, data privacy and data security seek to protect the company's data or information and the information relating to its customers, suppliers, and employees. Therefore, we can see privacy and security as essential elements of *information management*. This is about managing information of all kinds from various sources, including custody and disclosure of that information to those who need it, through to archiving or deletion as the case may be after usage by the company for the legitimate purposes of its business. The process will involve data quality, that is, accuracy, accessibility, and utility of the information, in addition to its storage in a safe and secure location.

Artificial intelligence

More and more companies recognize the potential benefits of using artificial intelligence (AI) to improve efficiency and productivity in the workplace. However, they must also acknowledge the importance of using AI responsibly and in an ethical manner, particularly in generating content of documents and communications.

Therefore companies should adopt guidelines for the responsible use of AI-generated content, including the need for proofing, editing, and fact-checking. The guidelines should include:

- Transparency – All AI-generated content must be clearly labelled as such, and the use of AI should be transparent to employees and customers.
- Data privacy – Personal or sensitive data used in AI content creation must handled with appropriate care and in compliance with data protection laws.
- Fairness – AI-generated content should not discriminate against any individual based on their race, gender, sexual orientation, age, or disability.
- Liability: The company must take responsibility for any harm caused by AI-generated content, and have insurance in place to protect against any potential claims.

ChatGPT

Chat Generative Pre-trained Transformer, or ChatGPT, is the most recent example of AI that could transform the world of work. ChatGPT is a language model-based chatbot developed by a company called OpenAI and launched in November 2022. It allows users to create a discussion of a desired length, format, style, level of detail, and language used.

ChatGPT is a technology that is designed to generate language based on the input it receives. The input consists of documents and other sources available on the internet. While ChatGPT is a sophisticated tool that can provide helpful insights and responses, it is not equipped to handle sensitive information. There is a risk that the information could be exposed or misused, either through a security breach or by unintended parties gaining access.

ChatGPT is not a legal entity and is not bound by the same confidentiality agreements or legal protections as human employees or contractors. Companies should be careful when sharing proprietary and confidential information with ChatGPT, as doing so could pose a security risk and compromise sensitive data. Ideally, every company should adopt a policy on employees' use of ChatGPT according to the company's specific business requirements.

Sample policy documents

1. Sample data protection policy

Below for reference is a sample data protection policy for use in the UK or an EU Member State:

DATA PROTECTION POLICY

[Insert company name]
Last updated:

Definitions:
"Company" means [insert company name], a company registered under number [company number, if applicable], having its place of business at [insert address of the company].
"DPA" means the UK Data Protection Act 2018 [or equivalent law in relevant EU Member State] which reflects or implements the EU General Data Protection Regulation 2016 ("GDPR").
"Responsible Person" means [insert name of person responsible for data protection within the company].
"Register of Systems" means a register of all systems in which personal data is processed by the Company.

1   Data protection principles

    The Company is committed to processing data in accordance with its responsibilities under the DPA.

DPA requires that personal data will be:

a processed lawfully, fairly and in a transparent manner in relation to individuals;
b collected for specified, explicit and legitimate purposes and not further processed in a manner that is incompatible with those purposes; further processing for archiving purposes in the public interest, scientific or historical research purposes or statistical purposes shall not be considered to be incompatible with the initial purposes;
c adequate, relevant and limited to what is necessary in relation to the purposes for which they are processed;
d accurate and, where necessary, kept up to date; every reasonable step must be taken to ensure that personal data that are inaccurate, having regard to the purposes for which they are processed, are erased or rectified without delay;
e kept in a form which permits identification of data subjects for no longer than is necessary for the purposes for which the personal data are processed; personal data may be stored for longer periods insofar as the personal data will be processed solely for archiving purposes in the public interest, scientific or historical research purposes or statistical purposes subject to implementation of the appropriate technical and organisational measures required by the DPA in order to safeguard the rights and freedoms of individuals; and
f processed in a manner that ensures appropriate security of the personal data, including protection against unauthorised or unlawful processing and against accidental loss, destruction or damage, using appropriate technical or organisational measures."

2 <u>General provisions</u>

a This policy applies to all personal data processed by the Company.
b The Responsible Person will be responsible for the Company's ongoing compliance with this policy.
c This policy will be reviewed at least annually.
d The Company will register with the [Information Commissioner's Office in the UK or equivalent authority in relevant EU Member State)] as an organisation that processes personal data.

3   Lawful, fair and transparent processing

   a   To ensure its processing of data is lawful, fair and transparent, the Company will maintain a Register of Systems.
   b   The Register of Systems will be reviewed at least annually.
   c   Individuals have the right to access their personal data and any such requests made to the Company will be dealt with in a timely manner and in accordance with the DPA.

4   Lawful purposes

   a   All data processed by the Company must be done on one of the following lawful bases: consent, contract, legal obligation, vital interests, public task or legitimate interests.
   b   The Company will note the appropriate lawful basis in the Register of Systems.
   c   Where consent is relied upon as a lawful basis for processing data, evidence of opt-in consent will be kept with the personal data.
   d   Where communications are sent to individuals based on their consent, the option for the individual to revoke their consent must be clearly available and systems should be in place to ensure such revocation is reflected accurately in the Company's systems.

5   Data minimisation

   a   The Company will ensure that personal data are adequate, relevant and limited to what is necessary in relation to the purposes for which it is processed.
   b   [Add relevant text to describe features/functions of the Company's systems that ensure data minimisation.]

6   Accuracy

   a   The Organisation will take reasonable steps to ensure personal data is accurate.
   b   Where necessary for the lawful basis on which data is processed, steps will be taken to ensure that personal data is kept up to date.
   c   [Add relevant text to describe features/functionality of the Company's systems that ensure accuracy.]

7 Archiving/removal

    a To ensure that personal data is kept for no longer than necessary, the Company will put in place an archiving policy for each area in which personal data is processed and review this process annually.

    b The archiving policy will set out what data must be retained and for how long and the reason(s) why.

8 Security

    a The Company will ensure that personal data is stored securely using modern software that is kept up to date.

    b Access to personal data will be limited to personnel who need access, and appropriate security must be in place to avoid unauthorised sharing of information.

    c When personal data is deleted this must be done safely such that the data is irrecoverable.

    d Appropriate back-up and disaster recovery solutions must be in place.

9 Breach

In the event of a breach of security leading to the accidental or unlawful destruction, loss, alteration, unauthorised disclosure of, or access to, personal data, the Company will promptly assess the risk to people's rights and freedoms and if appropriate report this breach to the [Information Commissioner's Office or relevant country's data protection authority]. The Company will also take steps to ensure the breach does not happen again.

Sample data security policy

Below for reference is a sample data security policy for use in the UK or an EU Member State:

DATA SECURITY POLICY

1 Introduction

    1.1 This Data Security Policy is [insert company name here] our policy regarding the safeguarding and protection of sensitive personal information and confidential information as is required by law (including, but not limited to, the UK Data Protection Act 2018 [or equivalent legislation in relevant EU Member State] that reflects or implements the EU General Data Protection Regulation 2016).

2 Purpose

2.1 The purpose of this document is to outline how we prevent data security breaches and how we react to them when prevention is not possible. By data breach we mean a security incident in which the confidentiality, integrity or availability of data is compromised. A breach can either be purposeful or accidental.

2.2 This Data Security Policy covers:

2.2.1 Physical access procedures;
2.2.2 Digital access procedures;
2.2.3 Access monitoring procedures;
2.2.4 Data security audit procedures;
2.2.5 Data security breach procedures.

3 Scope

3.1 This policy includes in its scope all data which we process either in hardcopy or digital copy, this includes special categories of data.

3.2 This policy applies to all staff, including temporary staff and contractors.

4 Physical access procedures

4.1 Physical access to records shall only be granted on a strict "need to know" basis.

4.2 During their induction each staff member who requires access to confidential information for their job role will be trained on the safe handling of all information and will be taught the procedures which govern how data is used, stored, shared and organised in our organisation.

4.3 Our staff must retain personal and confidential data securely in locked storage when not in use and keys should not be left unattended and in public view.

4.4 Insert locations where confidential information is stored, e.g. work stations, archive cupboards, admin office etc. All offices, when left unoccupied, must be locked unless all personal and confidential information has first been cleared off work stations/desks and secured in locked storage.

4.5 We will risk assess each storage location to ensure that the data is properly secured.

4.6 A record will be kept of who has access to each storage location.

4.7 An audit will be completed at least annually to ensure that information is secured properly and that access is restricted to those who have a legal requirement to use the information.

5 <u>Digital access procedures</u>

5.1 Access shall be granted using the principle of the least privilege required. This means that every program and every user of the system should operate using the least set of privileges necessary to complete their job.

5.2 We will ensure that each user is identified by a unique user ID so that users can be linked to and made responsible for their actions.

5.3 The use of group IDs is only permitted where they are suitable for the work carried out.

5.4 During their induction each staff member who requires access to digital systems for their job role will be trained on the use of the system, given their user login details, and they will be required to sign to indicate that they understand the conditions of access.

5.5 A record is kept of all users given access to the system.

5.6 In the instance that there are changes to user access requirements, these can only be authorised by the Data Security Lead or equivalent job role.

5.7 We will follow robust password management procedures and ensure that all staff are trained in password management.

5.8 As soon as an employee leaves, all their system logons are revoked.

5.9 As part of the employee termination process the Data Security Lead or equivalent job role is responsible for the removal of access rights from the computer system.

5.10 The Data Security Lead or equivalent job role will review all access rights on a regular basis, but in any event at least once a year. The review is designed to positively confirm all

DATA PROTECTION AND DATA SECURITY 59

system users. Any lapsed or unwanted logons which are identified are disabled immediately and deleted unless positively reconfirmed.

5.11 When not in use all screens will be locked and a clear screen policy will be followed.

6 Access monitoring procedures

6.1 The management of digital access rights is subject to regular compliance checks to ensure that these procedures are being followed and that staff are complying with their duty to use their access rights in an appropriate manner.

6.2 Areas considered in the compliance check include whether:

6.2.1 Allocation of administrator rights is restricted;
6.2.2 Access rights are regularly reviewed;
6.2.3 Whether there is any evidence of staff sharing their access rights;
6.2.4 Staff are appropriately logging out of the system;
6.2.5 Our password policy is being followed;
6.2.6 Staff understand how to report any security breaches.

7 Data security audit procedures

7.1 Confidentiality audits will focus on controls within electronic records management systems and paper record systems; the purpose being to discover whether confidentiality has been breached, or put at risk through deliberate misuse of systems, or as a result of insufficient controls. Audits of security and access arrangements within each area are to be conducted at least annually.

7.2 Audits will be carried out as required by some or all of these methods:

7.2.1 Unannounced spot checks to all work areas;
7.2.2 A series of interviews with management and staff, where a department or area of the organisation have been identified for a confidentiality audit;
7.2.3 Based on electronic reports – this may be from an ICT contractor or from our internal monitoring;
7.2.4 Based on electronic reports from care planning software or auditing of care plans – this may be from an ICT contractor or from our internal monitoring.

7.3 The following checks will be made during data security audits:

7.3.1 The record of processing operations has been reviewed, updated and signed off;
7.3.2 Failed attempts to access confidential information;
7.3.3 Repeated attempts to access confidential information;
7.3.4 Access of confidential information by unauthorised persons;
7.3.5 Previous confidentiality incidents and actions, including disciplinary, taken;
7.3.6 Staff awareness of policies and guidelines concerning confidentiality and understanding of their responsibilities with regard to confidentiality;
7.3.7 Appropriate communications with service users;
7.3.8 Appropriate recording and/or use of consent forms;
7.3.9 Appropriate allocation of access rights to confidential information, both hardcopy and digital;
7.3.10 Appropriate staff access to physical areas;
7.3.11 Storage of and access to filed hardcopy service user notes and information;
7.3.12 Correct process used to securely transfer personal information by post, fax or email;
7.3.13 Appropriate use and security of desktop computers and mobile devices in open areas;
7.3.14 Security applied to PCs, laptops and mobile electronic devices;
7.3.15 Evidence of secure waste disposal;
7.3.16 Appropriate transfer and data sharing arrangements are in place;
7.3.17 Security and arrangements for recording access to manual files both live and archive, e.g. storage in locked cabinets/locked rooms.
7.3.18 Appropriate staff use of computer systems, e.g. no excessive personal use, no attempting to download software without authorisation, use of social media, attempted connection of unauthorised devices etc.

8 Data security breach procedures

8.1 In order to mitigate the risks of a security breach we will:
8.1.1 Follow the physical access, digital access, access monitoring and data security Procedures;

8.1.2 Ensure our staff are trained to recognise a potential data breach whether it is a confidentiality, integrity or availability breach;

8.1.3 Ensure our staff understand the procedures to follow and how to escalate a security incident to the correct person in order to determine if a breach has taken place.

8.2 In the instance that it appears that a data security breach has taken place:

8.2.1 The staff member who notices the breach, or potential breach, will complete a Data Security Breach Incident Report Form without delay;

8.2.2 This form will be completed and handed to the Data Security Lead or equivalent job role or, if they are not available, to a member of senior management;

8.2.3 The Data Security Lead will complete the rest of the Incident Report Form and conduct a thorough investigation into the breach;

8.2.4 In the instance that the breach is a personal data breach and it is likely that there will be a risk to the rights and freedoms of an individual then the [Information Commissioner's Office or supervisory authority in relevant EU Member State] will be informed as soon as possible, but at least within 72 hours of our discovery of the breach.

8.2.5 As part of our report we will provide the following details:

8.2.5.1 The nature of the personal data breach, i.e. confidentiality, integrity, availability;

8.2.5.2 The approximate number of individuals concerned and the category of individual, e.g. employees, mailing lists, service users;

8.2.5.3 The categories and approximate number of personal data records concerned;

8.2.5.4 The name and details of our Data Security Lead or equivalent job role;

8.2.5.5 The likely consequences of the breach;

8.2.5.6 A description of the measures taken, or which we will take, to mitigate any possible adverse effects.

8.2.6 The Data Security Lead will inform any individual that their personal data has been breached if it is likely that there is a high risk to their rights and freedoms;

8.2.7 A data security breach must be marked on the data inventory and will prompt an audit of all processes in order to correct any procedure which led to the breach;

8.2.8 A record of all personal data breaches will be kept including those breaches which the [Information Commissioner's Office or supervisory authority in relevant EU Member State] was not required to be notified about.

9 <u>Responsibilities</u>

9.1 [Insert name here] is responsible for physical security;

9.2 [Insert name here] is responsible for updating and auditing the data inventory and record of processing operations;

9.3 [Insert name here] is responsible for digital access;

9.4 [Insert name here] is responsible for managing data breaches;

9.5 [Insert name here] is responsible for data security audits.

10 <u>Approval</u>

10.1 This policy has been approved by the undersigned and will be reviewed at least annually.

Name	
Signature	
Approval Date	
Review Date	

References

1 Directive 95/46/EC of the European Parliament and of the Council of 24 October 1995 on the protection of individuals with regard to the processing of personal data and on the free movement of such data, *Official Journal* L 281, 31–50.

2 Regulation (EU) 2016/679 of the European Parliament and of the Council of 27 April 2016 on the protection of natural persons with regard to the processing of personal data and on the free movement of such data, and repealing Directive 95/46/EC, *Official Journal* L 119, 1.

3. *Data Protection Act 2018*, C. 12. Available at: www.legislation.gov.uk/ukpga/2018/12/contents/enacted (Accessed: 15 September 2023).
4. Assembly Bill No. 375, Chapter 55, An act to add Title 1.81.5 (commencing with Section 1798.100) to Part 4 of Division 3 of the Civil Code, relating to privacy. Available at: https://leginfo.legislature.ca.gov/faces/billTextClient.xhtml?bill_id=201720180AB375 (Accessed: 15 September 2023).
5. Article 5, Regulation (EU) 2016/679 of the European Parliament and of the Council of 27 April 2016 on the protection of natural persons with regard to the processing of personal data and on the free movement of such data, and repealing Directive 95/46/EC, *Official Journal* L 119, 1.
6. Article 6, Regulation (EU) 2016/679 of the European Parliament and of the Council of 27 April 2016 on the protection of natural persons with regard to the processing of personal data and on the free movement of such data, and repealing Directive 95/46/EC, *Official Journal* L 119, 1.
7. Lloyd v Google LLC, [2021] UKSC 50. Available at: www.supremecourt.uk/cases/uksc-2019-0213.html (Accessed: 15 September 2023).
8. Assembly Bill No. 375, Chapter 55, An act to add Title 1.81.5 (commencing with Section 1798.100) to Part 4 of Division 3 of the Civil Code, relating to privacy. Available at: https://leginfo.legislature.ca.gov/faces/billTextClient.xhtml?bill_id=201720180AB375 (Accessed: 15 September 2023).
9. Proposal for a Regulation of the European Parliament and of the Council concerning the respect for private life and the protection of personal data in electronic communications and repealing Directive 2002/58/EC (Regulation on Privacy and Electronic Communications), COM(2017)010 final – 2017/03 (COD).
10. Proposal for a Regulation of the European Parliament and of the Council on harmonised rules on fair access to and use of data (Data Act) COM(2022)68 final – 2022/0047(COD).
11. International Standardization Organization 2013 *Information technology — Security techniques — Code of practice for information security controls*. Available at: https://www.iso.org/standard/54533.html (Accessed: 15 September 2023).
12. Vikki Davies, "Millions of South Africans affected by Debt-In data breach", Cyber, 27 September 2021, https://cybermagazine.com/cyber-security/millions-south-africans-affected-debt-data-breach.
13. Regulation (EU) 2016/679 of the European Parliament and of the Council of 27 April 2016 on the protection of natural persons with regard to the processing of personal data and on the free movement of such data, and repealing Directive 95/46/EC (2016) *Official Journal* L 119, 1.

14 Department for Digital, Culture, Media & Sport, 10 September 2021, "Data: A new direction", https://assets.publishing.service.gov.uk/government/uploads/system/uploads/attachment_data/file/1022315/Data_Reform_Consultation_Document__Accessible_.pdf.
15 Commission Delegated Regulation (EU) 2022/255 of 15 December 2021 amending Council Regulation (EEC) No 95/93 as regards the extension of measures for temporary relief from the slot utilisation rules due to the COVID-19 crisis (2022) *Official Journal* L 14 1.

6
CORPORATE SOCIAL RESPONSIBILITY

Introduction

Corporate social responsibility ("CSR") has come to mean anything and everything when it comes to describing the aspirations of many companies around the world to be good corporate citizens. It is almost akin to motherhood and apple pie. But what does it mean? CSR may be defined as a form of international business self-regulation that aims to contribute to society by philanthropic or charitable activities.[1] It consists of voluntary actions by individual companies and organizations and actions taken by them in accordance with industry standard practices at regional, national, and international levels. CSR may be understood as a strategic initiative that contributes to the company's reputation.[2] A company's implementation of CSR will go beyond compliance with legal and regulatory requirements, and will include "actions that appear to further some social good, beyond the interests of the firm and that which is required by law".[3]

Apart from any contribution to company profits, the benefits of CSR accrue through positive public relations and high ethical standards to reduce business and legal risks. In this way, CSR strategies encourage the company to make a positive impact on the environment and internal and external stakeholders including customers, suppliers, employees, and shareholders. From an ethical perspective, the company may adopt CSR policies and practices because of the ethical beliefs of senior management, for example to protect the environment.

The scope of CSR has greatly increased since the outbreak of COVID-19 which was declared a pandemic by the World Health Organization ("WHO") in March 2020. The number of people affected by the virus and its impact on CSR has transformed the way that businesses all over the world regard the communities in which they operate.

CSR acts as an aid to achieving the company's mission as well as serving as a guide to what the company represents for its customers. This will commit the company to what are called business ethics that examine ethical principles and moral or ethical problems that can arise in a business environment. As part of this approach, it will seek to comply with ISO 26000 which is the recognized international standard for CSR. (We will discuss this and other international standards later in the chapter.) Public sector organizations (the United Nations for example) adhere to what is referred to as the "triple bottom line" ("TBL"). TBL is an accounting framework with three parts: social, environmental, and financial. Some companies have adopted the TBL framework to evaluate their performance from a broader perspective to create greater business value.[4] It is widely accepted that CSR in the private sector adheres to similar principles but with no formal act of legislation.

Of course, CSR comes at a cost and some companies divert a percentage of their profits to charity, while others give their employees time off to help local charitable organizations. In 2014 Google committed to investing $1.5 billion in renewable energy and Disney invested $100 million in children's hospitals. Due to the costs involved, CSR is mainly a strategy for big companies. Small and medium-sized businesses may not have the same financial strength to allow them to divert a portion of their profits on a large scale. But regardless of strategy, all companies should at least be able to show their commitment to CSR to whatever extent that fits their business. A suitable policy document will outline the extent of this commitment.

Sustainability

Many corporate and business strategies now include sustainability as part of their CSR initiative. Sustainability is defined as the capacity to endure and sustain life on the planet in all its forms. At the present time it refers generally to the capacity for Earth's biosphere and human civilization to co-exist. In addition to the traditional environmental "green" sustainability concerns, business ethics practices have expanded to include social sustainability. This focuses on issues related to human capital in the business supply chain, such as worker's rights, child labour, and human trafficking. Some business sectors and industries are dedicated to verifying ethical delivery of products from start to finish such as the Kimberly Process which aims to stop the flow of conflict diamonds into international markets, or the Fair Wear Foundation dedicated to sustainability and fairness in the fashion business.

There are many different ways in which sustainability initiatives can be implemented:

1. Operations

    A company can implement sustainability initiatives by improving its operations and manufacturing process in order to make align it with environment, social, and governance requirements. For example, the pharmaceutical manufacturer Johnson & Johnson incorporates policies from the Universal Declaration of Human Rights, the International Covenant on Civil and Political Rights, and the International Covenant on Economic, Social and Cultural Rights, and applies these principles but also to its own internal operations.

2. Leadership

    The board of directors may decide to lower executive pay by a specific amount, and donate this amount to a charitable cause. This kind of initiative can only be implemented by the leadership as it will affect the pay of all executives in the company. However, it is usually the case that the board takes a uniform step on the company's behalf towards dealing with environment, social, and governance ("ESG") issues. This is most often done by establishing an ESG committee of the board.

3. Accountability

    Similar to the board and various committees that may deal with sustainability, the company may appoint senior managers who are identified as being accountable for meeting and if possible exceeding sustainability goals.

4   Remuneration

Remuneration incudes bonus schemes for executives who meet or exceed non-financial performance objectives such as safety targets, greenhouse gas emissions, emission reduction targets, and objectives to engage with stakeholders in order to help the company to determine an appropriate public policy position.

5   Engagement with stakeholders

Companies may decide to keep sustainability at the forefront of its strategy and objectives, presenting relevant information to shareholder meetings, and tracking metrics on sustainability. Companies such as PepsiCo and Heineken have taken steps in this direction to implement sustainability initiatives. Coca-Cola Inc. has tried to improve their efficiency of water usage, hiring external auditors to evaluate their water management approach.

6   Engagement with employees

Companies may also implement sustainability projects through direct engagement with employees. This involves integrating sustainability into the corporate culture, with recruitment practices and employee training. For example, General Electric Corp. in the US is taking the lead in implementing initiatives in this manner.

7   Supply chain

The company may establish requirements for not only its internal operations but also suppliers to help to ensure compliance with environmental and social requirements all along the supply chain. Companies such as Starbucks Inc. and Ford Motor Company have implemented requirements that suppliers must meet to win their business. Starbucks in particular has engaged with suppliers and local communities where they operate to accelerate investment in sustainable farming.

8   Transparency

By revealing data about its decision-making process in relation to sustainability, companies can share insights that can help suppliers and others to make more sustainable business decisions. For example, Nike Inc. launched its "making app" in 2013 which revealed data about the sustainability in the materials it was using. This ultimately allows other companies to make more sustainable design decisions and create products with a lower environmental impact.

Sustainability disclosure

The European Union has given force of law to these requirements. The Sustainable Finance Disclosure Regulation (Regulation (EU) 2019/2088) (the "SFDR") came into effect on 10 March 2021 on a phased basis for different providers financial services. The Regulation introduced sustainability disclosure requirements for financial market participants ("FMPs") and financial advisers.

Fund managers in the European Union and some non-EU fund managers were required to comply with certain SFDR requirements on or before 10 March 2021. These requirements include implementing a policy on integration of sustainability risks into the investment decision-making process, updating remuneration policies to integrate sustainability risks, making sustainability-related disclosures on websites and in fund documents, and periodic reporting in annual reports.

The pre-contractual disclosures for financial products with or without an ESG focus, include:

- disclosure on the integration of sustainability risk in investment decisions or an explanation where not deemed relevant; and
- disclosure of principal adverse impacts on a comply or explain basis.

Additional disclosures are required in respect of products with a specific ESG focus. (See Articles 8 and 9 SFDR.)

Other regulatory technical standards ("RTS") have been developed by regulatory bodies called the European Supervisory Authorities (the "ESAs") and relate to several disclosure obligations provided for by the SFDR. The RTS contain detailed specifications for the content, methodology, and presentation of SFDR disclosure requirements and mandatory templates for pre-contractual and periodic reporting disclosures. The SFDR has been amended by the EU's Corporate Sustainability Reporting Directive of November 2022, so as to apply to a wide range of companies (see Chapter 9).

International standards

There are several international standards for CSR in both the public and private sectors. Many organizations in the public sector, for example the United Nations, adhere to what is called the *triple bottom line* (TBL), as we discussed above. And ISO 26000, adopted by the International Standards Organization (ISO), is the recognized international standard for CSR for private companies and came into force on 1 November 2010. It aims to promote sustainable development around the world by encouraging businesses to practice social responsibility in their dealings with employees, society in general, and the environment.

The general principles of ISO 26000 are as follows:

- Accountability
- Transparency
- Ethical behaviour
- Respect for the interests of stakeholders
- Respect for the rule of law
- Respect for 'international norms of behaviour'
- Respect for human rights

Human rights

Human rights are increasingly relevant for companies who aspire to high standards of corporate social responsibility. They consist of moral principles or norms for certain standards of human behaviour and are protected by national and international laws. These rights are generally understood as inalienable fundamental rights to which an individual is entitled as a human being, regardless of age, ethnic origin, location, language, religion ethnicity or any other status. They are universal and egalitarian in the sense of being the same for everyone. The rule of law ensures they are enforced and cannot be taken away except as a result of due process based on specific circumstances.

The doctrine of human rights has been highly influential within international law and global and regional institutions. Actions by countries and non-governmental organizations form a basis of public policy worldwide. Human rights encompass a wide variety of rights such as the right to a fair trial, protection against slavery, prohibition of genocide, right to free speech and right to education. Many of the basic ideas of human rights movement developed in the aftermath of the Second World War, culminating in the adoption of the Universal Declaration of Human Rights in Paris by the United Nations General Assembly in 1948. The United Nations

Guiding Principles on Business and Human Rights adopted in 2011 provide specific rules for companies to comply with their human rights obligations.[5] An edited version of these Guiding Principles is at Appendix 1.

Sample policy

Below is a sample CSR policy:

CORPORATE SOCIAL RESPONSIBILITY POLICY

[Insert name of company]

Policy purpose

Our Corporate Social Responsibility (CSR) company policy refers to our responsibility toward our environment and the society in which we operate. Our company does not exist in a vacuum. We're part of a bigger system of people, values, other companies and organizations, and the natural world. The social responsibility of our business is to give back to the world just as it gives to us.

These are the values that underlie our CSR policy:

Integrity: Acting with honesty and professionalism, and respecting company policies
Collaboration: Working with colleagues and teams to meet joint objectives
Accountability: Taking responsibility for actions and decisions both in team and individual projects
Social responsibility: Integrating social and environmental solutions to business operations
Innovation: Implementing new ideas to improve the business
Customer orientation: Maximizing and maintaining customer satisfaction

What is corporate social responsibility?

Our Corporate Social Responsibility (CSR) company policy outlines our efforts to give back to the world as it gives to us.

Scope

This policy applies to our company and its subsidiaries. It may also refer to suppliers and partners as appropriate.

Policy elements

We want to be a responsible business that meets the highest standards of ethics and professionalism.

Our company's social responsibility falls under two categories: *compliance* and *proactiveness*. *Compliance* refers to our commitment to legality and willingness to observe community values. *Proactiveness* is every initiative to promote human rights, help communities, and protect the natural environment.

Compliance

Legality

Our company will:

- Respect the law
- Comply with our internal policies
- Ensure that all our business operations are legitimate
- Keep every partnership and collaboration open and transparent

Business ethics

We'll always conduct our business with integrity and respect to human rights. We'll promote:

- Safety and fair dealing
- Respect toward the customer
- Anti-bribery and anti-corruption practices

Examples of Corporate Social Responsibility

Protecting the environment

Our company recognizes the need to protect the natural environment. Keeping our environment clean and unpolluted is a benefit to all. We'll always follow best practices when disposing garbage and using chemical substances. Stewardship will also play an important role.

Protecting people

We'll ensure that we:

- Don't risk the health and safety of our employees and community.
- Avoid harming the lives of local and indigenous people.
- Support diversity and inclusion.

Human rights

Our company is dedicated to protecting human rights. We are a committed equal opportunity employer and will abide by all fair employment practices. We'll ensure that our activities do not directly or indirectly violate human rights in any country, e.g. forced labour.

Proactiveness

Donations and aid

Our company will maintain a budget to make monetary donations. These donations will aim to:

- Advance the arts, education and community events and
- Alleviate those in need

Volunteering

Our company will encourage its employees to volunteer. They can volunteer through programs organized internally or externally. Our company may sponsor volunteering events from other organizations.

Preserving the environment

Apart from legal obligations, our company will proactively protect the environment. Examples of relevant activities include:

- Recycling
- Conserving energy and
- Using environmentally-friendly technologies

Supporting the community

Our company may initiate and support community investment and educational programs. We may provide support to nonprofit organizations or movements to promote cultural and economic development of global and local communities.

Learning

We will actively invest in research and development as a priority. We will be open to suggestions and listen carefully to ideas. Our company will try to continuously improve the way it operates.

Our company is committed to the United Nations Global Compact. We'll readily act to promote our identity as a socially aware and responsible business. Management must communicate this policy on all levels. Managers are also responsible for resolving any CSR issues that are raised internally and externally.

References

1 Benedict Sheedy, "Defining CSR: Problems and Solutions", *Journal of Business Ethics*, 131, no. 3 (October 2015): 625–648.
2 Johnson, Zachary, Huifang Mao, Sarah Lefebvre, and Jaishankar Ganesh, "Good Guys Can Finish First: How Brand Reputation Affects Extension Evaluations", *Journal of Consumer Psychology*, 29, no. 4 (October 2019): 565–583, https://myscp.onlinelibrary.wiley.com/doi/abs/10.1002/jcpy.1109.
3 Abagail McWilliams and Donald Siegel, "Corporate social responsibility: A theory of the firm perspective". *Academy of Management Review*, 26, no. 1 (January 2001): 117–127, www.jstor.org/stable/259398.
4 Timothy F. Slaper and Tanya J. Hall, "The Triple Bottom Line: What Is It and How Does It Work?", *Indiana Business Review*, Spring 2011, 86, no. 1 (Spring 2011): 4–8, www.ibrc.indiana.edu/ibr/2011/spring/article2.html.
5 United Nations Human Rights, Office of the High Commissioner, Guiding Principles on Business and Human Rights", HR/PUB/11/04, (2011): www.ohchr.org/documents/publications/guidingprinciplesbusinesshr_en.pdf.

7

HEALTH AND SAFETY

Introduction

From a compliance point of view, "health and safety" refers to the many laws, regulations, and codes of practice that govern the welfare of employers and employees in the workplace. In the UK and in EU member states, employers have a legal duty to ensure as far as possible the health, safety and welfare of their employees while at work.[1] Many other countries have similar laws. But in a wider sense health and safety, or *occupational health and safety* to be exact, are about promoting wellbeing at work, that is comfort and contentment in the office or factory. In this sense health and safety goes beyond keeping workers safe from illness, disease, and accidents, and focuses on:

- Promoting and maintaining a high level of physical, mental and social wellbeing for workers;
- Preventing absence from work due to poor health caused by working conditions;

DOI: 10.4324/9781003258995-9

- Protecting workers from health risks at work; and
- Assessing the employee's working conditions, and adapting to his or her physical and mental needs.

According to the World Health Organisation, health means "a state of complete physical, mental and social wellbeing and not merely the absence of disease or infirmity". Obviously this is in the company's interests because employees with health problems are more likely to be absent from work, less productive while at work, and more likely to leave the company. The importance of health and safety can be seen from the global statistics. There are more than 2.7 million deaths in the workplace every year and 370 million work-related injuries. Health and safety problems are estimated to cost almost 4% of the world's Gross Domestic Product (GDP) every year.[2]

At a minimum, in order to comply with the legal requirements the business must identify any hazards within the workplace, assess the risks presented by these hazards, and implement control measures to mitigate those risks. In the UK this must be done in writing unless there are five employees or less.[3] (Hazards and risks are not the same. A hazard is anything that could cause injury or illness, e.g. stress, and risk is the likelihood of harm caused by a hazard.) There is also a legal requirement to have a written health and safety policy, including steps on how to implement the policy. The policy is important to ensure the company has done everything "reasonably practicable" as a business to ensure the safety of its employees. An employer is obliged by law to protect employees and others from harm.

Employers' duty

In the UK and many other countries, an employer's duty to provide a safe and healthy working environment arise from the core principles of negligence, contract, and numerous specific statutory duties. In particular, employers in the UK are obliged to:

- Publish a health and safety policy if they employ more than five people;
- Put in place an insurance policy to provide cover for employees against accidents and ill- health;
- Arrange for the appointment of health and safety representatives;
- Establish a health and safety committee if requested by a recognized trade union;

HEALTH AND SAFETY

- Appoint a competent person to evaluate risks and hazards;
- Arrange periodic risk assessments;
- Provide adequate safety training to address risks, as appropriate;
- Monitor and improve safety arrangements;
- Adapt work to the needs of employees, in particular the design of the workplace;
- Establish procedures to be followed in the event of serious and imminent danger to employees.

An employer must provide a system of work and a working environment that are as safe as possible and without risk to health. The duty extends to providing maintenance of safe equipment, information, training, supervision, and adequate support. An employer must also provide a safe place of work to employees and visitors to the premises. All organizations must take precautionary measures to control fire risks, provide fire escape routes and training, and carry out fire safety risk assessments. Under smoke-free legislation, display "no smoking" signs in all enclosed workplaces and shared vehicles. There are minimum standards for workplaces and work in or near buildings. These include: proper ventilation by ensuring a sufficient quantity of fresh and purified air; maintaining a reasonable temperature, and the provision of thermometers; suitable, sufficient, and natural light so far as possible.[4]

Every employer must undertake risk assessments on a regular basis. In a typical workplace such as a standard office, the assessment will be straightforward but it may be complicated in the case of serious hazards that occur in specific workplaces such as a nuclear power station, a chemical plant, laboratory, or an oil rig. A comprehensive risk assessment will include workstations, noise, specific hazards, and stress that may affect employees' mental health.

EU requirements

The European Union has implemented many rules and regulations about health and safety. The European Commission is committed to a Strategic Framework on Health and Safety at Work 2021–2027 that defines the key priorities and actions for improving workers' health and safety, addressing rapid changes in the economy, demography, and work patterns. A dedicated EU organization is responsible for these matters, the European Agency for Safety and Health at Work. The Agency has provided guidance on relevant subjects, including a return to work after COVID-19:[5]

> COVID-19: Resources for the workplace
>
> The COVID-19 pandemic is one of the biggest challenges that societies and businesses have faced. Overcoming this challenge will be possible only if we work together to stop the spread of this disease and provide a safe and healthy working environment for both home-based teleworkers and those returning to their usual workplaces. This section presents a collection of guidance documents, awareness-raising material and further links on the topic.
>
> At workplaces where workers can be exposed to a virus, which belongs to the category biological agents, employers have to carry out a workplace risk assessment and set appropriate measures. The guidance presented on this page is aimed at supporting employers in these duties. The minimum legal requirements are laid out in the Biological Agents Directive[6]
>
> What can workplaces do in practice to help tackle this pandemic and protect employees? Knowledge and awareness are key — everyone must be well informed about how the virus spreads, the symptoms of infection and how to minimise exposure. Our guidance helps organisations to provide workers with the information they need and put measures in place to prevent infection.

The COVID-19 pandemic has presented a unique challenge for companies in complying with health and safety requirements. This has led to many companies allowing their employees to work from home or some location away from the office. We will discuss remote working in Chapter 14.

ISO 45001

According to the International Labour Organization, more than 7,600 people around the world die from work-related accidents or diseases *every day*. An international standard for occupational health and safety (ISO 45001) aims to help companies and organisations to improve employee safety and health, reduce workplace risks, and create better, safer working conditions for everyone.[7] Any company that aspires to complying with the standard will need to:

1   Perform an analysis of the operations of interested parties, i.e. those individuals or organizations that can affect the company's operations, as well as internal and external factors that may affect the company's

business. How can these risks be controlled through the health and safety management system?
2   Establish the scope of the system, while considering what the system is designed to achieve.
3   Based on steps 1 and 2, establish the company's health and safety processes, risk evaluation/assessment and set the key performance indicators (KPIs) for these processes.

The benefits of implementing ISO 45001 are many if done correctly. While the standard requires that health and safety risks be addressed and controlled, it adopts a risk-based approach to the health and safety management system itself in order to ensure that it is effective and that it is being continually improved to meet an organization's ever-changing needs. Moreover, it ensures compliance with current legislation worldwide. All of these measures can establish the company's reputation as a safe place to work and a host of benefits, from lower insurance costs to improved employee morale.

ISO 45001 certification is not mandatory but operates as an endorsement that demonstrates to third parties such as customers and suppliers that the company has achieved compliance with a recognized international standard. ISO 45001 provides many benefits for companies who achieve certification of compliance with the standard. Certification will enable companies to:

- Develop and implement a comprehensive health and safety policy;
- Establish robust processes to deal with health and safety risks with the legal requirements;
- Establish operational controls to mitigate the risks that have been identified;
- Increase awareness of health and safety among the company's employees;
- Evaluate the company's performance and seek to improve it;
- Reduce the number and cost of work accidents incidents; and
- Reduce absenteeism and staff turnover.

Health and safety policy

A health and safety policy should demonstrate the company's commitment to managing health and safety in an effective manner. The policy will operate as statement of intent to provide a safe and healthy working environment. It must be workable and easily accessible and communicated to all employees. Specific responsibilities should be assigned to named individuals or roles. The document should include risk assessments and arrangements for employee consultation, maintaining equipment, and safe handling of substances if necessary.

Ideally the policy should be prepared and adopted following consultation with employees and a survey of employee attitudes to health and safety. The policy should be applied uniformly throughout the organization and there should be a process to ensure regular monitoring and review of the policy to ensure that it complies with current legislation.

In addition to best practice, the law in many countries requires that every company must have a formal policy for health and safety. At a minimum, the policy will set out the company's approach in general terms, how it will manage health and safety in the organization, and who does what. However, a comprehensive health and safety policy will address all matters we have discussed in this chapter.

Sample health and safety policy

Below is a template for a health and safety policy[8] provided by the Health and Safety Executive UK.

Part 1: Statement of intent
This is the health and safety policy statement of: [name of company]
   Our health and safety policy is to: [description of company's commitment and approach]

Signed: Date:
Print name:
Review date:

Part 2: Responsibilities for health and safety
1   Overall and final responsibility for health and safety: [name(s)/position(s)]
2   Day-to-day responsibility for ensuring this policy is put into practice: [name(s)/position(s)]

3   To ensure health and safety standards are maintained/improved, the following people have responsibility in the following areas: [names]
4   All employees should:

- co-operate with supervisors and managers on health and safety matters;
- take reasonable care of their own health and safety; and
- report all health and safety concerns to an appropriate person (as detailed above).

Part 3: Arrangements for health and safety
Risk assessment:
Training:
Consultation:
Evaluation:

References

1. Workplace (Health, Safety and Welfare) Regulations 1992, No. 3004. Available at: /www.legislation.gov.uk/uksi/1992/3004/contents/made (Accessed: 13 September 2023).
2. International Labour Organization, "ILO: Work Hazards Kill Millions, Cost Billions", 23 May 2023, www.ilo.org/global/about-the-ilo/newsroom/news/WCMS_075615/lang--en/index.htm.
3. Management of Health and Safety at Work Regulations 1999, No. 3242. Available at: www.legislation.gov.uk/uksi/1999/3242/contents/made (Accessed: 13 September 2023).
4. Workplace (Health, Safety and Welfare) Regulations 1992, No. 3004. Available at: www.legislation.gov.uk/uksi/1992/3004/contents/made (Accessed: 13 September 2023).
5. European Agency for Safety and Health at Work, "Healthy Workplaces Stop the Pandemic", ttps://osha.europa.eu/en/themes/covid-19-resources-workplace#pk_campaign=ban_homecw.
6. Directive 2000/54/EC of the European Parliament and of the Council of 18 September 2000 on the protection of workers from risks related to exposure to biological agents at work (seventh individual directive within the meaning of Article 16(1) of Directive 89/391/EEC) (2000) *Official Journal* L 262 17.10.2000, p. 21, Amended by: Commission Directive (EU) 2019/1833 of 24 October 2019, *Official Journal* L 279, p. 54; and Commission Directive (EU) 2020/739 of 3 June 2020 (2020) *Official Journal* L 175 11.

7 International Organization for Standardization, 2018, *ISO 45001 – All you need to know*. Available at: www.iso.org/news/ref2271.html (Accessed: 13 September 2023).
8 Reproduced in accordance with UK Open Government Licence at www.nationalarchives.gov.uk/doc/open-government-licence/version/3/.

8

FAIR EMPLOYMENT

Introduction

Every company wants to be seen as a good corporate citizen. This is essential for its reputation and therefore its business. No-one wants to buy from a company that damages the environment or its partners and suppliers and is seen to behave in this way. An important part of the public perception of the company is how the company treats its employees and prospective employees. Does it treat people fairly when hiring and firing and everything in between? Fair employment means treating people on a basis of equality without discrimination or segregation, especially because of race, colour, or religion. What is the company's policy on all of this?

Employment law

As in the case of many other policy commitments, the starting point is the law. A substantial body of laws in the UK, EU member states, and many other countries protect people in the workplace against unfair treatment such as discrimination and harassment. In the UK it is unlawful to discriminate against a person on grounds of age, disability, gender, marriage and civil partnership, race, religion, pregnancy and maternity, or sexual orientation. These are referred to as the "protected characteristics". The main legislation is the Equality Act 2010 which outlaws discrimination in access to education, public services, private goods and services, transport or premises as well as employment. Discrimination on the grounds of work status, that is, part-time, fixed-term, agency worker or union membership is banned by other UK legislation. This reflects to a large extent EU directives and regulations that applied to the UK pre-Brexit.

What conduct amounts to unlawful discrimination? Discrimination is unlawful when an employer makes an adverse decision about an employee or a group of employees on the basis of a protected characteristic, except for age. (There may be a legitimate business reason to discriminate on the basis of age.) The decision may be recruitment, promotion, demotion, or dismissal. Another exception is an "occupational requirement", so that for instance a female role in a play or film may be refused to a male actor. Conduct may amount to harassment or even victimization if it meets the legal definitions.[1] Harassment is unwanted conduct related to one or more of someone's protected characteristics and that has the purpose or effect of violating that person's dignity or creating an intimidating, hostile, degrading, humiliating, or offensive environment for him or her. Victimization means subjecting someone to harassment after they try to complain about discrimination.

Employees are entitled to "reasonable notice" before dismissal after one month's employment. They can only be dismissed after two years for a "fair" reason and are entitled to a redundancy payment if their job was no longer necessary. If the company is sold or an employee's role is outsourced, specific legislation provides that terms and conditions of employment cannot suffer without good reason.[2] All of these rights seek to protect security of employment and a decent standard of living for employees.

Fair employment policy

The company's fair employment policy will confirm its commitment to fairness and industry best practice, in addition to compliance with all of the legal and regulatory obligations outlined in this chapter. The policy should state the company's commitment to diversity and inclusion, equality and the modern slavery legislation. The policy may be a stand-alone document or form part of an employee handbook or similar document given to all employees.

At the end of this chapter is a sample fair employment policy to ensure compliance with best practice and with relevant legal and regulatory obligations.

Diversity and Inclusion

"Our employees are the company's greatest asset." This is an oft-repeated statement in annual reports and press releases, and is designed to show how much the company values its workforce. But the question remains as to the make-up of the workforce itself. In addition to treating employees fairly and obeying the law, has the company taken steps to ensure diversity and inclusion?

Diversity and inclusion are concepts that have much in common but they are quite distinct. Diversity aims to ensure that the workforce represents all sorts of people – different ages, genders, nationalities, and sexual orientations. Inclusion is about giving everyone an equal opportunity to contribute to all parts of the business, and valuing the contributions of everyone in equal measure. So inclusion goes further to see that everyone in a diverse workplace can contribute and be valued.

There are many benefits from a diverse and inclusive workforce:[3]

- Revenue growth – employees in a trusting, caring workplace are 44% more likely to work for a company with above-average revenue growth.
- Innovation – diverse teams inspire each other to generate new ideas.
- Recruitment – greater ability to recruit a diverse talent pool. Like attracts like.
- Retention – 5.4 times higher employee retention than industry standard

Diversity and inclusion do not only apply to managers and employees. The company's directors should also reflect the diversity of people in our society and should also have an equal opportunity to contribute to the business. The UK Corporate Governance Code 2018 provides for the selection and performance of directors in this regard:[4]

The annual report should describe the work of the nomination committee, including:

- *the process used in relation to appointments, its approach to succession planning and how both support developing a diverse pipeline;*
- *how the board evaluation has been conducted, the nature and extent of an external evaluator's contact with the board and individual directors, the outcomes and actions taken, and how it has or will influence board composition;*
- *the policy on diversity and inclusion, its objectives and linkage to company strategy, how it has been implemented and progress on achieving the objectives.*

Modern Slavery

Some of us might believe that slavery disappeared with the American Civil War or the slums of Dickensian London. Sadly this is not so. Fifty million people were living in modern slavery in 2021, according to the latest Global Estimates of Modern Slavery. Of these people, 28 million were in forced labour and 22 million were trapped in forced marriage.

The number of people in modern slavery has risen significantly in the last five years. 10 million more people were in modern slavery in 2021 compared to 2016 global estimates. Women and children remain disproportionately vulnerable.

Modern slavery occurs in almost every country in the world, and cuts across ethnic, cultural, and religious lines. More than half (52 per cent) of all forced labour and a quarter of all forced marriages can be found in upper-middle income or high-income countries. In 2019, 40 million people approximately throughout the world, a quarter of them children, were slaves even though it is illegal, apart from being immoral and inhuman.[5] More than half of all enslaved people perform forced labour in the factories and sweatshops of many countries.[6] Slavery is the state of being of someone who is forbidden to quit their labour or service for another person, while treated as that person's property. Typically the slave is forced to perform some form of work dictated by his or her "owner".

Human trafficking is a modern version of slavery. This is the trade of human beings for the purpose of forced labour or commercial or sexual exploitation. It constitutes a crime against the person because of a violation of the rights of free movement and freedom to work or provide services. *Modern slavery* is the term used to refer to slavery that continues to exist in the 21st century. The UK government took the lead in legislative terms by introducing the Modern Slavery Act 2015 which was designed to combat modern slavery in the UK. This legislation was supported by other UK legislation such as the Criminal Finances Act 2017 which focused on money laundering offences related to modern slavery and tax evasion attributed to the modern slave trade.

The 2015 Act provides that companies and organizations of a certain size must publish a statement of their compliance with the legal requirements, that is, businesses over a certain size must disclose each year what action they have taken to ensure there is no modern slavery in their business or supply chains. This applies to companies with an annual global turnover of more than £36 million. The Act provides the tools to fight modern slavery, ensured that guilty parties receive severe punishment for their crimes, and enhance support and protection for victims. The Act also provides for courts to make reparation orders to compensate victims where assets are confiscated from the guilty party.

At the end of this chapter is a sample statement in line with the requirements of the 2015 Act.

Sample policy documents

Fair Employment Policy

Objective
[company name] is an equal opportunity employer. In accordance with equality and anti-discrimination laws, it is the purpose of this policy to ensure full compliance with the principles underlying these legal requirements. [company name] prohibits discrimination and harassment of any kind and affords equal employment opportunities to employees and applicants without regard to race, colour, religion, sex, sexual orientation, gender identity or expression, pregnancy, age, national origin, disability status, genetic information, protected veteran status, or any other characteristic protected by law. [company name] conforms to the spirit as well as to the letter of all applicable laws and regulations.

Scope

The policy of equal employment opportunity and anti-discrimination applies to all aspects of the relationship between [company name] and its employees, including:

- Recruitment
- Employment
- Promotion
- Transfer
- Training
- Working conditions
- Wages and salary administration and
- Employee benefits and application of policies.

The policies and principles of fair employment also apply to the selection and treatment of independent contractors, personnel working on our premises who are employed by temporary agencies and any other persons or firms doing business for or with [company name].

Dissemination and implementation of policy

The directors and officers of [company name] will be responsible for the dissemination of this policy. Directors, managers, and supervisors are responsible for implementing fair employment practices within each department. The HR department is responsible for compliance and will maintain personnel records in compliance with applicable laws and regulations.

Procedures

[company name] administers our fair employment policy fairly and consistently by:

- Posting all required notices regarding employee rights under applicable laws in areas highly visible to employees;
- Advertising for job openings with the statement "*We are an equal opportunity employer and all qualified applicants will receive consideration for employment without regard to race, colour, religion, sex, sexual orientation, gender identity or expression, pregnancy, age, national origin, disability status, genetic information, protected veteran status, or any other characteristic protected by law*";

- Posting all required job openings with the appropriate state agencies and other third parties;
- Forbidding retaliation against any individual who makes a complaint of discrimination, opposes a practice believed to be unlawful discrimination, reports harassment, or assists, testifies, or participates in any proceedings to do with fair employment;
- Requires employees to report to a member of management, an HR representative or the legal department any apparent discrimination or harassment. The report should be made within 48 hours of the incident;
- Promptly notifies the legal department of all incidents or reports of discrimination or harassment and takes other appropriate measures to resolve the situation.

Harassment
Harassment is a form of unlawful discrimination and violates [company name] policy. Prohibited sexual harassment, for example, is defined as unwelcome sexual advances, request for sexual favours, and other verbal or physical conduct of a sexual nature when:

- Submission to such conduct is made either explicitly or implicitly a term or condition of an individual's employment;
- Submission to or rejection of such conduct by an individual is used as the basis for employment decisions affecting that individual; or
- Such conduct has the purpose or effect of substantially interfering with an individual's work performance or creating an intimidating, hostile or offensive working environment.

Harassment also includes unwelcome conduct that is based on race, colour, religion, sex, sexual orientation, gender identity or expression, pregnancy, age, national origin, disability status, genetic information, protected veteran status, or any other characteristic protected by law. Harassment becomes unlawful where:

- Enduring the offensive conduct becomes a condition of continued employment; or
- The conduct is severe or pervasive enough to create a work environment that a reasonable person would consider intimidating, hostile, or abusive.

[company name] encourages employees to report all incidents of harassment to a member of management or the HR department. [company name] conducts harassment prevention training for all employees, and maintains and enforces a separate policy on harassment prevention, complaint procedures and penalties for violations. [company name] investigates all complaints of harassment promptly and fairly, and, when appropriate, takes immediate corrective action to stop the harassment and prevent it from recurring.

Remedies
Violations of this policy, regardless of whether an actual law has been violated, will not be tolerated. [company name] will promptly, thoroughly, and fairly investigate every issue that is brought to its attention in this area and will take disciplinary action, when appropriate, up to and including termination of employment.

Modern Slavery Statement

[company name] has taken steps to ensure that slavery and human trafficking is not taking place in any part of our business or in any third party we do business with.

The UK Modern Slavery Act 2015 provides as follows:

Transparency in supply chains, etc.

(1) A commercial organisation within subsection (2) must prepare a slavery and human trafficking statement for each financial year of the organisation.
(2) A commercial organisation is within this subsection if it—
  (a) supplies goods or services, and
  (b) has a total turnover of not less than an amount prescribed by regulations made by the Secretary of State.
(3) For the purposes of subsection (2)(b), an organisation's total turnover is to be determined in accordance with regulations made by the Secretary of State.
(4) A slavery and human trafficking statement for a financial year is—

(a) a statement of the steps the organisation has taken during the financial year to ensure that slavery and human trafficking is not taking place—
   (i) in any of its supply chains, and
   (ii) in any part of its own business, or
(b) a statement that the organisation has taken no such steps.

(5) An organisation's slavery and human trafficking statement may include information about—

(a) the organisation's structure, its business and its supply chains;
(b) its policies in relation to slavery and human trafficking;
(c) its due diligence processes in relation to slavery and human trafficking in its business and supply chains;
(d) the parts of its business and supply chains where there is a risk of slavery and human trafficking taking place, and the steps it has taken to assess and manage that risk;
(e) its effectiveness in ensuring that slavery and human trafficking is not taking place in its business or supply chains, measured against such performance indicators as it considers appropriate;
(f) the training about slavery and human trafficking available to its staff.

(6) A slavery and human trafficking statement—

(a) if the organisation is a body corporate other than a limited liability partnership, must be approved by the board of directors (or equivalent management body) and signed by a director (or equivalent);
(b) if the organisation is a limited liability partnership, must be approved by the members and signed by a designated member;
(c) if the organisation is a limited partnership registered under the Limited Partnerships Act 1907, must be signed by a general partner;
(d) if the organisation is any other kind of partnership, must be signed by a partner.

(7) If the organisation has a website, it must—

(a) publish the slavery and human trafficking statement on that website, and
(b) include a link to the slavery and human trafficking statement in a prominent place on that website's homepage.

(8) If the organisation does not have a website, it must provide a copy of the slavery and human trafficking statement to anyone who makes a written request for one, and must do so before the end of the period of 30 days beginning with the day on which the request is received.

This statement sets out the steps that [company name] has taken to ensure that slavery and human trafficking does not take place in our supply chains or in any part of our business. This statement is in respect of the company's financial year ended [date of year end] and was approved by the Board of Directors on [date of approval].

Overview
The Modern Slavery Act 2015 requires commercial organisations supplying goods or services with a turnover of more than £36 million to prepare and publish an annual slavery and human trafficking statement. The statement must set out the steps an organisation has taken, if any, during its financial year to ensure that slavery or human trafficking is not taking place in its business or supply chain.

What is modern slavery?
Modern slavery is an international crime, affecting millions of people around the world – a growing global issue that transcends age, gender, and race. Vulnerable people from overseas as well as across the UK, are forced to work illegally against their will across many different sectors from agriculture, construction, hospitality, retail, manufacturing, and more.

Organisation structure and supply chain
[name of company] is a private company registered in [name of country].

Our business employs a wide range of people with different skills and experiences either as full-time employees, part-time employees, or independent contractors. Our policies ensure fair treatment of all employees and contractors.

Our external suppliers are mostly UK, EU, and US-based companies in low-risk sectors such as professional services, as well as suppliers in other sectors such as events and travel which are potentially higher risk.

Our policies in relation to slavery and human trafficking
[company name] has established a zero-tolerance position on violations to the UK anti-human trafficking and anti-modern slavery laws. If we find

breaches of these laws within our supply chain, we will work with these companies in their efforts to comply with the legislation.

The values of collaboration, leadership, excellence, agility, respect, and responsibility are the pillars of our culture. They embody everything that we do at [company name] and how we do business. They outline the expectation of our people's behaviour with colleagues, customers and suppliers.

We seek to treat everyone fairly and consistently, creating a workplace and business environment that is open, transparent, and trusted. Our policies and procedures relating to the Modern Slavery Act are in line with our culture and values.

Our specific procedures to address modern slavery risk include:

- A modern slavery policy for our people, which sets out the key issues and how we should respond including a process for raising concerns internally;
- An ethics hotline that allows for anonymous reports to be submitted by our people;
- A process for handling complaints raised by people outside the company;
- Employment policies that protect our people from unfair treatment and promote a fair and inclusive workplace;
- Robust recruitment processes in line with relevant employment laws;
- Market-related pay and rewards reviewed annually;
- Wellbeing strategy and initiatives to support our people's physical and mental wellbeing and lifestyle choices;
- A procurement policy for how we deal with suppliers and a supplier code of conduct making clear the standards we expect.

Due diligence processes, risk assessment and management

The implementation of our policies and procedures includes due diligence on suppliers that we engage with, in accordance with our procurement policy. A heightened risk area is the use of hotel and conference facilities and providers of travel services. To mitigate against this risk, we assess the companies that we deal with as part of the decision-making process for events and travel.

<u>Key performance indicators to measure the effectiveness of steps being taken</u>
We log complaints received via our ethics hotline system or through other sources, together with the actions taken.

<u>Training on modern slavery and trafficking</u>
[company name] provides periodic training to our people on the subject of modern slavery and our policies to address the risks to help increase education and awareness.

<u>Review and update</u>
[company name] takes responsibility for this Statement and its related objectives and will review and update it in accordance with the relevant legislation.

References

1. *Equality Act 2010*, c.15. Available at: www.legislation.gov.uk/ukpga/2010/15/contents (Accessed: 13 September 2023).
2. Transfer of Undertakings (Protection of Employment) Regulations 2006, S.I. 2006/246. Available at: https://en.wikipedia.org/wiki/Transfer_of_Undertakings_(Protection_of_Employment)_Regulations_2006 (Accessed: 13 September 2023).
3. Great Place to Work Institute, "Why is Diversity and Inclusion in the Workplace Important?", www.greatplacetowork.com/resources/blog/why-is-diversity-inclusion-in-the-workplace-important.
4. Financial Reporting Council, "The UK Corporate Governance Code", July 2018, www.frc.org.uk/directors/corporate-governance/uk-corporate-governance-code#:~:text=UK%20Corporate%20Governance%20Code%202018%20(Current%20edition),-UK%20Corporate%20Governance&text=The%20Code%20is%20separated%20into,'comply%20or%20explain'%20basis.
5. International Labour Organization, "50 Million People Worldwide in Modern Slavery", 12 September 2022, www.ilo.org/global/about-the-ilo/newsroom/news/WCMS_855019/lang--en/index.htm.
6. Annie Kelly, "Fifty Million People Now Trapped in Modern Slavery in a 'Surge of Exploitation'", *The Guardian*, 12 September 2022, www.theguardian.com/global-development/2022/sep/12/ten-million-more-people-now-trapped-in-slavery-report-says.

9

ENVIRONMENT AND SUSTAINABILITY

Introduction

The environment dominates not only the media and public debate but also all of our concerns about the future of the planet. Without a healthy planet, there is no mankind or any other species. In November 2022 the world's elite gathered at the COP27 climate conference in Sharm el-Sheikh in Egypt in yet another "last-ditch" effort to reach an agreement and avoid disaster. The rest of us could only hope and pray they succeeded, and then do our bit for the sake of the planet and ourselves. In this chapter, we consider the policy implications of environmental damage and what commitments can be made by companies to play their part as good corporate citizens.

This global conference came at a difficult time in the aftermath of the COVID-19 pandemic. Among other things, the COP27 conference tried to set ambitious climate targets and overhaul the status quo on energy production and use. World leaders descended on Sharm el-Sheikh for the conference that was billed as the "last, best chance" to curb carbon emissions and slow global warming. This was the 27th COP, or Conference of the Parties. It aimed at reaching an agreement on compensation for environmental loss and damage, and an agreement to hold companies and organizations to account for their environmental impact, all the while continuing international efforts to reach net zero carbon emissions by 2050 and to limit global warming to 1.5 degrees Celsius above pre-industrial levels. .

An edited version of the Sharm el-Sheikh Implementation Plan 2022 is at Appendix 2.

It is perhaps the greatest truism of all that the environment is all around us, both the natural environment and man-made. And it surrounds us not only as individuals in our own lives but also the companies and organizations that must operate within the constraints imposed by it. We have no choice but to respect the natural environment and as we approach the middle of the 21st century we are finally learning the lesson that a heavy price will be paid if we continue to carry on regardless of the consequences of our actions, individual and corporate. In July 2021 many parts of western Germany were subject to heavy floods, and Siberia of all places endured a heat wave that severely damaged the flora and fauna of that region. And in June 2023 Sardinia and Sicily saw temperatures of 48 degrees Celsius, the highest ever recorded in Europe. Science tells us these and other events are not normal and are directly caused by human activity.

The natural environment encompasses all living things in the world that occur naturally and not by artificial or man-made means. It represents the interaction of all species of animals and plants, the climate, weather, and natural resources that affect human survival and economic activity. "Habitat" is a word often used to describe the natural resources of an area that support a species of animal or plant. There are two components of the natural environment:

- "Ecological units" that function as natural systems with defined boundaries, including vegetation, soil, and the atmosphere; and
- Natural resources such as air, water, and climate, as well as energy, radiation, and magnetism, i.e. magnetic interaction between elements.

The built environment consists of urban and rural landscapes where humans have effectively created a *human environment* out of the natural world. In this way, part of the natural environment has become an artificial one.

In addition to the natural environment on land, we have made a lasting impact on the oceans, lakes, and rivers. Humans have modified rivers through dams and diversions, building cities and planting forests beside them. These have affected water levels and water quality and prevented the migration of fish. The effects of *global warming* have also been well documented. These include climate change and its interaction with the release of greenhouse gases such as carbon dioxide and methane, which trap heat inside the Earth's atmosphere and turn it back towards the Earth. Global warming is also responsible for the extinction of natural habitats, which has damaged the wildlife population of the world.

Mankind seems to have woken up at last to the damage it is doing to the natural world. The so-called environmental movement aims to:

- Eliminate pollution and toxins in air, water and soil;
- Preserve biodiversity and protect endangered species of plants and animals;
- Conserve and use natural resources such as water, land, and air in a sustainable manner;
- Halt global warming, which causes pollution and is a threat to biodiversity;
- Move from fossil fuels such as coal and oil to renewable energy in electricity, heating, and transport;
- Manage and reduce waste by various means such as recycling – a key element of the "circular economy"; and
- Reducing unnecessary consumption.

All of these objectives form part of what is often referred to by the acronym ESG – environment, social, and governance. ESG sets out specific criteria to define environmental, social, and governance objectives. (Many of these objectives are discussed in other chapters of this book.)

> <u>Environmental</u> – Materials, energy use, greenhouse gas emissions, water use, waste, biodiversity, pollution;
> <u>Social</u> – Human rights, employment rights, health and safety, diversity and inclusion, training and development, responsible sourcing, community engagement, product safety, customer safety, access and affordability, responsible marketing/advertising/labelling;

Governance – Livelihoods, procurement, legal and compliance, business ethics, legal and compliance, business ethics, data protection/privacy, tax transparency, risk management.

Sustainability

The concept of *sustainability* underlies all three elements of ESG. In a business context, sustainability can mean different things to different businesses and is applied as an umbrella term of simply doing good in the world. This means doing good for the environment and society, and putting in place the necessary checks and balances, that is, corporate governance, to ensure a sustainable business.

A generally accepted definition of sustainability is as follows:

> Sustainable development is development that meets the needs of the present without compromising the ability of future generations to meet their own needs.
> (*Our Common Future*, United Nations 1987)

The United Nations has adopted a set of Sustainable Development Goals[1] as follows:

1. *No Poverty*: Access to basic human needs of health, education, sanitation
2. *Zero Hunger*: Providing food and humanitarian relief, establishing sustainable food production
3. *Good Health and Wellbeing*: Better, more accessible health systems to increase life-expectancy
4. *Quality Education*: Inclusive education to enable upward social mobility and end poverty
5. *Gender Equality*: Education regardless of gender, advancement of equality laws, fairer representation of women
6. *Clean Water and Sanitation*: Improving access for billions of people who lack these basic facilities
7. *Affordable and Clean Energy*: Access to renewable, safe, and widely available energy sources for all
8. *Decent Work and Economic Growth*: Creating jobs for all to improve living standards, providing sustainable economic growth

9 *Industry, Innovation, and Infrastructure*: Generating employment and income through innovation
10 *Reduced Inequalities*: Reducing income and other inequalities, within and between countries
11 *Sustainable Cities and Communities*: Making cities safe, inclusive, resilient, and sustainable
12 *Responsible Consumption and Production*: Reversing current consumption trends and promoting a more sustainable future
13 *Climate Action*: Regulating and reducing emissions and promoting renewable energy
14 *Life Below Water*: Conservation, promoting marine diversity and regulating fishing practices
15 *Life on Land*: Reversing man-made deforestation and desertification to sustain all life on earth
16 *Peace, Justice and Strong Institutions*: Inclusive societies, strong institutions, and equal access to justice
17 *Partnerships for the Goals*: Revitalize strong global partnerships for sustainable development

European Union

The European Union (EU) may have the most advanced environmental laws of any country or group of countries. These laws address matters such as acid rain, the thinning of the ozone layer, air quality, noise pollution, waste, water pollution, and sustainable energy. And the EU has some of the world's highest environmental standards aimed at making the EU economy become more environmentally friendly, protect Europe's natural resources, and safeguard the health and wellbeing of people living in the Union. The EU implements a wide range of policies on climate change and is committed to ensuring the successful implementation of the Paris Agreement and the EU's Emissions Trading System. The Paris Agreement, often referred to as the Paris Accords or the Paris Climate Accords, is an international treaty on climate change, adopted in 2015. It covers climate change mitigation and adaptation. The fight against climate change is an explicit objective of EU environmental policy.[2]

The EU has recognized that climate change and environmental degradation are an existential threat to Europe and the world. To overcome these challenges, the European Green Deal will transform the EU into a modern, resource-efficient and competitive economy, ensuring:

- no net emissions of greenhouse gases by 2050;
- economic growth decoupled from resource use; and
- "no person and no place left behind".

The European Commission has adopted a set of proposals designed to ensure that the EU's climate, energy, transport, and taxation policies contribute to reducing net greenhouse gas emissions by at least 55%.

EU law requires certain large companies to disclose information on the way they operate and manage social and environmental challenges. This helps investors, civil society organizations, consumers, policy makers, and other stakeholders to evaluate the non-financial performance of large companies and encourages these companies to develop a responsible approach to business. An EU Directive of 2014[3] – also called the Non-Financial Reporting Directive (NFRD) – lays down the rules on disclosure of non-financial and diversity information by certain large companies. (This Directive amended the Accounting Directive of 2013.[4])

EU rules on non-financial reporting currently apply to large public-interest companies with more than 500 employees. This covers approximately 11,700 large companies and groups across the EU, including:

- listed companies
- banks
- insurance companies and
- other companies designated by national authorities as "public-interest entities".

The NFRD provides that all of these large companies must publish information related to:

- environmental matters
- social matters and treatment of employees
- respect for human rights
- anti-corruption and bribery and
- diversity on company boards (in terms of age, gender, educational and professional background).

In June, 2017 the European Commission published its guidelines to help companies to disclose environmental and social information in accordance with the NFRD. These guidelines were not mandatory and companies could decide to use international, European, or national guidelines according to their own characteristics or business environment. In June 2019 the Commission published guidelines on reporting climate-related information, which in practice consisted of a supplement to the existing guidelines on non-financial reporting, which remained applicable.

Corporate Sustainability Reporting Directive

In April 2021 the Commission adopted a proposal for a Corporate Sustainability Reporting Directive (CSRD) which would amend the reporting requirements of the NFRD. The proposal:

- extended the scope to all large companies and all companies listed on regulated markets;
- required the audit of reported information;
- introduced more detailed reporting requirements and a requirement to report according to mandatory EU sustainability reporting standards; and
- required companies to digitally "tag" the reported information, so it is machine readable and feeds into the European single access point envisaged in the capital markets union action plan.

The Commission's proposal for a CSRD envisages the adoption of EU sustainability reporting standards. The draft standards would be developed by the European Financial Reporting Advisory Group (EFRAG). The standards were tailored to EU policies, while building on and contributing to international standardisation initiatives.

In November, 2022 the European Parliament adopted these standards and the Commission's proposal for the CSRD. These expanded the scope of the reporting requirements from approximately 11,700 entities under the NFRD to approximately 49,000 entities under the CSRD. The CSRD amends and updates the NFRD not only by expanding the number of companies but also by widening the reporting requirements to include environmental matters. The CSRD came into force on 18 December 2022.[5]

Unlike the NFRD, the CSRD specifies the format of disclosure and standards that companies must use for their reports. The CSRD also emphasises "double materiality", that is, that companies will have to detail both their impacts on the environment and the climate-related risks they face in their operations.

The CSRD will apply to:

(i) all large companies incorporated in an EU member state, including EU subsidiaries of non-EU companies. A "large company" is an entity that meets at least two of the following three criteria:

   (a) a net turnover of more than €40 million;
   (b) balance sheet total assets greater than €20 million; and/or
   (c) more than 250 employees;

(ii) parent companies incorporated in an EU member state, where the group of companies collectively meet the large company criteria;

(iii) non-EU incorporated companies if they meet the following criteria:

   (a) the company carries on substantial activity in the EU, meaning the company's net turnover in the EU in two consecutive financial years was over €150 million per annum; and
   (b) the company has at least one branch in the EU that has a net turnover of at least €40 million, or a subsidiary in the EU that meets at least two of the "large company" requirements above;

(iv) companies listed on an EU-regulated market, including small and medium-sized companies (SMEs[6]) but excluding "micro companies";[7] and

(v) captive insurance companies (companies that insure other companies in the same group), "reinsurance undertakings" (companies that insure other insurance companies) as well as small financial institutions.

When will the CSRD come into force? EU member states will phase in the CSRD, applying the Directive first to companies most likely to be able to comply, as follows:

- Starting 1 January, 2024: any company already subject to the NFRD for Financial Year 2024 with reports due in 2025;
- Starting 1 January, 2025: large listed companies and others mentioned above for Financial Year 2025 with reports due in 2026; and
- Starting 1 January, 2026: SMEs for Financial Year 2026; however, listed SMEs may opt out of the CSRD until 2028.

The information that a company is required to provide under the CSRD must include information about the company's own operations and its suppliers. However, the EC has acknowledged the difficulties in gathering this information. Accordingly, if a company cannot provide the information, the company should explain the efforts it has made to provide it, state the reasons why the information could not be provided, and explain how the company intends to provide it in the future.

In November 2022 EFRAG submitted the first set of 12 draft European Sustainability Reporting Standards (ESRS) outlining the reporting requirements for the CSRD. The standards are divided into two so-called "cross-cutting standards" and 10 "topical standards". The cross-cutting standards set out general requirements that will apply across all of the matters covered by the CSRD, while the topical standards are further divided to apply separately to environmental, social, and governance issues.

In contrast to reporting protocols under the NFRD, companies that are affected by the CSRD will need to report sustainability information in a clearly identifiable section of their management reports (not in separate sustainability reports). The CSRD require sustainability reporting to be checked externally. Companies will need to seek "limited" audit or assurance of the sustainability information. Where a non-EU company is subject to the CSRD, the company should certify its reporting either by a European auditor or an independent auditor from a third country.

Are there any exemptions from the Directive? A company will be exempt from the CSRD reporting requirements as a member of a group of companies if the consolidated management sustainability report of a parent company has included the report of the parent company and its subsidiaries. The exemption will be available if a group's consolidated management report has been drawn up in a manner that may be considered equivalent with the CSRD, based on an equivalency mechanism yet to be decided by the EU.

Taxonomy Regulation

The question arises as to how the CSRD will sit alongside the EU Taxonomy Regulation 2020.[8] EU taxonomy is a cornerstone of the EU's sustainable finance framework and an important market transparency tool. It helps direct investments to the economic activities most needed in order to meet the European Green Deal objectives set out above. The taxonomy is a classification system that defines criteria for economic activities that are aligned with net zero carbon emissions by 2050 and the broader environmental goals apart from climate. Companies that are within the scope of the CSRD will also have to comply with the EU Taxonomy Regulation.

The EU taxonomy allows financial and non-financial companies to share a common definition of economic activities that can be considered environmentally sustainable. In this way, it plays an important role in helping the EU to increase sustainable investment, by creating security for investors, protecting private investors from "greenwashing", that is, companies pretending to be greener than they are, and helping companies to become more climate-friendly.

The EU Taxonomy Regulation sets out six environmental objectives:

1   climate change mitigation to lessen its impact;
2   climate change adaptation to cope with the changes;
3   sustainable use and protection of water and marine resources;
4   transition to a "circular economy", e.g. recycling;
5   pollution prevention and control; and
6   protection and restoration of biodiversity and ecosystems.

The Taxonomy Regulation entered into force in July 2020. It established the basis for the EU taxonomy by setting out the four conditions that an economic activity has to meet in order to qualify as environmentally sustainable. These are as follows:

- the activity contributes to the environmental objectives of the Regulation;
- the activity does not significantly harm any of the environmental objectives of the Regulation;
- a company carries out the activity in compliance with the minimum safeguards set out in the Regulation; and
- the activity complies with the technical screening criteria established by the EU in accordance with the Regulation.

What are the disclosure requirements? A company must disclose:

- how and to what extent its activities are associated with environmentally sustainable economic activities; and
- information on the proportion of its turnover, capital expenditure and operating expenditure that are derived from products or services associated with environmentally sustainable economic activities.

If a company is exempt from reporting under the CSRD as set out above, the company will also be exempt from reporting under the Taxonomy Regulation. The Regulation does not provide for any other exemptions. As we have seen, a company will be exempt from CSRD reporting requirements if, as a member of a group of companies, the consolidated management report of its parent company has included the results of the company and its subsidiaries. The exemption will be available if a group's consolidated management report has been drawn up in a manner that may be considered equivalent with the CSRD, based on an equivalency mechanism yet to be decided by the EU.

United Kingdom

In the wake of Brexit, there is similar legislation in the United Kingdom. In April 2022 the Companies (Strategic Report) (Climate-Related Financial Disclosure) Regulations 2021 came into force, and amended the UK Companies Act 2006. The Regulations make sustainability reporting in accordance with the Task Force on Climate-Related Financial Disclosures (TCFD) compulsory for a number of UK companies as part of their strategic reporting. Companies are required to disclose sustainability-related information in the non-financial information section of their strategic reports.

The 2021 Regulations apply to the following UK companies:

- listed companies;
- banking companies;
- insurance companies; and
- high-turnover companies, provided that the company has more than 500 employees (or, if it is a parent company, that it together with its subsidiaries has more than 500 employees).

A company that is otherwise subject to the Regulations does not need to publish an annual climate-related disclosure report if the company is a subsidiary and is included in its parent company's group strategic report. The Regulations propose mandatory disclosure of material information in all four of the TCFD's core categories: 1. Governance; 2. Strategy; 3. Risk Management; and 4. Metrics and Targets. The disclosure requirements are similar to those provided for by the CSRD and the Taxonomy Regulation for EU member states.

ISO 14001

In addition to environmental laws and regulations, the International Standards Organization (ISO) has implemented a standard called ISO 14001 that sets out best practice for companies and organizations that wish to minimise their impact on the environment. They can do this by adopting an effective environmental management system. ISO 14001 sets out the key elements of this system and the process for certification of compliance. By achieving certification, the company can be assured that its impact on the environment impact is being measured and improved. As at 2019, there were more than 312,000 certifications to ISO 14001 in 171 countries around the world.[9]

What are the benefits of a strategic approach to environmental impact, leading to certification of compliance? The company will be in a position to:

- Demonstrate compliance with legal and regulatory requirements;
- Ensure engagement of leaders and employees;
- Secure the company's reputation and the confidence of internal and external stakeholders through effective communication;
- Achieve strategic objectives aims by incorporating environmental issues;
- Obtain a competitive advantage through improved efficiencies and reduced costs; and
- Encourage better performance by suppliers in their environmental impact.

What are the requirements for ISO 14001?[10]

1 The company must keep documented evidence that its environmental management system (EMS) meets the required standard. The documentation will show that robust environmental processes are in place and that everyone in the company is aware of and working towards its

environmental objectives. This documentation will include an environment policy, as we discuss below. The policy should describe the company's commitment to take responsibility for the effects on the wider environment and any legal requirements. It should include a clear commitment to prevent pollution, and to continually improve the way the company seeks to deliver upon its environmental objectives.

2 "Evaluation of Environmental Risks and Opportunities" – outlines the environmental risks and opportunities that may be encountered by the company's operations. This will include any opportunities to make changes and improvements. The evaluation will explain the methodology and approach, together with documented evidence such as a business plan, strategy or operational plan.

3 "Evaluation of Environmental Aspects" – evaluates the activities that result in an impact on the environment. These include utilities such as water, electricity, gas, and so on, generation of waste, emissions, and effluents. The evaluation will determine the potential impact on the environment and the risk of occurrence of an adverse event.

4 "Environmental Objectives and Plans" – sets out the company's environmental objectives, and a plan for how these objectives can be achieved. Where possible, objectives should be measurable, for example recording of electricity consumption per month, time-bound, and "owned" by a named individual or team. This will help the management team to make informed decisions and hold someone responsible.

5 "Operational Control Procedures" – defines the company's operational controls appropriate to the sector where it operates. These controls will ensure that:

- all legal and compliance requirements are being met;
- environmental objectives have been assessed and set;
- internal, external, and outsourced processes have been defined; and
- any training requirements have been assessed, implemented, and reviewed.

6 "Procedure for Emergency Preparedness and Response" – to show the company's ability to respond to an emergency event or an event that affects the environment to a significant extent.

7 "List of Interested Parties, Legal and Other Requirements" – identifies parties who are essential to the company's operations, for example,

customers who have placed orders for the company's products or services. There are legal obligations on the company to deliver.
8. "Competence Records" – records of training and competence of employees in order to track any upskilling that may be needed. These will also help to show that everyone in the company is competent as to their environmental responsibilities.
9. "Evidence of Communication" – required to show the company is sending clear internal and external communications.
10. "Monitoring Performance Information" – evidence the company has considered what to measure, how and when, and that the outcomes of any measurement feed into effective process control.
11. "Compliance Obligations Record" – the relevant legal requirements the company must comply with.
12. "Internal Audit Programme and Results" – demonstrate the company's compliance with its own environment policy and procedures.
13. "Management Review Results" – the EMS should be reviewed on a regular basis to ensure that it remains effective.
14. "Nonconformities and Corrective Action" – records any non-conformities in the company's environmental processes, and the corrective actions taken.

Environment policy

All of these concerns for the environment and compliance with relevant laws, regulations, and standards, must be reflected in a company's policy as appropriate to the nature of the business. In a general sense, environmental policy is the commitment of an organization to the laws, regulations, and other policy mechanisms concerning environmental issues. These issues are, as we have seen, the harmful effects of human activity on the environment, for example air and water pollution. Accordingly, the company's policy will be aimed at regulating the activities of employees so as to prevent adverse effects on the environment and its natural resources.

The policy is only one part of an environmental management framework or system but it is essential for the implementation of a recognized standard such as ISO 14001. And it will demonstrate to customers and other stakeholders that the company is committed to managing its environmental impact in a responsible way.

A comprehensive environmental policy will set out the key objectives and principles for the company to achieve the best possible impact on the natural world. However, the benefits are not limited to the company's operations. By demonstrating a commitment to the environment, this will foster good relations with external stakeholders such as customers and suppliers and lead to an improved reputation in the company's markets. An effective EMS will deliver these policy objectives and principles. Certification of the company's EMS in turn will help it to demonstrate to all stakeholders that its policy statements are credible, reliable, and have been independently verified.[11]

Format and content

Ideally the policy should contain a series of statements about the following:

- The company's mission and some information about its operations;
- A commitment to improve its environmental performance by effectively managing its environmental impact;
- The company's expectations of its suppliers and contractors;
- Undertaking to comply with all relevant environmental laws, regulations, and standards;
- Training of employees in environmental matters as they affect the business of the company;
- Monitoring and review of environmental performance; and
- A commitment to communicate its environmental objectives and principles to employees and to external stakeholders.

Review

The company should carry out a regular review of the policy to check that it still reflects the company's operations – and that the operations comply with it. This may be done every year or at least every two years. Obviously the longer the interval between reviews, the greater the risk of non-compliance. The company's operations may change at any time and this may require an immediate review of the environment policy.

Scope of the policy

The environmental policy, or any policy, does not exist in isolation. It forms part of the company's endeavour to act as a good corporate citizen and be seen to do so. The scope of the policy may be extended to address corporate social responsibility (CSR) and sustainable development. By encompassing CSR in particular, the company demonstrates that it will deal with its suppliers and other third parties in a responsible way, for example by being open and honest about its products and services. Sustainable development, as we have seen, has an obvious link to the environment, and requires the company to consider the life cycle of its products among other requirements. It also places an obligation on the company to reduce waste.

Sample environment and sustainability policies

Below are a couple of sample policy statements for a company to show its commitment to comply with environment and sustainability obligations. These are the minimum requirements and may be supplemented by commitments to specific obligations under national and international laws. To assist, these commitments may be mapped to the United Nations Sustainable Development Goals set out above.

---

1. XYZ Limited

XYZ Limited is committed to leading the industry in minimising the impact of its activities on the environment.

The key points of its strategy to achieve this are:

- Minimise waste by evaluating operations and ensuring they are as efficient as possible.
- Minimise toxic emissions through the selection and use of its fleet and the source of its power requirement.
- Actively promote recycling both internally and amongst its customers and suppliers.
- Source and promote a product range to minimise the environmental impact of both production and distribution.

- Meet or exceed all the environmental legislation that relates to the company.
- Use an accredited program to offset the greenhouse gas emissions generated by our activities.

(Source: Environmentalpolicy.org.uk)

2. Newly-Enlightened Co.

Newly-Enlightened Co accepts responsibility for the harmful effects its operations have on both the local and global environment and is committed to reducing them.

Newly-Enlightened Co will measure its impact on the environment and set targets for ongoing improvement.

The Company will comply with all relevant environmental legislation.

The Company will implement a training program for its staff to raise awareness of environmental issues and enlist their support in improving the Company's performance.

Newly-Enlightened Co will encourage the adoption of similar principles by its suppliers.

(Source: Environmentalpolicy.org.uk)

References

1 United Nations Department of Economic and Social Affairs, "The 17 Goals", https://sdgs.un.org/goals.
2 Treaty on the Functioning of the European Union 2009 *Official Journal* C 202, 132–133.
3 Directive 2014/95/EU of the European Parliament and of the Council of 22 October 2014 amending Directive 2013/34/EU as regards disclosure of non-financial and diversity information by certain large undertakings and groups (2014) *Official Journal* L 330, 1–9.
4 Directive 2013/34/EU of the European Parliament and of the Council of 26 June 2013 on the annual financial statements, consolidated financial statements and related reports of certain types of undertakings, amending Directive 2006/43/EC of the European Parliament and of the Council and repealing Council Directives 78/660/EEC and 83/349/EEC (2013) *Official Journal* L 182, 19–74.

5 Directive (EU) 2022/2464 of the European Parliament and of the Council of 14 December 2022 amending Regulation (EU) No 537/2014, Directive 2004/109/EC, Directive 2006/43/EC and Directive 2013/34/EU, as regards corporate sustainability reporting (2022) *Official Journal* L 322, 15–80.
6 SMEs are companies that on their balance sheet do not exceed at least two of the following three criteria: (i) an annual balance sheet total not exceeding €20 million; (ii) net turnover not exceeding €40 million; and (iii) an average number of employees for the financial year not exceeding 250.
7 Micro companies are company that on their balance sheet do not exceed at least two of the following three criteria: (i) an annual balance sheet not exceeding €350,000; (ii) net turnover not exceeding €700,000; and (iii) an average number of employees for the financial year not exceeding 10.
8 Regulation (EU) 2020/852 of the European Parliament and of the Council of 18 June 2020 on the establishment of a framework to facilitate sustainable investment, and amending Regulation (EU) 2019/2088 (2020) *Official Journal* L 198, 13–43.
9 International Standardization Organization, "The ISO Survey of Management System Standard Certifications" – 2019 – Explanatory Note, September 2020, https://isotc.iso.org/livelink/livelink/fetch/8853493/8853511/8853520/18808772/0._Explanatory_note_and_overview_on_ISO_Survey_2019_results.pdf?nodeid=21413237&vernum=-2.
10 British Assessment Bureau, "What are the ISO 14001 requirements?", 16 June 2021, www.british-assessment.co.uk/insights/what-are-the-iso-14001-requirements/.
11 Info-Entrepreneurs, "How to Write an Environmental Policy", 2009, www.infoentrepreneurs.org/en/guides/how-to-write-an-environmental-policy/.

PART III

INDIVIDUAL CONDUCT

These are policies that primarily regulate the conduct of individuals employed by the company, whether as full-time permanent employees or on a temporary, as-needed basis such as consultants or contractors. These policies may also provide for corporate conduct, but they are aimed mainly at employees.

10

ANTI-BRIBERY AND CORRUPTION

Introduction

Bribery and corruption may be nefarious activities that we associate with dictators and oligarchs in developing countries rather than the respectable citizens of our corporate world. But politics does not have a monopoly on dark deeds when it comes to cutting corners to get things done. Sadly the business world has its share of charlatans. Human nature is human nature, whether dressed in a business suit or a military-style uniform. In this chapter, we discuss the meaning of bribery and corruption and how they should be addressed in policy terms. This includes the practice of bribery and corruption or any other improper activities by third parties that have a relationship with the company, whether as partners, suppliers, or indeed customers.

Bribery

Before we can decide what to include in a comprehensive anti-bribery policy, we must first define what we mean by bribery itself. According to

Black's Law Dictionary, this is the "offering, giving, receiving or soliciting of any item of value to influence the actions of an official, or other person, in charge of a public or legal duty".[1] Bribery in the political sphere is a specific form of activity that has been defined as "[c]orrupt solicitation, acceptance, or transfer of value in exchange for official action".[2] A gift of money or other item of value which is not made for dishonest purposes does not amount to bribery. For example, offering a discount or a refund to purchasers of a consumer item may be a rebate and is not bribery. It may arise from a promotion available to all customers or to customers of a specific product or service, and offered to them all equally or otherwise *bona fides*.

If bribery is the act of giving or receiving something of value, what is that something? In other words, what is a bribe? This is an illegal or unethical gift or lobbying effort made in order to influence the conduct of the person who receives it. It may be in the form of cash, goods, other property, legal right, advantage or privilege, or merely a promise to influence the actions of a person in an official or public capacity.[3] A common form of bribery is what is sometimes called a "kickback", a reward to someone who performs or allows favourable treatment to someone else for no good reason. An obvious example is the purchasing manager of a department store who accepts payment for placing an order with a particular supplier.

Corruption

Corruption is wider than bribery and encompasses any unlawful or improper behaviour that seeks to gain an advantage through illegitimate means. (This behaviour of course includes giving or receiving a bribe.) The World Bank has defined corruption as "a form of dishonesty or a criminal offense which is undertaken by a person or an organization which is entrusted with a position of authority, in order to acquire illicit benefits or abuse power for one's private gain". Corruption may involve, as we have seen, many activities such as bribery or embezzlement are a form of fraud, and may also involve activities that are legal in some countries. Just because something is unethical or improper does not necessarily mean it is against the law. The United Nations has set a target in its Sustainable Development Goal No. 16 to substantially reduce corruption and bribery of all forms as part of an international effort in order to ensure peace, justice, and strong institutions. This is one of the UN's 17 Sustainable Development Goals (SDGs), with a target date of 2030 for Goal No. 16 to be achieved. (See Chapter 9 for details of all the SDGs.)

UK Bribery Act

As we have seen, bribery can undermine democracy and the rule of law and poses serious threats to sustained economic progress in developing and emerging economies and to the proper operation of free markets. The UK Bribery Act 2010[4] is intended to respond to these threats and to the wide range of ways that bribery can be committed. It does this by providing robust offences, enhanced sentencing powers for the courts (raising the maximum sentence for bribery committed by an individual from 7 to 10 years' imprisonment), and wide jurisdictional powers.

The Act contains two general offences which are the offering, promising, or giving of a bribe (active bribery) and the requesting of, agreeing to receive, or accepting a bribe (passive bribery). It also sets out two further offences which specifically address commercial bribery. Section 6 of the Act creates an offence relating to bribery of a foreign public official in order to obtain or retain business or an advantage in the conduct of business, and section 7 creates a new form of corporate liability for failing to prevent bribery on behalf of a commercial organization.

US Foreign Corrupt Practices Act

The United States has perhaps the most advanced legislation on this subject of any country in the world. The Foreign Corrupt Practices Act of 1977 (FCPA) prohibits US citizens and organizations from bribing foreign government officials for the benefit of their business interests.[5] The main objective of the Act is to prevent companies and their officers, that is, directors and other officeholders, from influencing foreign officials with any personal payments or rewards. The FCPA applies to any person who has a connection to the US and to US companies and foreign companies listed in the US, that is, listed on a stock exchange. The Act applies throughout the world and specifically to listed companies and their directors, employees, and shareholders with the necessary US connection. The Act was amended in 1998 to apply to foreign companies and individuals who carry out or facilitate corrupt payments in US territory. Every company listed in the US is subject to various accounting requirements for accurate and transparent financial records and internal accounting controls.

European Union

In May 2023 the EU proposed new legislation[6] to prevent corruption within the member states. The EU aims to ensure that a high level of security, including through the prevention and combating of crime and the approximation of criminal laws throughout the Union. Corruption is designated as a "euro-crime" which is a particularly serious crime with a cross-border dimension. Bribery remains at the core of the new legislation but many other forms of corruption threaten citizens and damage our society. The proposed legislation will:

- Step up corruption prevention by raising awareness of the negative impact of corruption on citizens and our society to address corruption before it happens or promote a culture of integrity;
- Extend the definitions of criminal corruption beyond the narrow bribery offences, including misappropriation, trading in influence, abuse of functions, as well as obstruction of justice and illicit enrichment related to corruption offences;
- Introduce minimum criminal penalties for corruption offences to ensure a level playing field in all EU member states;
- Extend the statute of limitation to prosecute corruption in courts; and
- Ensure that law enforcement and prosecutors have appropriate investigative tools and resources to fight corruption.

With this proposal, the EU plans to modernize the current fragmented EU-level framework on corruption and implements international obligations under the UN Convention Against Corruption.

ISO 37001

In order to enable companies and organizations to deal with bribery, and comply with the legal requirements, the International Standards Organization (ISO) introduced a standard in 2021 for a management system to do just that. ISO 37001 provides for a system to demonstrate the company's credibility to its customers, suppliers, and other parties, based on transparency and trust. The standard sets out the requirements to establish, implement, and maintain an anti-bribery management system (ABMS). It also provides guidance on the actions that organizations can take to adhere to the requirements of the standard.

ISO 37001 is the International Standard that allows companies and organizations of all kinds to detect and prevent the practice of bribery. This is done by adopting an anti-bribery policy, appointing someone responsible to oversee:

- Anti-bribery compliance
- Training
- Risk assessments and due diligence on projects
- Financial and business controls and
- Reporting and investigation procedures.

So the starting point is a robust anti-bribery and anti-corruption policy. The objective is to embed a culture of honesty and integrity throughout the organization. But the policy is only one element of a management system intended to help organizations in the fight against bribery by establishing the policies, procedures, and controls to foster a culture of compliance. The anti-bribery management system may be stand-alone or integrated into an existing management system such as the Quality Management System ISO 9001 or other systems relating to environment and safety.

Anti-bribery and corruption policy

Below is a sample policy document on bribery and corruption:

[company name]

Introduction

[Company name] is committed to conducting its business ethically and in compliance with all applicable laws and regulations, including the US Foreign Corrupt Practices Act (FCPA), the UK Bribery Act (UKBA) and similar laws in other countries that prohibit improper payments to obtain a business advantage. This document describes our policy prohibiting bribery and other improper payments in the conduct of our business operations and employee responsibilities for ensuring implementation of the policy. Questions about the policy or its applicability to particular circumstances should be directed to [compliance officer or equivalent].

Policy overview

[Company name] strictly prohibits bribery or other improper payments in any of its business operations. This prohibition applies to all business activities, anywhere in the world, whether involving government officials or other commercial enterprises. A bribe or other improper payment to secure a business advantage is never acceptable and can expose individuals and [company name] to possible criminal prosecution, reputational harm or other serious consequences.

This policy applies to everyone at [company name], including all officers, employees and agents or other intermediaries acting on our behalf. Each officer and employee of [company name] has a personal responsibility and obligation to conduct our business activities ethically and in compliance with all applicable laws based on the countries wherein [company name] does business. Failure to do so may result in disciplinary action, up to and including dismissal. Improper payments prohibited by this policy include bribes, kickbacks, excessive gifts or entertainment, or any other payment made or offered to obtain an undue business advantage. These payments should not be confused with reasonable and limited expenditures for gifts, business entertainment and other legitimate activities directly related to the conduct of our business.

[Company name] has developed a comprehensive program for implementing this policy, through appropriate guidance, training, investigation and oversight. [Compliance officer or equivalent] has overall responsibility for the program, supported by our executive leadership. [Compliance officer or equivalent] is responsible for giving advice on the interpretation and application of this policy, supporting training and education, and responding to reported concerns.

The prohibition on bribery and other improper payments applies to all business activities, but is particularly important when dealing with government officials. The FCPA and similar laws in other countries strictly prohibit improper payments to gain a business advantage and impose severe penalties for violations. The following summary is intended to provide personnel engaged in international activities a basic familiarity with applicable rules so that inadvertent violations can be avoided and potential issues recognized in time to be properly addressed.

Common questions about anti-bribery laws

What do anti-bribery laws prohibit?

The FCPA, UKBA and other anti-bribery laws make it unlawful to bribe a foreign official to gain an "improper business advantage". An improper business advantage may involve efforts to obtain or retain business, as in the awarding of a government contract, but also can involve regulatory actions such as licensing or approvals. Examples of prohibited regulatory bribery include paying a foreign official to ignore an applicable customs requirement. A violation can occur even if an improper payment is only offered or promised and not actually made, it is made but fails to achieve the desired result, or the result benefits someone other than the giver (for example, directing business to a third party). Also, it does not matter that the foreign official may have suggested or demanded the bribe, or that a company feels that it is already entitled to the government action.

Who is a "foreign official"?

A "foreign official" can be anyone who exercises governmental authority. This includes any officer or employee of a foreign government department or agency, whether in the executive, legislative or judicial branch of government, and whether at the national, state or local level. Officials and employees of government-owned or controlled enterprises also are covered, as are private citizens who act in an official governmental capacity. Foreign official status often will be apparent, but not always. In some instances, individuals may not consider themselves officials or be treated as such by their own governments but nevertheless exercise authority that would make them a "foreign official" for purposes of anti-bribery laws.

Personnel engaged in international activities are responsible under this policy for inquiring whether a proposed activity could involve a foreign official or an entity owned or controlled by a foreign government, and should consult with [compliance officer or equivalent] when questions about status arise.

What types of payments are prohibited?
The FCPA prohibits offering, promising or giving "anything of value" to a foreign official to gain an improper business advantage. In addition to cash payments, "anything of value" may include:

- Gifts, entertainment, or other business promotional activities;
- Covering or reimbursing an official's expenses;
- Offers of employment or other benefits to a family member or friend of a foreign official;
- Political party and candidate contributions;
- Charitable contributions and sponsorships.

Other less obvious items provided to a foreign official can also violate anti-bribery laws. Examples include in-kind contributions, investment opportunities, stock options or positions in joint ventures, and favourable sub-contracts. The prohibition applies whether an item would benefit the official directly or another person, such as a family member, friend, or business associate. Under the law, [company name] and individual officials or employees may be held liable for improper payments by an agent or other intermediary if there is actual knowledge or reason to know that a bribe will be paid. All employees therefore must be alert to potential "red flags" in transactions with third parties. [Company name] and its affiliates must keep accurate books and records that reflect transactions and asset dispositions in reasonable detail, supported by a proper system of internal accounting controls. These requirements are implemented through our standard accounting rules and procedures, which all personnel are required to follow without exception. Special care must be exercised when transactions may involve payments to foreign officials. Off-the-books accounts should never be used. Facilitation or other payments to foreign officials should be promptly reported and properly recorded, with respect to purpose, amount, and other relevant factors. Requests for false invoices or payment of expenses that are unusual, excessive, or inadequately described must be rejected and promptly reported.

[Company name] has established detailed standards and procedures for the selection, appointment, and monitoring of agents, consultants, and other third parties. These standards and procedures must be followed in all cases, with particular attention to "red flags" that may indicate possible legal or ethical violations. Due diligence ordinarily will include appropriate reference and background checks, written contract provisions that confirm a business partner's responsibilities, and appropriate monitoring controls. Personnel working with agents and other third parties should pay particular attention to unusual or suspicious circumstances that may indicate possible legal or ethics concerns, commonly referred to as "red flags". The presence of red flags in a relationship or transaction requires greater scrutiny and implementation of safeguards to prevent and detect improper conduct.

This policy imposes on all personnel specific responsibilities and obligations that will be enforced through standard disciplinary measures and properly reflected in personnel evaluations. All officers, employees, and agents are responsible for understanding and complying with the policy, as it relates to their jobs. Every employee has an obligation to:

- Be familiar with applicable aspects of the Policy and communicate them to subordinates;
- Ask questions if the policy or action required to take in a particular situation is unclear;
- Properly manage and monitor business activities conducted through third parties;
- Be alert to indications or evidence of possible wrongdoing; and
- Promptly report violations or suspected violations through appropriate channels.

Any employee who has reason to believe that a violation of this policy has occurred, or may occur, must promptly report this information to his or her supervisor, the next level of supervision,

> or [compliance officer or equivalent]. Alternatively, information may be reported in confidence by calling the [company hotline]. Retaliation in any form against an employee who has, in good faith, reported a violation or possible violation of this policy is strictly prohibited. Employees who violate this policy will be subject to disciplinary action, up to and including dismissal. Violations can also result in prosecution by law enforcement authorities and serious criminal and civil penalties.

References

1 Bryan A. Garner, *Black's Law Dictionary, 11th Edition* (Sweet & Maxwell).
2 Legal Information Institute, Cornell Law School, www.law.cornell.edu/wex/bribery.
3 T. Markus Funk, "Don't Pay for the Misdeeds of Others: Intro to Avoiding Third-Party FCPA Liability," Perkins Coie (11 January 2011), www.perkinscoie.com/en/news-insights/don-t-pay-for-the-misdeeds-of-others-intro-to-avoiding-foreign.html.
4 Bribery Act 2010 c. 23. Available at: www.legislation.gov.uk/ukpga/2010/23 (Accessed: 16 September 2023).
5 United States Code, 2018 Edition, Supplement 3, Title 15 - COMMERCE AND TRADE, tle15-chap2B-sec78dd-1. Available at: https://www.govinfo.gov/app/details/USCODE-2021-title15/USCODE-2021-title15-chap2B-sec78dd-1 (Accessed: 16 September 2023).
6 Proposal for a Directive of the European Parliament and of the Council on combating corruption, replacing Council Framework Decision 2003/568/JHA and the Convention on the fight against corruption involving officials of the European Communities or officials of Member States of the European Union and amending Directive (EU) 2017/1371 of the European Parliament and of the Council, COM(2023) 234 final 2023/0135(COD).

11

CONDUCT AND CONFLICTS OF INTEREST

Introduction

In this chapter we discuss the need for a comprehensive code of conduct or ethics for employees or contractors of the company, and a conflicts of interest policy to address any such conflicts that might arise in the course of their work. Good conduct of course is central to the life of any employee or contractor and not just their work for the company. But the company has a vested interest in seeing to it that employees and contractors behave themselves on the job, whatever they get up to outside working hours.

The conflicts of interest policy may be incorporated into the code of conduct or stand as a separate document. They are so closely related that we can deal with both of them in the same chapter. Both the code and policy will focus mainly on the individual conduct of employees and contractors rather than the company itself but some of the requirements involved will apply to the company as well.

Code of conduct/ethics

Of course the company wants to do the right thing, and be seen to do it. This commitment may be stated in concrete terms, in a code of conduct or ethics. A code in this context is a set of rules for employees/contractors in order to protect the company and inform them of how they are expected to behave. These rules will be reflected in a set of principles or values designed to ensure that individuals conduct themselves with honesty and integrity.

What do we mean by *ethics* here? Ethics seeks to resolve questions of morality by defining ideas such as good and evil, and right and wrong. In the corporate context, this means trying to determine the company's values so as to guide it towards doing good or at least avoiding evil. In fact Google included 'Don't do evil' in its code of conduct until 2018 when the words were removed after several employees resigned due to Google's alleged links with the US military at the time.

In considering the role of a company's code of conduct, we should note that it's not all about ethics and good behaviour. There can be legal implications as well. In a case in the US in 2013, *Morgan Stanley v. Skowran*,[1] an employee of a company that operated a hedge fund engaged in insider trading contrary to the company's code of conduct. The court in New York held that the employee should have reported his misconduct, as required by the code, and ordered him to repay $31 million to the company. This was in accordance with the "faithless servant" doctrine in US law that employees who act unfaithfully to their employers must forfeit all compensation received during the period of disloyalty.

A code of conduct plays a central role in creating a culture of compliance throughout the organization. However, it does not ensure compliance by itself. A healthy culture of compliance and doing the right thing is created by the directors and senior managers who should demonstrate their commitment to ethical conduct in their own roles. The effective implementation of a code of conduct is part of a learning process that requires training, consistent enforcement, and continuous measurement and improvement.[2]

Even the act of preparing a code of conduct has a value:

> Corporate codes have certain usefulness and there are several advantages to developing them. First, the very exercise of doing so in itself is worthwhile, especially if it forces a large number of people in the

firm to think through, in a fresh way, their mission and the important obligations they as a group and as individuals have to the firm, to each other, to their clients and customers, and to society as a whole. Second, once adopted a code can be used to generate continuing discussion and possible modification to the code. Third, it could help to inculcate in new employees at all levels the perspective of responsibility, the need to think in moral terms about their actions, and the importance of developing the virtues appropriate to their position.[3]

We have considered the importance of a corporate culture of compliance in Chapter 3.

Conflicts of interest

There are an infinite number of scenarios where a conflict of interest might arise in the business world. Everyone has an interest of one kind or another, usually financial, in the success or failure of an enterprise, and sometimes these interests collide with the interests of other people or the enterprise itself. Conflicts of interest are a complex and difficult subject and give rise to more disputes perhaps than any other subject of company policy. This is because of the number and complexity of possible scenarios as well as the difficulty in recognizing a conflict in some of them. If we don't recognize that a conflict or potential conflict exists, we can't take steps to prevent it or at least deal with it after the damage has been done. And prevention is always better than cure.

We must be clear about what we mean by a conflict of interest before we discuss the ideal structure and contents of an appropriate policy. A conflict for this purpose is a situation where an individual or an organization has a number of interests in a decision or transaction, and these interests conflict with each other. These situations usually arise when someone's personal interests may affect his or her duty to a third party. (The third party may be the individual's employer or client or someone else who is owed a duty of care.) For example, an employee might own shares in a competitor and this might lead him or her to take certain actions against the interests of the company. Or he or she might have a personal interest in a supplier to the company: the employee might be tempted to treat the supplier in a way that works to the company's disadvantage.

What is an interest?

What is an *interest* for this purpose? It has been defined as a "commitment, obligation, duty or goal associated with a particular social role or practice".[4] Therefore a conflict arises when an individual or an organization is subject to two or more interests that are in conflict with each other. The situation must be avoided, or managed if it cannot be avoided, because an important decision or transaction may be made or carried out for improper reasons, leading to an unjust or even illegal outcome. For example, a company director owes a duty of care, called a *fiduciary* duty, to the company. He or she may own shares in a supplier to the company or maybe even a competitor. If so, he or she may be influenced by personal interest in making decisions or carrying out transactions that involve the two companies. As we have seen, a decision by the director may benefit the supplier or competitor at the expense of the company. This is a clear conflict of interests. Ideally the director should not find himself or herself in this position but if it arises the conflict must be managed to ensure that personal interests play no part in the outcome. The conflict must be disclosed to all concerned and the appropriate procedures followed to protect the integrity of the decision or transaction. The individual concerned may either resign as a director or step aside from the decision or transaction, as the case may be.

The interests involved may or may not be financial. And the question whether a conflict exists is a question of fact and not a state of mind. The individual's intentions are irrelevant. What is relevant are the circumstances and whether they could reasonably give rise to a risk of undue influence over the decision-maker. Essentially the question is: do the circumstances cause a reasonable suspicion that the decision or transaction may be affected by a conflict of interests on the part of the individuals involved?

Below are some common forms of conflict of interests:

- Self-dealing – A company official or representative of the company enters into a transaction on its behalf with himself or herself or with another company for his or her benefit. The same individual is on both sides of the deal. In legal terms, self-dealing consists of conduct by a trustee, corporate officer or other person in a fiduciary position regarding the company in taking advantage of their position and acting in their own interests rather than the interests of the company.

- Double-jobbing – The interests of one job conflict with another, whether due to the demands of each job or sensitive information available to the individual that may lead to a benefit for one company at the expense of the other.
- Nepotism – A spouse, child or other close relative is employed by an individual on behalf of the company, or goods and services for the company are purchased from a relative of the individual or from a supplier controlled by a relative. To avoid nepotism, applicants for employment may be asked if they are related to any company employee.
- Gifts – Friends who also do business with the person receiving a gift or from individuals or companies who do business with the company where the recipient is employed, run the risk of putting the recipient in a conflict of interests. These gifts may be tangible benefits such as jewellery or house ornaments or non-tangible items of value such as entertainment or leisure.
- "Pump and dump" – A stockbroker who owns shares in a company inflates the price by spreading positive information about the company and then sells the shares at a large profit.

Sample code of conduct/ethics and conflicts of interest policy

Below is a sample code of conduct for employees and contractors:

Employee code of conduct

Overview

At [company name] we require that all of our employees conduct themselves according to the highest standards of ethics, integrity, and behaviour when dealing with our clients, colleagues and other stakeholders. This includes, but is not necessarily limited to, full compliance with all legal obligations imposed by statute or any other source of law. This Code establishes the standards of behaviour that must be met by all employees. Where these standards are not met, appropriate disciplinary action will be taken. In cases where the breach involves serious misconduct, this may result in summary dismissal. In cases where a breach of the policy involves a breach of any law, then the relevant government authorities or the police may be notified.

Operation

The purpose of this policy is to make it clear what the company expects from employees, and employees are required to be familiar with and comply with the terms of this policy at all times. Failure to do so may result in disciplinary action, including termination of employment. In so far as this policy imposes any obligations on the company, those obligations are not contractual and do not give rise to any contractual rights. To the extent that this policy describes benefits and entitlements for employees, they are discretionary in nature and are also not intended to be contractual. The company may unilaterally introduce, vary, remove or replace this policy at any time.

Standards of conduct

The standards expected of employees include:

- Compliance with all Company and workplace policies, procedures, rules, regulations and contracts;
- Compliance with all applicable laws and regulations;
- Compliance with all reasonable and lawful instructions given by or on behalf of the Company;
- Devotion of the employee's entire time, attention and skill during normal working hours and at other times as reasonably necessary for the employee to perform their duties;
- To be honest and fair in dealings with customers, clients, co-workers, company management and the general public, and to treat them with courtesy and respect;
- To be faithful and diligent, and actively pursue the Company's best interests at all times;
- To work in a safe and compliant manner, and to observe all workplace health and work responsibilities;
- Refraining from any discriminatory, bullying or harassing behaviour toward customers, clients, co-workers, company management and the general public;

- To not make any statements to the media about the Company's business, unless expressly authorised to do so by the company. Requests for media statements should be referred to [responsible employee name];
- To not make any statements about the Company on social media, or any other public platform, that may harm the Company's reputation;
- To not, in connection with the employee's employment, accept any financial or other benefit from any entity other than the Company – unless acceptance of such benefit is in accordance with the Company's other workplace policies or is otherwise disclosed to the Company and expressly permitted by the Company;
- To not engage in any employment or provide any services to any person or entity other than the Company that may interfere with or affect the employee's work for the Company, except with the Company's prior written consent;
- To not engage in any employment or provide any services to a supplier or competitor of the Company, except with the Company's prior written consent;
- Immediately disclosing any potential, perceived or actual conflict of interest (whether direct or indirect) that may give rise to a conflict with the performance of the employee's obligations to the Company, or the Company's business, confidential information or reputational interests. The Company may direct employees to take action to eliminate or reduce any such conflict, and employees must comply with such directions;
- To not engage in conduct, whether during or after work hours, that in the reasonable opinion of the Company causes or may cause damage or potential damage to the Company's property or reputation;
- To not use in the course of your work, or come to work, while affected by use of prohibited drugs or alcohol;
- To not discriminate on the basis of personal characteristics including (but not limited to) sex, race, disability, pregnancy, age, marital status or sexual orientation;
- To ensure and maintain punctuality in attending at the Company's offices and any meetings there;
- To respect the Company's property;
- To dress in an appropriate manner in accordance with any applicable dress code and to ensure that appearance is presentable, clean, neat

- and tidy (including but not limited to wearing any uniform that is reasonably required of you by the Company);
- To not misuse Company internet to access and/or download sexually explicit material or other offensive material;
- To not use Company email to send sexually explicit or suggestive material, or other offensive or harassing material;
- To maintain both during employment and after termination of employment with the Company, the confidentiality of any confidential information, records or other materials acquired during the course of employment;
- At all times, behave in a way that upholds the Company's core values and the integrity and good reputation of the Company; and
- Reporting any conduct of other workplace participants which is in breach of any of the above, or potentially in breach of any of the above, without delay.

References

1 Morgan Stanley v. Joseph F. "Chip" Skowron (2013) United States District Court, S.D. New York, 989 F. Supp. 2d 356 (S.D.N.Y. 2013). Available at: https://casetext.com/case/stanley-v-skowron. (Accessed: 17 September 2023).
2 Alan Doig and John Wilson, "The Effectiveness of Codes of Conduct", *Business Ethics, the Environment & Responsibility*, July 1998, 140–149.
3 Paul A. Komesaroff, Ian Kerridge, and Wendy Lipworth, "Conflicts of Interest: New Thinking, New Processes", *Internal Medicine Journal*, May 2019, 574–577.
4 Richard T. DeGeorge, "The Status of Business Ethics: Past and Future", *Journal of Business Ethics*, April 1987, 207–208.

12

SOCIAL MEDIA

Introduction

We live in a world of social media. People are communicating every day on social media platforms such as Facebook, X (formerly Twitter), and LinkedIn. It may be about politics or current affairs or even holidays with family and friends. And we're also doing it as part of our job or at least on company time, and so the company should have a policy. With more than 2.7 billion monthly active users as of June 2021, Facebook is the most popular social media worldwide. During the second quarter of 2023, the number of *daily* active users on Facebook reached 2 billion.[1] When compared with the number of daily active users in the second quarter of 2022, the platform gained almost 100 million users. X had 240 million daily active users worldwide in Q2 2022[2] and LinkedIn had more than 740 million active users in 2021.[3]

So what do we mean by social media for this purpose? These are digital, interactive forms of media that allow the creation and exchange of information and ideas online. The content is user-generated such as text messages, photos, and videos. They also connect a user's profile to connect him or her with other individuals or groups and so form online social networks. In general, users access social media through apps on their desktop or laptop device or mobile phone. So these media are based on computer technology that allows the sharing of ideas and information through *virtual*, that is, online, networks and communities. In this way, social media plays a crucial role in connecting people and developing relationships, not only with key influencers involved in a specific industry or sector but also providing an opportunity to establish solid customer relationships by direct contact with them.

Therefore "social media" is a collective term for websites and applications that focus on communication, community-based input, interaction, content-sharing, and collaboration. Social media has an enormous impact all over the world and mobile applications make these platforms easily accessible. People use social media to stay in touch and interact with friends, family and various communities.

Social media have challenged the traditional media of newspapers, radio, and TV, and overtaken them in some countries. There have been positive and negative effects. While social media can help to connect people with real or online communities and can act as an effective communication tool for companies and organizations, the same media are often used by those involved in political movements to communicate and organize at times of social unrest, for example, the *gilets jaunes* (yellow vests) protests in France in 2018 against new taxes on petrol and diesel. As a new technology, there has been little research into the long-term consequences but many studies have established a link between constant use of social media and an increased risk of depression, anxiety, and loneliness.

Some social media sites have the potential for content posted there to spread *virally* over social networks. The term is analogous to the concept of viral infections, which can spread rapidly from individual to individual. In a social media context, content or websites that are "viral" (or which "go viral") are those with a greater likelihood that users will re-share content posted (by another user) to their social network, leading to further sharing. In some cases, posts containing popular content or fast-breaking news have been rapidly shared and re-shared by a huge number of users. Many social media sites provide specific functionality to help users re-share (also known as re-blogging) content, such as X's "retweet" button, Pinterest's "pin" function, Facebook's "share" option, or Tumblr's "re-blog" function. Re-sharing (or, in this case, retweeting) is an especially popular component and feature of X, allowing its users to keep up with important events and stay connected with their peers, as well as contributing in various ways throughout social media. When certain posts become popular, they start to get retweeted over and over again, becoming viral. "Hashtags", or online X addresses, can be used in tweets, and can also be used to count how many people have used that hashtag.

Forms of social media

These are the main forms of social media:

- Social networks
  People use these networks to connect with one another and share information, thoughts, and ideas. The focus of these networks is usually on the user. User profiles help participants identify other users with common interests or concerns. Facebook and LinkedIn are good examples. Facebook is a free social networking website where registered users create profiles, upload photos and videos, send messages, and keep in touch with friends, family, and colleagues. LinkedIn is a social networking site designed for the business community. Registered LinkedIn members can create networks of people they know and trust professionally.
- Media-sharing networks
  These networks' focus is on content. For example, on YouTube, interaction is around videos that users create. Other media-sharing networks are TikTok and Instagram. Streaming platforms like Twitch are considered a subset of this category. Pinterest is a social curation website for sharing and categorizing images found online. The main focus of Pinterest is visual, although it does call for brief descriptions of images. Clicking on an image will take a user to the original source.
- Community-based networks
  The focus of this type of social network is in-depth discussion, much like a blog forum. Users leave prompts for discussion that spiral into detailed comment threads. Communities often form around select topics. Reddit is an example of a community-based network. X is a

(mainly) free microblogging service for registered members to broadcast short posts called tweets. X members can broadcast tweets and follow other active users' tweets using several platforms and devices. Wikipedia is a free, open content encyclopaedia created through a collaborative community. Anyone registered on Wikipedia can create an article for publication; registration is not required to edit articles.

- Review board networks
  With these networks, the focus is on a review, usually of a product or service. For example, on Yelp, users can write reviews on restaurants and endorse each other's reviews to boost visibility.

Social media for business

Businesses use social media applications to market and promote their products and track customer concerns in relation to complaints and general queries. Business-to-consumer (B2C) websites include social components, such as comment fields for users. Various tools help companies to track, measure, and analyse the attention the company gets from social media, including brand perception and customer insight.

Companies have a particular interest in viral marketing because a viral campaign can achieve widespread advertising coverage, particularly if the viral reposting itself attracts news coverage, for a fraction of the cost of a traditional marketing campaign, which typically uses printed materials, like newspapers, magazines, mailings, and billboards, and television and radio commercials. Non-profit organizations and activists may have similar interests in posting content on social media sites with the aim of it going viral.

Social media is also used for *crowdsourcing*. That's the practice of using social networking to gather knowledge, goods, or services. Companies use crowdsourcing to get ideas from employees, customers, and the general public for improving products and services or developing future products and services.

Examples of business-to-business (B2B) applications include the following:

- Social media analytics: This is the practice of gathering and analysing data from blogs and social media websites to assist in making business decisions. The most common use of social media analytics is to do customer sentiment analysis.

- Social media marketing (SMM): This application increases a company's brand exposure and customer reach. The goal is to create compelling content that social media users will share with their social networks. A key component of SMM is social media optimization (SMO). Like search engine optimization (SEO), SMO is a strategy for drawing new visitors to a website. Social media links and share buttons are added to content and activities are promoted via status updates, tweets, and blogs.
- Social customer relationship marketing (CRM): CRM is a powerful business tool. For example, a Facebook page lets people who like a company's brand to like the business's page. This, in turn, creates ways to communicate, market, and network. Social media sites give users the option to follow conversations about a product or brand to get real-time market data and feedback.
- Recruiting: Social recruiting has become a key part of employee recruitment strategies. It is a fast way to reach a lot of potential candidates, both active job seekers and people who were not thinking about a job change until they saw the recruitment post.
- Enterprise social networking: Companies also use enterprise social networking to connect people who share similar interests or activities. These applications include internal intranets and collaboration tools, such as Yammer, Slack and Microsoft Teams, that give employees access to information and communication capabilities. Externally, public social media platforms let organizations stay close to customers and make it easy to conduct market research.

Benefits of social media

Social media provides several benefits, including:

- User visibility: Social platforms let people easily communicate and exchange ideas or content.
- Business and product marketing: These platforms enable businesses to quickly publicize their products and services to a broad audience. Businesses can also use social media to maintain a following and test new markets. In some cases, the content created on social media is the product.
- Audience building: Social media helps entrepreneurs and artists build an audience for their work. In some cases, social media has eliminated

the need for a distributor, because anyone can upload their content and transact business online. For example, an amateur musician can post a song on Facebook, and get instant visibility among their network of friends, who in turn share it on their networks.

Challenges of social media

To balance against these benefits, companies face similar and yet unique social media challenges as follows:

- Offensive posts: Conversations on intranets and enterprise collaboration tools can veer off into non-work-related subjects. When that happens, there is potential for co-workers to disagree or be offended. Controlling such conversations and filtering for offensive content can be difficult.
- Security and retention: Traditional data security and retention policies may not work with the features available in collaboration tools. This can raise security risks and compliance issues that companies must deal with.
- Productivity concerns: Social interaction, whether online or in person, is distracting and can affect employees' productivity.

It is vital for companies to have a social media strategy and to establish social media goals. These help to build trust, educate their target audience, and create brand awareness. They also enable people – potential customers – to find and learn about a business.

Social media strategy

In order to deal with these challenges and to avail of all the benefits, the company should have a social media strategy in place. This will consist of a comprehensive policy and a set of procedures and best practices throughout the organization.

Below are a set of social media best practices for companies to follow:

- Establish social media policies that set expectations for appropriate employee social behaviour. These policies should also ensure social media posts do not expose the company to legal problems or public embarrassment. Guidelines should include directives for when an

employee must identify them self as a company representative and rules for what type of information can be shared.
- Focus on platforms geared to B2B marketing, such as X and LinkedIn.
- Put in place an engaging, customer-centric strategy in social media campaigns. An example would be to use X to field questions from customers.
- Include rich media, such as pictures and video, in content to make it more compelling and appealing to users.
- Use social media analytics tools to measure user engagement with content and to keep on top of trends.
- Use a conversational voice in posts that comes across as professional but not rigid.
- Simplify long form content to make it social friendly. Lists and audio and video snippets are good examples.
- Embrace employees and customers talking positively about the organization and repost that content.
- Check in on analytics and management tools frequently as well as the social media accounts.

Sample social media policy

In terms of policy, the document should set out how the company and its employees should conduct themselves online. This is an essential tool for any organization that uses social media. The policy should include non-disclosure of confidential information, non-use of defamatory or insulting content, including information or pictures that might suggest illegal or improper conduct.

Social media policy

[Company name]

I. Purpose

The purpose of this policy is to establish guidelines for staff, contractors, stakeholders, and other individuals. This policy covers the conduct and expectations, policies, definitions, standards, guidelines, and examples for employees, contractors, and members of the public when participating in [company name] social media or social networking platforms. [Company name] must ensure the use of social media communications maintains our brand, identity, integrity, and reputation while minimizing legal risks, inside or outside of the workplace. Social media can move quickly and be challenging and is to be used to convey information about company products and services, promote and raise awareness of [company name] brand, search for potential new markets, communicate with employees and customers to brainstorm, issue or respond to breaking news or negative publicity, and discuss corporate, business-unit, and department-specific activities and events.

II. Definitions

Social media or social networking includes all forms of online publishing and discussion, including but not limited to: blogs, wikis, file-sharing, user-generated video and audio, social networks and other social networking applications. At present, many organizations are fully engaged with social media websites such as Facebook, X, YouTube, and LinkedIn, and most intend to embrace all new social media environments that may appear in the future.

III. Company policy and guidelines

1. **Authorized users:**

   - Employees must be authorized by [company name] manager, based on employee job responsibilities, to engage in work-time social media sites.
   - All employees must identify themselves as employees of [company name] or their affiliation and expertise when posting to [company name] social media.

2. **Content guidelines:**

   - For social media including [company name], content must be relevant, meet specified goals or purposes and add value to [company name] brand.

- Any copyrighted or confidential information requires written or verbal authorization [company name] before it can be published and should be properly attributed.
- All content must conform to all appropriate laws and regulations, as well as guidelines adopted by and governing the industry, such as privacy laws.
- Content must be polite and respectful. All messaging should maintain the same tone as if interacting with someone in person on behalf of the organization.

3. **Editorial control:**

- [Company name] is authorized to remove any content that does not meet the rules and guidelines of the aforementioned policy or may be illegal or offensive. Removal of such information will be done without permission of the author or advance warning.
- [Company name] expects all public users (non-employees, non-members, non-stakeholders) to abide by all guidelines of the company policy mentioned above and
- [Company name] reserves the right to take the same action as mentioned above in removing offensive or illegal content.

Social media comments from public users that require response will be addressed in a timely but thoughtful, and respectful manner.

IV. *Personal Rules & Guidelines*

Employees are expected to follow the guidelines and policies set forth below to provide a clear line between you as the individual and you as the employee of [company name].

- [Company name] respects the right of employees to use social media forums for self-publishing and self-expression on personal time but unless specifically authorized by department head or manager, employees are not permitted to use forms of social media during working hours or at any time on Company computers or any other Company-supplied devices, unless the employee is authorized to speak on the Company's behalf.
- Social networking sites have blurred the line between private and public activity. In many ways, today's social media pages have

replaced the written letters of the past but are more visible. Your social media posts – even if you intend them to be solely personal messages to your friends or family – can be easily circulated beyond your intended audience. This content, therefore, represents you and the Company to the outside world.

- Employees will be held personally liable for any commentary that is considered defamatory, obscene, proprietary, or libellous by any offended party up to and including [company name] when on the Company's time or using Company computers or Company-supplied devices.
- Employees are prohibited from harassing, discriminating, or disparaging against any employee or anyone affiliated with or doing business with [company name].
- Employees are prohibited from posting the Company's name, trademark or logo, or any company-privileged information, including but not limited to: copyrighted information or company-issued documents, unless authorized by [company name].
- Employees are prohibited from promoting personal projects or endorsing other brands, causes or opinions without the use of a disclaimer to separate employee's personal uses with those of [company name].
- Employees shall use discretion in responding to public users through social media and use a respectful and courteous tone.

V. *Enforcement*

Violations of this policy will be enforced under current employee personnel policies regarding personal conduct, supervisory discipline, reprimand, performance evaluation and/or employment termination.

References

1 Statistica, "Number of Daily Active Facebook Users Worldwide as of 2nd Quarter 2023", July 2023, www.statista.com/statistics/346167/facebook-global-dau/.
2 Statistica, "Number of Monetizable Daily Active X (formerly Twitter) Users (mDAU) Worldwide from 1st Quarter 2017 to 2nd Quarter 2022", July 2022, www.statista.com/statistics/970920/monetizable-daily-active-twitter-users-worldwide/.
3 Pamela Bump, "31 LinkedIn Stats That Marketers Need to Know in 2021", 22 March 2021, https://blog.hubspot.com/marketing/linkedin-stats.

13
REMOTE WORKING

Introduction

One of the many benefits of technology is that most of us can work from almost anywhere. No longer do we have to be at a specific address or in a specific town or city or even country. We're not chained to a desk anymore. But remote working has come into sharper focus with the advent of the COVID-19 pandemic. Since the early months of 2020, a previously unknown virus became a global pandemic and changed the world of work almost completely. For many workers, COVID-19 abolished the daily commute to the office or factory, the water cooler chat, and not least their access to the stash of chocolate bars and biscuits in their bottom drawer. As a result, a remote working policy is now essential for the many companies and organizations that have employees working from home because, although the office may not be off-limits after the pandemic, it may be subject to restrictions. The policy will help to ensure that employees can work productively and securely from anywhere.

DOI: 10.4324/9781003258995-16

Remote working is not the same as working from home. 'Working from home' usually means that employees have the option to go to an office but choose to work from their home for a specific day or several days. Strictly speaking, 'remote working' means that an employee does not have that option and so works from home or elsewhere every day. An employee can work from somewhere other than the company's offices but not necessarily from his or her home. Some employees have jobs that allow remote flexibility or allow them to work from home at least some of the time. Others may work in a different city, district, or even country from the company's head office.

Many companies have seen the benefits of the facility of remote working for their staff even before the COVID-19 pandemic. For example, a survey in the US in 2017 showed that staff turnover at companies that offered remote working was 25% less than at companies that did not.[1] So it can safely be said that remote working has a beneficial effect on the 21st-century workplace. By enabling its employees to work in this way, the company shows that it cares about their work-life balance and trusts them to do what is best for the company and for themselves. The question of whether working from home or remote working is better for performance/productivity is another question altogether.

COVID-19

It has become apparent, and maybe it was inevitable, that the pandemic changed the world of work. The long-term effects remain to be seen. McKinsey management consultants have carried out extensive research into the effects, in particular how employees may be affected in the way they work and where they work:

> we find that about 20 to 25 percent of the workforces in advanced economies could work from home between three and five days a week. This represents four to five times more remote work than before the pandemic and could prompt a large change in the geography of work, as individuals and companies shift out of large cities into suburbs and small cities. We found that some work that technically can be done remotely is best done in person. Negotiations, critical business decisions, brainstorming sessions, providing sensitive feedback, and

onboarding new employees are examples of activities that may lose some effectiveness when done remotely.[2]

In June, 2021 Facebook in Ireland announced a significant change in its policy on remote working that would send ripples through workplaces everywhere. The tech giant employs 6,000 people approx. in Dublin and decided that it would allow permanent remote working after the COVID-19 pandemic. Facebook employees would have the option of keeping their job while working in another country in Europe.[3]

The COVID-19 pandemic was one of the biggest challenges that societies and businesses have faced. Overcoming this challenge was possible only if everyone worked together to stop the spread of this disease and provide a safe and healthy working environment for both home-based workers and those returning to their usual workplaces.

Although the worst effects of COVID-19 seem to have passed, in workplaces where workers can be exposed to a virus (which belongs to the category of biological agents) employers should carry out a workplace risk assessment and put in place appropriate measures. The minimum EU legal requirements are laid out in the Biological Agents Directive.[4]

The UK Department for Business, Energy & Industrial Strategy and Department for Digital, Culture, Media & Sport published detailed guidance[5] in July 2021. This relates to the necessary steps that businesses should take to protect their employees and customers.

1. Complete a health and safety risk assessment that includes the risk from COVID-19.
    Complete a risk assessment, considering the measures set out in this guidance. Also consider reasonable adjustments needed for staff and customers with disabilities. Share it with all your staff. Keep it updated.
2. Provide adequate ventilation.
    You should make sure there is a supply of fresh air to indoor spaces where there are people present. This can be natural ventilation through opening windows, doors, and vents, mechanical ventilation using fans and ducts, or a combination of both. You should identify any poorly ventilated spaces in your premises and take steps to improve fresh air flow in these areas. In some places, a CO_2 monitor can help identify if the space is poorly ventilated.

3   Clean more often.
    It's especially important to clean surfaces that people touch a lot. You should ask your staff and your customers to use hand sanitiser and to clean their hands frequently.
4   Turn away people with COVID-19 symptoms.
    Staff members or customers should self-isolate if they have a high temperature, a new continuous cough, or a loss or change to their sense of smell or taste. They must also self-isolate if they:

- have tested positive for COVID-19
- live in a household with someone who has symptoms, unless they're exempt from self-isolation
- have been told to self-isolate by NHS Test and Trace.

If you know that a worker is legally required to self-isolate, you must not allow them to come to work. It's an offence to do this.

5   Enable people to check in at your venue.
    You're no longer legally required to collect customer contact details, but doing so will support NHS Test and Trace to contact those who may have been exposed to COVID-19 so that they can book a test. You can enable people to check in to your venue by displaying an NHS QR code poster. You do not have to ask people to check in or turn people away if they refuse. If you choose to display a QR code, you should also have a system in place to record contact details for people who want to check in but do not have the app.
6   Communicate and train
    Keep all your workers, contractors and visitors up-to-date on how you're using and updating safety measures.

The European Union also published guidance in 2020 for a safe return to work after COVID-19. An edited version of the guidance is at Appendix 4.

Remote working policy

Having put the appropriate measures in place as set out in this chapter, the company needs to put a comprehensive policy in place. A remote work policy can be defined as an agreement between the company and its employees that sets out how and when they can work from locations other than the office. The policy may be temporary or permanent. We have to assume that COVID-19 will not always be with us, and so the company must be flexible in its approach to the health of its employees and everyone they come into contact with. The policy will identify who can work remotely, how they should go about it, and their legal rights and obligations while doing it, including working hours and security requirements.

1. Determine how employees will work remotely.
   The policy should ensure that everyone can work from home, regardless of their role. For example, an HR role that conducts in-person interviews and training sessions might not fit as well into the remote environment as a software programmer. If possible, the remote working policy should set out how these meetings can be conducted safely and securely.
2. Provide the right tools for safe and secure work.
   For some employees, a laptop and a Wi-Fi connection might not be enough. They might also need a printer or other hardware. Remote employees need equipment and technology that makes them feel engaged and part of the team. To address security concerns, the company might need a Virtual Private Network (VPN) or other form of security for confidential company information. The policy should provide for all of these concerns and also whether, and to what extent, the company will pay for any equipment and technology the employee requires.
3. Establish clear rules about working from home.
   Many employees believe they can be more productive in a remote environment but distractions abound at home and other locations away from the office. The TV or the sunny back garden are obvious examples. And children and pets don't always behave as they should. The policy should be clear about when employees are expected to be available online and what the boundaries are, if any, to accommodate personal matters.
4. Plan time for collaborating and socializing.
   The policy should include some provision for time for team-building and conversations that do not relate to work matters. We are social animals whatever our job.
5. Clearly outline employees' legal rights and obligations.
   Remote workers have the same legal rights and obligations as in-office workers. The policy should be specific about the legal position as regards working hours (including compliance with any working time

regulations), payment for equipment and technology if applicable, any tax implications, and any other matters arising from the employee's location away from company premises such as health and safety and information security.

Sample remote working policy

Below is a template with guidance for a suitable remote working policy[6] from ACAS, the UK government's Advisory, Conciliation and Arbitration Service.

Homeworking policy
    The main features of a policy for staff working from home are set out below.

Introduction	
Opening Statement	The employer should set out its commitment to flexibility with the aim of meeting both its and employees' needs. It should also make clear that while homeworking is categorised as a type of flexible working, employees should not assume that other aspects of flexible working (such as amended hours) are automatically part of a homeworking arrangement.
Define homeworking	The employer should set out types of homeworking that the policy will cover and whether home or the employer's business premises will be the main place of work. For example, the types might include: • Home as the main place of work. • Flexible homeworking with time split between home and the office. • Mobile working with a base at home to travel to the employer's different premises and customers. • The office as the main place of work with working from home occasionally.

How an employee should apply	The employer should ask an employee to apply in writing, outline the process to be followed and factors to be considered in assessing their application (preferably linking to a flexible working policy), say who will make the decision, and the grounds on which the employee can appeal if their request is refused. To find out more, see ACAS Guide: The Right To Request Flexible Working.
Business Case	
Is the role suitable for homeworking?	The employer should set the factors for assessing whether the role can be done just as well away from the business base by someone working on their own.
Is the jobholder eligible?	The employer should set out who will be eligible. For example: • Those requesting it as a reasonable adjustment. • Those making a flexible working request. • Those who have completed a certain length of service or satisfactorily completed their training and achieved satisfactory in their last annual performance review.
Is the jobholder suitable?	Personal qualities required are likely to include: • Self-motivation and discipline. • Ability to work without direct supervision. • Ability to complete work to deadline.
Is the home suitable?	Homeworkers need a safe and reasonable space, security and privacy in which to work, and for office-type tasks an internet connection able to support work systems.
Will homeworking be beneficial?	An arrangement should meet business needs and the employee's needs so it is favourable for both.
Other Important Practicalities	
Health and safety risk assessments	The employer has a duty of care to its employees and should carry out a risk assessment before homeworking can be approved. It should set out what will happen if the risk assessment identifies concerns including who will make and pay for changes to bring the home up to standard, and what timescale will be allowed.

	It should also set out what will happen if concerns are not addressed and reserve the right to refuse a homeworking application.
Setting up the employee to work from home	The employer should set out: - What the company will provide, for example, furniture, phone, phone line, broadband, printer, fire extinguisher, paper. - What the employee is expected to provide, for example, heating and lighting. - Who will pay for any installation and other necessary costs, and, if required and agreed, how costs can be claimed back. - Who the equipment belongs to, who is responsible for maintaining/moving it and how this will be done, and whether it can, or cannot, be used for personal matters by the homeworker or their family.
Running costs and expenses	The employer should state whether it will contribute towards costs in working from home – for example, heating and lighting – and expenses. If so, it should state how much, what can be claimed and how, and what is taxable.
Taxation	The employer should set out the implications of homeworking on tax. To find out more, see HMRC's guidance.
Mortgage, lease and insurance issues	The employee should tell their mortgage provider or landlord and home insurer of their intention to work from home. They should check that there isn't anything preventing them from working at home – for example, in their mortgage agreement, lease, or insurance. The employee should obtain from their home insurer confirmation of cover should work equipment cause damage and for a claim from a third party. The employer should say if it will pay the extra if the employee's premium rises as a result. Work property and a claim by a third party should be covered by the employer's insurance policy.

The employer's access to the employee's home	The employer should say how frequently and in what circumstances it would require access to the home. For example: • Initial set-up. • Maintenance of equipment. • Health and safety assessment. • Electrical equipment testing. • One-to-one meetings with managers/colleagues/clients.
If the employee moves home?	The employer should set out what will happen if a homeworker wants to move house.
Managing The Homeworker	
Employee Performance	The employer should set out how employees who work from home will be managed consistently with office staff, and given the same opportunities for training, development, and promotion. It should also refer to its policies relating to: • Health and safety. • Monitoring and performance. • Team working. • Communication. • Training, development and support. The employer should ensure that employees who work from home are clear about their hours and the core hours when they should be at work.
The employee's attendance at the main office/base	The employer should set out how frequently, for how long, where, and for what reasons the employee's attendance at the organisation's premises will be required.
Security including information	The employer should set out how staff working from home should store and transmit documents and information.

References

[1] Owl Labs, "Remote Work Distribution by Department and Role", 2017, https://resources.owllabs.com/state-of-remote-work/2017.

2 McKinsey Global Institute, "The future of work after COVID-19", February 18, 2021, www.mckinsey.com/featured-insights/future-of-work/the-future-of-work-after-covid-19, 18 February 2021.
3 Jonathan Keane, "Could Facebook's remote working policy upend Dublin's tech hub?", *Silicon Republic,* 14 June 2021, www.siliconrepublic.com/careers/facebook-remote-working-policy-dublin.
4 Directive 2000/54/EC – biological agents at work of the European Parliament and of the Council of 18 September 2000 on the protection of workers from risks related to exposure to biological agents at work (seventh individual directive within the meaning of Article 16(1) of Directive 89/391/EEC) (2000), *Official Journal* L 262 21.
5 UK Health Security Agency, "Guidance – Reducing the spread of respiratory infections, including COVID-19, in the workplace", 10 June 2022, www.gov.uk/guidance/working-safely-during-covid-19/offices-factories-and-labs.
6 National Government Archives, *Open Government Licence for public sector information,* www.nationalarchives.gov.uk/doc/open-government-licence/version/3/.

14

SPEAK UP/WHISTLEBLOWING

Introduction

Whistleblowing is one of those words that describes what it means in a concrete way. Blowing a whistle is the act of bringing attention to something illegal or improper, or both. The referee in a football match blows the whistle to stop the match for foul play. In the context of corporate conduct, it means disclosure of information or activity within the company that may indicate illegal or improper behaviour.

The whistleblower, who is usually an employee, may decide to make the disclosure either inside or outside the company. An internal disclosure may or may not be made anonymously if the company provides that facility through a *hotline* or something similar. Indeed, research has shown that employees are more likely to take action to report unacceptable behaviour internally if it can be done in strict confidence.[1] The anti-bribery management systems standard ISO 37001 includes anonymous reporting as one of the criteria. ISO 37001 is a management system standard published by the International Standards Organization (ISO) in 2016 and it sets out

DOI: 10.4324/9781003258995-17

the requirements for the establishment and operation of an anti-bribery management system. On the other hand, an employee may decide to report misconduct to someone outside the company. It may be the company has appointed an external agency to create a secure and anonymous channel for its employees to report wrongdoing.

In both cases the whistleblower must be protected from any retaliation against him or her for a disclosure made in good faith. This may take the form of dismissal, a change to working conditions, or harassment in various ways, including bullying.[2] Obviously the whistleblower must have credible evidence of wrongdoing in order to be seen to act in good faith and to oblige the company or a regulatory agency, as the case may be, to investigate the disclosure and if necessary, hold the company to account.

From an ethical point of view, whistleblowing can be regarded as simply telling the truth to stop illegal or improper behaviour. Seen from the company's perspective, however, blowing the whistle may be seen as an act of disloyalty and breach of confidentiality regarding the company's affairs. Although the laws of many countries seek to protect the whistleblower who acts in good faith, these may or may not be enforced and can leave the individual in a vulnerable position. As a result, an employee must still weigh his or her options. They can either expose the company and stand on the moral high ground or expose the company and lose their job, their reputation, and maybe even their career. According to a study at the University of Pennsylvania, US, 69% chose the first option and they were either fired or were forced to retire after taking the moral high ground.[3]

In a healthy corporate culture, everyone in the company will be encouraged to speak up or "blow the whistle" in the event of any wrongdoing. This wrongdoing may take the form of fraud or damage to the environment or a breach of any of the legal obligations discussed in this book. Ideally the company will have in place a policy document that sets out the employees' responsibilities to report wrongdoing and how to go about it. However, while most companies have a set of core policies in place, or at least perhaps a staff handbook, few of them have produced a specific policy on whistleblowing and what employees should do if they suspect there is wrongdoing within their organization. As we will see, legislation in some countries such as the UK and Ireland protects whistleblowers against retaliation for their actions.

What is whistleblowing?

Whistleblowing is the act of reporting certain types of wrongdoing within an organization. The wrongdoing that a whistleblower reports must be in the public interest, meaning that it must affect others, for example the general public. Employees can raise their concerns at any time and are protected by law but they may be afraid to come forward for fear they will lose their job or be treated unfairly shortly after they have disclosed an issue.

Legal protection

The law protects whistleblowers if they report any of the following:

- a criminal offence, e.g. fraud;
- an individual's health and safety is in danger;
- damage or risk of damage to the environment;
- a miscarriage of justice;
- the company is breaking the law, e.g. failure to have any required insurance; and cover-up of wrongdoing.

In the UK, specific legislation since the 1990s has for some time protected the positions of those who report instances of wrongdoing or suspected wrongdoing. The Employment Rights Act 1996 as amended by the Public Interest Disclosure Act 1998 provides protection for employees from any retaliation or ill-treatment due to making a disclosure. A whistleblowing policy is not required by law but it is considered best practice for employers to have one in place.

A disclosure that the whistleblower makes to his or her employer or any other person, for example a regulator, is protected. In addition, the disclosure must be one that the whistleblower "reasonably believes" constitutes: a criminal offence, a failure to comply with legal obligations, a miscarriage of justice, danger to the health and safety of employees, damage to the environment, or hiding any information that would show any of these. The disclosure does not have to consist of confidential information, and it can be the disclosure of information about actions that have already occurred, are occurring, or may occur in the future.

An employee will be protected if he "makes a disclosure in good faith" to one of these people, and "reasonably believes that the relevant failure ... is a matter in respect of which the person is prescribed and the information is substantially true".

If an employee makes such a disclosure he or she must not suffer any action to their detriment in their employment as a result. This includes both negative action and the absence of action and so covers discipline, dismissal, or failing to gain a pay rise or access to facilities that would otherwise have been provided. If an employee suffers a detriment, he or she is permitted to make a complaint before an employment tribunal. If an employee has been dismissed for making a protected disclosure, this dismissal is automatically considered to be unfair. Similarly, an employee cannot be given priority for redundancy simply because he made a disclosure. A non-disclosure agreement (NDA) between an employer and employee, often a condition of compensation for loss of employment for whatever reason, does not remove a worker's right to make a protected disclosure, that is, to blow the whistle.

The UK legislation applies to Crown servants, except for employees of MI5, MI6 or GCHQ. The legislation does not apply to serving police officers and those employed outside the UK.

In Ireland, the Protected Disclosures Act 2014 aims to protect people who raise concerns about wrongdoing in the workplace. (Some parts of the public service were already subject to relevant legislation.) The Act provides for redress for workers who have been dismissed or otherwise penalized for having made a disclosure. The definition of "worker" includes:

- Employee or former employee;
- Trainee;
- Someone working under a contract for services;
- Independent contractor;
- Agency worker; and
- Someone on work experience, e.g. an intern or similar.

What is a "protected disclosure" for purposes of the Act? One can make a protected disclosure if he or she is a "worker" as defined and disclose "relevant information" in a particular way. Information is relevant if it came to the worker's attention in connection with their work and he or she reasonably believe that it may constitute wrongdoing as defined. Similar to the UK legislation, "wrongdoing" includes:

- Commission of a criminal offence;
- Failure to comply with a legal obligation;
- Endangering the health and safety of individuals;
- Damaging the environment;
- Miscarriage of justice;
- Misuse of public funds;
- Oppressive, discriminatory, grossly negligent, or grossly mismanaged acts or omissions by a public body; and
- Concealment or destruction of information about any of the above wrongdoing.

When assessing a claim taken under the 2014 Act, the first issue that arises is whether a protected disclosure has been made. In a case in 2019, *A Civil Servant v. A Government Department*,[4] a civil servant reported concerns about inaccuracies in various official forms that he claimed had potentially serious adverse consequences. He alleged this constituted a disclosure of gross negligence and gross mismanagement as defined in the Act. The Irish Workplace Relations Commission found that the matters reported could have serious consequences and that the forms were in need of change but they did not arise from "wrongdoing" as defined, either in their nature or degree of gravity. In a case in 2020, *A Concierge v. A Hotel*,[5] an employee reported a colleague for breaching the employer's policies by accepting commission payments. The employee who made the complaint was on probation at the time and was called into meetings with the hotel's management some months later when he was cautioned about his timekeeping. He was told this could result in the extension of his probation, and he was due to have a follow-up meeting a week later when he was suddenly dismissed. The Workplace Relations Commission decided that his disclosure did not provide enough detail about the alleged wrongdoing to meet the definition of a protected disclosure, nor was a breach of the employer's policy serious enough to be considered a "relevant wrongdoing".

Global perspective

Whistleblowing has been mainly concerned with bribery and corruption (see Chapter 10). The 2022 Corruption Perceptions Index[6] (CPI) produced by Transparency International, a non-profit organization that fights corruption around the world, shows that most countries are failing in their efforts to stop corrupt activities. The CPI ranks 180 countries and territories around the world by their perceived levels of public sector corruption, scoring on a scale of 0 (highly corrupt) to 100 (very clean).

The global average is 43 out of 100. More than two-thirds of countries score below 50, while 26 countries have fallen to their lowest scores yet. Despite concerted efforts and hard-won gains by some countries, 155 of them have made no significant progress against corruption or have declined in their rankings.

The Top 10 are as follows:

Country	Rank	Score
Denmark	1	90
Finland	2 (joint)	87
New Zealand	2 (joint)	87
Norway	4	84
Singapore	5 (joint)	83
Sweden	5 (joint)	83
Switzerland	7	82
Netherlands	8	80
Germany	9	79
Ireland	10 (joint)	77
Luxembourg	10 (joint)	77

The Bottom 10 are as follows:

Country	Rank	Score
Burundi	171 (joint)	17
Equatorial Guinea	171 (joint)	17
Haiti	171 (joint)	17
North Korea	171 (joint)	17
Libya	171 (joint)	17
Yemen	176	16
Venezuela	177	14

Country	Rank	Score
South Sudan	178 (joint)	13
Syria	178 (joint)	13
Somalia	180	12

European Union

The global financial crisis of 2007 brought to light serious mismanagement in many financial institutions and the Volkswagen scandal in 2015 arose from a corporate decision to cheating emissions tests on vehicles in the US. These events may have been avoided by an effective whistleblowing policy in place within the organization. Because of serious concerns about the position of the whistleblower, the European Union introduced an EU-wide standard to protect him or her. This was the Directive adopted in 2019 and which EU member states were obliged to implement before the end of 2021.

Whistleblowers are vital for maintaining an open and transparent society, as they expose misconduct or hidden threats. To ensure that they are better protected against negative consequences, the new EU Directive came into force on 16 December 2019.

The essential elements of the Directive[7] are:

- Protection not only for employees who report their concerns, but also for job applicants, former employees, and any third parties involved;
- Protection from dismissal, degradation, and other discrimination;
- Protection applies only to reports of wrongdoing in relation to EU law, such as tax fraud, money laundering, public procurement, product safety, environmental protection, public health, and consumer and data protection; and
- The whistleblower can decide whether to make a report internally within the company or, if he or she believes it is in the public interest, directly to a third party such as a regulatory authority or the media.

Whistleblower protection refers to the reporting of wrongdoing related to EU law, such as tax fraud, money laundering, or offences related to public procurement, product and transport safety, environmental protection, public health, and consumer and data protection. Companies with 250 or more employees are expected to comply within two years of adoption of the new Directive, whereas companies with employees between 50 and 250 have another two years after that to comply. Whistleblowers should be able to submit reports either in writing via an online system, a mailbox, or by post and/or orally via a telephone hotline or answering machine.

Responsibilities

Companies must determine the "most suitable" person to receive and follow up on reports internally. According to the Directive, this could be:

- Compliance officer or equivalent;
- Head of HR;
- Legal counsel;
- Chief Financial Officer; or
- Executive board member or member of senior management.

Companies can also outsource the processing of reports, for example to an external ombudsman.

Processing times

The company is obliged to confirm receipt of the report to the whistleblower within seven days. The whistleblower must be informed of any action taken within three months, the status of the internal investigation and its outcome.

Duty to inform

Companies are required to provide information on the internal reporting process as well as on the reporting channel(s) to the competent authority. This information must be easily understandable and accessible, not only to employees, but also to suppliers, service providers, and business partners.

Data storage

All reports received must be kept in a secure place so that they can be used as evidence, if necessary.

Exceptions

Companies with between 50 and 250 employees may use a shared reporting channel to obtain and identify evidence, provided that all obligations outlined are met.

Sanctions

The new Directive also includes details on sanctions. Companies that obstruct the reporting of concerns or attempt to obstruct them will face penalties. The same applies if companies fail to keep the identity of the whistleblower confidential. Retaliatory measures against whistleblowers will also be punished. It is the job of national legislators to determine the severity of these sanctions.

Benefits

While the Directive clearly benefits whistleblowers we also believe there are significant benefits for organizations. Most importantly, by ensuring that effective whistleblowing arrangements are in place, employees and other stakeholders are encouraged to raise concerns internally.

By doing so, organizations have an opportunity to identify and manage risk at an early stage, helping to avoid or limit financial and reputational damage.

An edited version of the Directive is set out at Appendix 3.

Scope

The new Directive will broaden the scope of the Protection Disclosures Act 2014 in Ireland and its equivalent in other EU member states. (As the UK has left the EU, the new Directive may or may not be adopted by the UK government to update its own legislation. The UK-EU Trade and Co-operation Agreement requires that the UK maintain the same level of employment protection as the EU. The UK government may decide to amend UK law to keep an equivalence with EU worker rights and best practice.)

EU Member States will be obliged by the Directive to offer full immunity to whistleblowers in judicial proceedings, including disclosure of trade secrets. The Directive outlines minimum standards to protect whistleblowers reporting breaches of Union law specifically, although it is likely that as it is implemented it will broaden the scope of protections provided to whistleblowers reporting under the relevant legislation. The main changes are as follows:

- Burden of proof: One of the most significant changes the Directive will make is reversal of the burden of proof in legal claims brought for penalization. At present, whistleblowers who take legal action if they have been penalized must prove that they would not have been penalized but for the fact that they had made a protected disclosure. Under the Directive, however, the employer has to prove that any detrimental action taken against a whistleblower was based on "duly justified grounds".
- Definition of "worker": The Directive significantly expands the range of people who are protected. Volunteers, shareholders, and non-executive directors will be able to make protected disclosures. The Directive protects people reporting "information acquired in a work-based relationship", which can include job applicants where they encounter information about relevant wrongdoings during recruitment or pre-contractual negotiations.
- Obligation to have policies and procedures: At present, only public bodies must have policies and procedures for making protected disclosures. The Directive extends this to all workplaces with 50 or more employees, though EU Member States may decide to extend this further. Companies working in areas governed by EU law on financial services, products and markets, prevention of money laundering and terrorist financing, transport safety, and protection of the environment will have to maintain these procedures regardless of their size or number of employees.
- Tighter timeframes on investigation and response: The Directive will oblige "competent authorities" and companies required to adopt whistleblowing procedures to process protected disclosures within specific timeframes. They will have to acknowledge receipt within seven days and "diligently follow-up on disclosures". They will have to give the whistleblower feedback within three to six months, although this may not necessarily be the outcome of an investigation.
- New rules for "competent authorities": The Directive places new obligations on these authorities who will have to provide a variety of

reporting channels, with dedicated and trained staff who are obliged to stay in touch with the whistleblower. They will have to maintain secure systems for receiving and recording these reports. Competent authorities will be obliged to keep in touch with the whistleblower and must acknowledge receipt of a disclosure within seven days unless the whistleblower requests otherwise, or they believe that acknowledging the report would jeopardize the whistleblower's confidentiality. They will also have to give the whistleblower some information on what actions are being taken.

Code of practice

In March, 2015 the UK Department for Business Innovation & Skills introduced a Code of Practice[8] (below) for companies and organizations to ensure their compliance with best practice and the relevant laws.

Whistleblowing Code of Practice

It is important that employers encourage whistleblowing as a way to report wrongdoing and manage risks to the organisation. Employers also need to be well equipped for handling any such concerns raised by workers. It is considered best practice for an employer to:

- Have a whistleblowing policy or appropriate written procedures in place.
- Ensure the whistleblowing policy or procedures are easily accessible to all workers.
- Raise awareness of the policy or procedures through all available means such as staff engagement, intranet sites, and other marketing communications.
- Provide training to all workers on how disclosures should be raised and how they will be acted upon.
- Provide training to managers on how to deal with disclosures.
- Create an understanding that all staff at all levels of the organisation should demonstrate that they support and encourage whistleblowing.
- Confirm that any clauses in settlement agreements do not prevent workers from making disclosures in the public interest.
- Ensure the organisation's whistleblowing policy or procedures clearly identify who can be approached by workers that want to raise a

disclosure. Organisations should ensure a range of alternative persons who a whistleblower can approach in the event a worker feels unable to approach their manager. If your organisation works with a recognised union, a representative from that union could be an appropriate contact for a worker to approach.
- Create an organisational culture where workers feel safe to raise a disclosure in the knowledge that they will not face any detriment from the organisation as a result of speaking up.
- Undertake that any detriment towards an individual who raises a disclosure is not acceptable.
- Make a commitment that all disclosures raised will be dealt with appropriately, consistently, fairly, and professionally.
- Undertake to protect the identity of the worker raising a disclosure, unless required by law to reveal it and to offer support throughout with access to mentoring, advice and counselling.
- Provide feedback to the worker who raised the disclosure where possible and appropriate subject to other legal requirements. Feedback should include an indication of timings for any actions or next steps.

A robust whistleblowing policy will authorize employees to raise a concern if they come across any kind of illegal or improper act such as bribery, fraud, harassment, and so on.

> Measuring the effectiveness of a whistleblowing policy can also be useful to boards in assessing how effectively a culture is embedded. A healthy 'speak up' culture breaks down the barriers than can often exist between the workforce and the board. External publication of the data can also give investors confidence that a genuine culture of openness exists and where it does not that the board knows about it. Demonstrating how the policy is working can also inspire employees to speak up in other ways and the culture becomes self-reinforcing.[9]

The policy should be clear, simple, and easily understood. It should encourage anyone who has serious concerns about any aspect of work to come forward and voice these concerns. It should include a commitment to training employees in relation to whistleblowing. The policy should set out what action will be taken if a whistleblower is victimized or if any malicious allegations are made or if anyone knowingly provides false information. However, it should make clear that no disciplinary action will be taken against anyone who makes a disclosure in good faith. Their position at work will remain unaffected by the disclosure. Finally, any information disclosed should be treated as confidential.

Sample speak up/whistleblowing policy

Below is a sample speak up/whistleblowing for use by companies in Ireland and other EU member states (and elsewhere with adaptations):

[Name of company]

What is whistleblowing?

Whistleblowing occurs when an employee raises a concern or discloses information that relates to wrongdoing, illegal practices, or unethical conduct that has come to his/her attention through work. This whistleblowing policy is intended to encourage and enable [name of company] employees to raise concerns within the workplace rather than overlooking a problem or feeling that appropriate channels do not exist internally to allow reporting in confidence. Under this policy, an employee is entitled to "speak up", that is, raise concerns or disclose information, without fear of penalization or threat of less favourable treatment, discrimination, or disadvantage.

This policy has been created, and has been subsequently reviewed and updated, in the context of applicable whistleblowing legislation as applies to member companies in the UK and Ireland (and their staff members and other relevant individuals, as noted later in the policy).

Our commitment

[Company name] is committed to maintaining an open culture with the highest standards of honesty and accountability where our employees are encouraged to speak up if they have any concerns in confidence. This policy applies to all of our employees and extends to partners, principals, board members, trainees, and job applicants. It is important to note that should you have a concern in relation to your own employment or personal circumstances in the workplace it may be more appropriate to utilize the grievance procedure

Likewise, concerns arising concerning workplace relationships should generally be dealt with through the Dignity and Respect at Work Policy. Please note that this policy does not replace any legal reporting or disclosure requirements. Where statutory reporting requirements and procedures apply, these must be complied with in full.

Aims of the policy

- To encourage you to feel confident and safe in raising concerns and disclosing information;
- To provide avenues for you to raise concerns in confidence and receive feedback on any action taken;
- To ensure that you receive a response where possible to your concerns and information disclosed; and
- To assure you that you will be protected from penalization or any threat of penalization.

Staff members may refer to the employee handbook or the HR page on the staff intranet and/or consult with HR for further details.

This policy also complements the provisions of [company name] Ethics and Quality Control Manual.

What disclosures can be made?

A concern or disclosure should relate to a relevant wrongdoing such as possible fraud, crime, danger, or failure to comply with any legal obligation which has come to your attention in connection with your employment and about which you have a reasonable belief of wrongdoing. A relevant wrongdoing also includes breaches relating to the internal market, competition law and state aid, corporate tax law, public procurement, financial services, protection and welfare, risks to public health and to consumer protection, and privacy and protection of personal data.

Such disclosures are considered to be "protected disclosures" and which are subject to the protections set out in this policy, including protections from incurring liability for a breach of confidentiality pursuant to the disclosure meeting the requirements set out in this policy.

What disclosures should not be made?

A personal concern, for example a grievance around your own contract of employment, would not be regarded as a whistleblowing concern and would be more appropriately processed through the [company name] grievance procedure. In addition, there are other reporting channels in relation to disclosures such as (but not necessarily limited to) money laundering and terrorist financing, and fraud related reporting procedures, and data protection breach related reporting. The whistleblowing reporting provisions set out in this policy are not intended as replacement or alternative reporting channels unless the specific case allegedly involves relevant wrongdoing by [company name] and/ or the reporting individual feels they need or want to make use of the anonymous reporting functionality. The applicable processes for the existing reporting channels will also be reviewed and updated to ensure that "protected disclosures" that are potentially reported via the existing reporting channels are correctly identified and treated in line with the provisions of this policy.

Protected disclosures – safeguards and penalization

An employee who makes a "protected disclosure" and has a reasonable belief of wrongdoing will not be penalized by [company name] as a result of making such a disclosure, even if the concerns or disclosure turn out to be unfounded. Penalization means any act or omission that affects a worker to the worker's detriment, including the following:

- suspension, lay-off, or dismissal;
- discrimination, disadvantage, or unfair treatment;
- failure to renew or early termination of a temporary employment contract;
- demotion or loss of opportunity for promotion;
- injury, damage, or loss;
- harm, including to the person's reputation, particularly in social media, or financial loss, including loss of business and loss of income;
- transfer of duties, change of location of place of work, reduction in wages or change in working hours;

- threat of reprisal – blacklisting on the basis of a sector or industry-wide informal or formal agreement, which may entail that the person will not, in the future, find employment in the sector or industry;
- the imposition or administering of any discipline, reprimand or withholding of training;
- early termination or cancellation of a contract for goods and services;
- other penalty (including a financial penalty);
- unfair treatment;
- a negative performance assessment or employment reference;
- cancellation of a licence or permit;
- coercion, intimidation, or harassment; and
- failure to convert a temporary employment contract into a permanent one, where the worker had legitimate expectations that he or she would be offered permanent employment.

Psychiatric or medical referrals

[Company name] will keep its HR and other relevant policies and processes under ongoing review to ensure that they are aligned with this policy and with the need to protect individuals that have undertaken "protected disclosures" from such penalization.

These policies include but are not limited to the Dignity and Respect at Work Policy (available to staff as an appendix to their employee handbook). If you believe that you are being subjected to penalization as a result of making a disclosure under this procedure, you should inform your manager immediately. Employees who penalize or retaliate against those who have raised concerns under this policy will be subject to disciplinary action. Employees are not expected to prove the truth of an allegation. However, they must have a reasonable belief that there are grounds for their concern. It should be noted that appropriate disciplinary action may be taken against any employee who is found to have raised a concern or raised a disclosure with malicious intent.

The provisions of this policy in relation to protections for individuals having made "protected disclosures" are to be read in the context of the disciplinary procedure (available to staff as an appendix to their employee handbook).

Confidentiality

[Company name] is committed to protecting the identity of the employees raising a concern and ensures that relevant disclosures are treated in confidence. The focus will be on the wrongdoing rather than the person making the disclosure. However, there are circumstances, as outlined in the associated legislation, where confidentiality cannot be maintained particularly in a situation where the employee is participating in an investigation into the matter being disclosed. Should such a situation arise, we will make every effort to inform the employee that his/her identity may be disclosed.

[Company name] will not disclose to another person beyond such persons authorized to receive or follow up on the disclosure concerned any information that might identify the person by whom the protected disclosure was made. Where the identity of the reporting person is disclosed to another person, the reporting person shall be informed before their identity is disclosed unless such information would jeopardize the related investigations or judicial proceedings. This policy will be implemented in line with the provisions of the applicable data protection legislation. Any processing of personal data carried out pursuant to this policy, including the exchange or transmission of personal data, shall be carried out in accordance with the applicable data protection legislation.

Raising a concern anonymously

A concern may be raised anonymously through our whistleblowing reporting system. However, on a practical level it may be difficult to investigate such a concern and [company name] has limited obligations to accept or follow up on anonymous reports. [Company name] would encourage employees to put their names to allegations, with our assurance of confidentiality where possible, in order to facilitate appropriate follow-up. This will make it easier for us to assess the disclosure and take appropriate action including an investigation if necessary. Any person who reports anonymously is still protected by the provisions of this policy (and the underlying legislation that implements the EU Whistleblowing Directive) if their identity is subsequently revealed and they are potentially subject to penalization.

Raising a concern – who should you raise your concern with?

All employees wishing to speak up or blow the whistle should do so by making a report through our internal reporting system, available at: [link]. All reports made will be handled by [head of relevant function]. Where ethical issues are identified, [head of relevant function] will be consulted and will have final approval on the appropriate actions to be taken.

Raising a concern – how to raise a concern

Concerns may be raised via our internal reporting system, our hotline at [hotline number], or in writing. Should you raise a concern verbally through the hotline, this will be transcribed and input into (and managed via) the reporting system. Should you raise a concern in writing we would ask you to give the background and history of the concern, giving relevant details, insofar as is possible, such as dates, sequence of events, and description of circumstances. The earlier you express the concern, the easier it will be for us to deal with the matter quickly. Having raised your concern with us, we will acknowledge receipt of the report within seven days, and feedback and follow-up will be provided within three months from the date of report received. If your concern has been raised anonymously through the reporting system, you will be provided with a pin code to re-access your report and allow for follow-up communication.

We will need to clarify at this point if the concern is appropriate to this procedure or is a matter more appropriate to our other procedures, for example the grievance procedures or the Dignity and Respect at Work Policy. If an associated meeting is agreed, you can choose whether or not you want to be accompanied by a colleague or a representative. In regard to confidentiality, it is important that there should be an awareness of respecting sensitive company information, which, while unrelated to the disclosure, may be disclosed in the course of a consultation or investigation process.

Raising a concern – how we will deal with your disclosure

Having met with you, or communicated with you via the internal reporting system, in regard to your concern and clarified that the matter is in fact appropriate to this procedure, we will carry out an initial assessment to examine what actions we need to take to deal with the matter. This may involve simply clarifying certain matters, clearing up misunderstandings, or resolving the matter by agreed action without the need for an investigation. If, on foot of the initial assessment, we conclude there are grounds for concern that cannot be dealt with at this point, we will conduct an investigation which will be carried out fairly and objectively.

The form and scope of the investigation will depend on the subject matter of the disclosure. Disclosures may, in the light of the seriousness of the matters raised, be referred immediately to the appropriate authorities. Likewise, if urgent action is required this action will be taken. It is important that you feel assured that a disclosure made by you under this policy is taken seriously and that you are kept informed of steps being taken by us in response to your disclosure. In this regard we undertake to communicate with you as follows:

- We will acknowledge receipt of your disclosure and arrange to meet with you as outlined above;
- We will inform you of how we propose to investigate the matter and keep you informed of actions, where possible, in that regard including the outcome of any investigation, and, should it be the case, why no further investigation will take place. However, it is important to note that sometimes the need for confidentiality and legal considerations may prevent us from giving you specific details of an investigation;
- We will inform you of the likely timelines in regard to each of the steps being taken but in any event we commit to dealing with the matter as quickly as practicable. It is possible that in the course of an investigation you may be asked to clarify certain matters. To maximize confidentiality, such a meeting can take place off-site and you can choose whether or not to be accompanied by a colleague or representative. Where a concern is raised or a disclosure is made in accordance with this policy, but the allegation is subsequently not upheld by an investigation, no action will be taken against you and you will be protected against any penalization. It is important to note, however, that if an unfounded allegation is found to have been made with malicious intent, then disciplinary action may be taken.

> **Raising a concern – how the matter can be taken further**
>
> The aim of this policy is to provide an avenue within this workplace to deal with concerns or disclosures in regard to wrongdoing. [Company name] is confident that concerns or disclosures can be dealt with internally and we strongly encourage employees to report such concerns though our reporting system. We acknowledge there may be circumstances where an employee wants to make a disclosure externally, and the relevant legislation provides for a number of avenues in this regard. It is important to note, however, that while you need only have a reasonable belief as to wrongdoing to make a disclosure internally, if you are considering an external disclosure, different and potentially more onerous obligations apply depending on the party to whom the disclosure is made.

References

1 Mary Rowe, "Options and Choice for Conflict Resolution in the Workplace", in *Negotiation: Strategies for Mutual Gain*, ed. Lavinia Hall (Sage Publications, 1993), 105–119.
2 Wim Vandekerchkove, *Whistleblowing and Organizational Social Responsibility: A Global Assessment* (Routledge, 2006).
3 O.C. Ferrell, John Fraedrich, and Linda Ferrell, *Business Ethics: Ethical Decision Making and Case* (Cengage Learning, 2015), 193.
4 A Civil Servant v. A Government Department (2019) Workplace Relations Commission, ADJ-00021748. www.workplacerelations.ie. Available at: www.workplacerelations.ie/en/cases/2019/october/adj-00021748.html (Accessed: 18 September 2023).
5 A Concierge v. A Hotel (2020) Workplace Relations Commission, ADJ-00023901. www.workplacerelations.ie. Available at: www.workplacerelations.ie/en/cases/2020/february/adj-00023901.html (Accessed: 18 September 2023).
6 Transparency International, "Corruption Perceptions Index", 2022, www.transparency.org/en/cpi/2022/index/nor.
7 Directive (EU) 2019/1937 of the European Parliament and of the Council of 23 October 2019 on the protection of persons who report breaches of Union law (2019) *Official Journal* L 305, 17–56.

8 Department for Business Innovation & Skills, "Whistleblowing Guidance for Employers and Code of Practice" March, 2015). Available at: https://assets.publishing.service.gov.uk/government/uploads/system/uploads/attachment_data/file/415175/bis-15-200-whistleblowing-guidance-for-employers-and-code-of-practice.pdf#:~:text=Whistleblowing%20law%20is%20located%20in%20the%20Employment%20Rights,their%20job%20because%20they%20have%20%E2%80%98blown%20the%20whistle%E2%80%99. (Accessed: September 18 2023).
9 Financial Reporting Council (UK), "Corporate Culture and the Role of Boards Reporting of Observations", July 2016, 26, www.frc.org.uk/getattachment/3851b9c5-92d3-4695-aeb2-87c9052dc8c1/Corporate-Culture-and-the-Role-of-Boards-Report-of-Observations.pdf.

PART IV

FINANCE

Finance policies are a separate category concerned with corporate and individual conduct related to accounting and reporting of financial results for the company. Typically, they will provide a set of principles or rules about money and how the company accounts for, and reports on, money matters.

PART IV

FINANCE

15

ANTI-FRAUD

Introduction

Fraud is an emotive word and conjures up images of smooth-talking men in suits drawing up fictitious documents, and their hapless victims on the street who have lost everything. And that sequence of events is not entirely without foundation. Bernie Madoff and his infamous Ponzi scheme in the US in the 2000s is the best known example. Madoff was a US financier who convinced thousands of investors to hand over their savings and falsely promised consistent profits in return. In 2009 he was convicted of fraud, money laundering, perjury, and theft, and sentenced to 150 years in prison and ordered to pay compensation of $170 billion.

In legal terms, fraud is an intentional deception to secure unfair or unlawful gain, or to deprive a victim of a legal right. Intention was defined in an English criminal case in 1976[1] as "the decision to bring about a prohibited consequence". The mental element, or *mens rea*, of murder, for example, is traditionally expressed as malice aforethought, and the interpretations of "malice", "maliciously" and "wilful" vary between pure intent and recklessness or negligence depending on the country where the crime was committed and the seriousness of the offence. A person intends a consequence when they foresee that it will happen if their series of acts or omissions continue, and desire it to happen.

Civil and criminal fraud

It may be a civil matter in that the victim can sue the perpetrator to avoid the fraud if that is possible, or obtain compensation after the event. Or it may be a matter for the criminal law in the sense of a prosecution that results in the imprisonment of the perpetrator. The purpose of fraud may be monetary gain or some other benefit such as a passport, visa or driver's licence or in the case of mortgage fraud the perpetrator may attempt to qualify for a mortgage by way of false documentation.

As a civil matter, fraud is a wrong done or in technical terms a tort. The essential elements are that someone made an intentional deception or misrepresentation on which someone else relied, or it was intended that he or she should rely, to his or her detriment. Proving fraud is difficult because there must be an intention to defraud. In the US, proof is even more difficult because of the specific need for "clear and convincing evidence". Not all evidence produced in a courtroom comes up to that standard. If the fraud is proven, a court can rescind, that is, terminate, an agreement or transaction, and award compensation to the innocent party. In extreme cases the compensation can amount to what are called punitive damages to deter others who may be tempted to engage in the same behaviour.

As a criminal matter, fraud takes many different forms. It may be theft by false pretences in general or a specific fraud such as bank fraud, insurance fraud, or forgery of documents. If proven beyond a reasonable doubt – which is a higher standard than the balance of probabilities on a preponderance of the evidence – the perpetrator may be convicted of a criminal offence and imprisoned. The Fraud Act 2006 in the UK provides for three classes of fraud:

- False representation, i.e. lying;
- Failing to disclose information, i.e. concealment; and
- Abuse of position of trust.

Fraud by an employee might consist of one or more of these classifications. The severity of the fraudulent action will depend on a number of factors, including the amount of money involved, whether it was an isolated incident or one of a series of incidents, and whether the employee was in a position of trust such as a director or other senior position with wide responsibilities.

Common types of employee fraud include:

1. Theft of cash – In a bar or restaurant, the cashier keeps the register open and does not enter details of a purchase. The manager in a department store steals from the register and provides a false receipt by another manager or a false refund to a customer.
2. Unauthorized billing, money transfers, and overpayments–- An employee overstates an invoice amount and transfers the excess to his or her personal account. An employee creates a fictitious supplier and generates false invoices to the company for non-existent services, in order to conceal transfers to the employee's account.
3. Kickbacks and bribery – An employee takes payments or benefits in exchange for providing advantages to customers or suppliers to the company.
4. Benefits fraud – An employee submits a false claim for a massage or other treatment covered by a company insurance plan that they did not receive.
5. Compensation fraud – An employee exaggerates an injury or a disability or invents an injury that did not occur in order to receive compensation.
6. Asset misappropriation – This is theft of company assets by an employee, including use of a company credit card for personal items or using company assets for personal gain, for example a company car.
7. Payroll fraud – This involves an employee misusing the company's payroll system, such as paying a non-existent employee and diverting payment to himself or herself, or producing false time sheets to inflate the number of hours worked.
8. Data or intellectual property theft – An employee steals company data or intellectual property. This many involve sale of the data or property to a competitor.

The monetary value of fraud in the UK was £2.11 billion in 2017, according to a study published in the Financial Times in January, 2018. The average amount stolen in each incident of fraud increased from £1.5 million in 2003 to £3.66 million in 2017. The Crime Survey of England and Wales in October, 2015 revealed there had been 5.1 million incidents of fraud in England and Wales in the previous year, and these involved one in 12 adults. These figures make fraud the most common form of crime in the UK and this may be true of other countries as well.

Anti-fraud measures

There are a number of measures that will protect the organization from the various forms of fraud. These include:

1   Internal controls

Establish internal controls specifically designed to prevent and detect fraud. A code of ethics or code of conduct will set the tone that the company will not tolerate any unethical behaviour. An employee reporting system, such as an anonymous hotline, will help to uncover fraud.

2   Hiring procedures

Formal employment procedures when hiring staff should include thorough background investigations, education, credit and employment history as well as references from previous employers if appropriate. Evaluation of an employee's compliance with company ethics should be incorporated in performance reviews.

3   Training for fraud prevention

All employees should be trained in fraud prevention. Are employees aware of procedures for reporting suspicious activity by customers or co-workers? Do employees know the warning signs of fraud? All staff should know at least some basic fraud prevention measures.

4   Regular audits

Routine and non-routine audits should target high-risk areas such as finance and procurement.

5   External resources

The company may not have the internal resources to deal effectively with an actual or suspected fraud. When a fraud is revealed or suspected it may be necessary to hire the anti-fraud expertise of a third party such as an accountant or lawyer or other professional.

Fraud policy

As with all company policies and initiatives, the tone must be set from the top. Employees must know that the board of directors and senior management take fraud seriously and that wrongdoers will be punished. The company must be prepared to take strong action if needs be, and show that it will do so. A robust fraud policy is an effective way to show the company's commitment to combating fraud and corruption wherever they are found. This will also raise awareness of the danger and so promote an "anti-fraud culture" within the organization. As with any policy, the document should set out roles and responsibilities and the procedures to be followed in order to ensuring the right decisions are made.

A fraud policy should include these key elements:

- Specific actions that are fraudulent;
- Responsibility for the management of fraud in the organization;
- Explicit statement that all appropriate measures will be taken to prevent fraud;
- Formal procedures for investigation and reporting which employees should follow if a fraud is suspected; and
- Explicit statement that offenders will be prosecuted and all necessary steps will be taken to recover any ill-gotten gains.

Sample fraud policy

[company name]

Objective

The objective of this fraud policy is to implement monetary and risk controls that will help to detect and prevent fraud against [company name]. It is the intention of [company name] to promote good behaviour and to uphold the highest standards of moral and ethics while conducting its business.

Scope and applicability

This policy applies to all employees as well as shareholders, consultants, vendors, contractors, outside agencies doing business with employees of such agencies, and/or any other parties with a business relationship with [company name].

The policy applies to any and all act(s) or omission(s) that constitute(s) fraudulent or suspected fraudulent activity, including monetary items such as cash, funds, stock, proprietary information, intellectual property, material of value, content, data, assets, properties, consumables, office articles and supplies including stationery, contracts, bribes, gifts, favours, influencing, undue prioritisation, and so on for personal gains either individually or collectively by its employees or associates.

Actions that constitute fraud

The terms misappropriation and other fiscal irregularities refer to, but are not limited to:

- Any dishonest or fraudulent act, including forgery, falsification of documents and instruments, misrepresentation, impersonation and other activities;
- Misappropriation of funds, securities, supplies, or other assets;
- Impropriety in handling or reporting of money or financial transactions;
- Profiteering as a result of insider knowledge of company activities;

- Disclosing confidential and proprietary information to outside parties;
- Disclosing to other persons the security activities engaged in or contemplated by the company;
- Accepting or seeking anything of material value from contractors, vendors, or persons providing services / materials to the company;
- Destruction, removal, or inappropriate use of records, furniture, fixtures, and equipment and/or;
- Any similar or related irregularity.

Responsibility

Management is responsible for the detection and prevention of fraud, misappropriations, and other irregularities. Fraud is defined as the intentional, false representation, or concealment of a material fact for the purpose of gain, profiteering, or inducing another to perform fraudulent acts alone or in partnership. It is a breach of trust and gross violation of our high standards of behaviour.

Any irregularity that is detected or suspected must be reported immediately to [designated person] who will co-ordinate any investigation and appropriate action that may be required.

[name of department/function] has the primary responsibility for the investigation of all suspected fraudulent acts as defined in this policy. If the investigation confirms that fraud has occurred, the [name of department/function] will issue reports to appropriate designated personnel and, if appropriate, to the board of directors.

Any decision to prosecute or refer the investigation results to the appropriate law enforcement and/or regulatory agencies will be made in conjunction with legal counsel if necessary and Management.

The [name of department/function] treats all information received confidentially. Any employee who suspects dishonest or fraudulent activity must notify the [name of department/function] immediately and should not attempt to personally conduct investigations or interviews related to any suspected fraudulent act. Investigation results will not be disclosed or discussed with anyone other than those who have a legitimate need to know. This is important in order to avoid damaging the reputation of persons suspected but subsequently found innocent of wrongful conduct.

Authorization

Members of the Investigation team will have:

- Free and unrestricted access to all company records and premises, whether owned or rented; and
- The authority to examine, copy, and/or remove all or any portion of the contents of files, desks, cabinets, and other storage facilities on the premises without prior knowledge or consent of any individual who might use or have custody of any such items or facilities when it is within the scope of their investigation.

Employees under investigation may be asked not to enter the company's premises or to access any company web pages, drives, or links either personally or through colleagues or other means, until the investigation is complete. The company reserves the right to question the employee's colleagues, friends, relatives, associates, or service providers, whom the company or its investigation team suspects of their involvement.

Reporting

Great care must be taken in the investigation of suspected fraud so as to avoid mistaken accusations or alerting suspected individuals that an investigation is underway. An employee who discovers or suspects fraudulent activity must contact the [name of department or function] immediately. The employee or other complainant may remain anonymous. All inquiries concerning the activity under investigation from the suspected individual, his or her representative, or any other inquirer should be directed to the [name of department or function]. No information concerning the status of an investigation will be disclosed.

The individual who reports a fraud should be made aware of the following:

- Do not contact the suspected individual in an effort to determine the facts.
- Do not discuss the case, facts, suspicions, or allegations with anyone unless specifically asked to do so by [name of department or function].

Termination

If an investigation results in a decision to terminate an individual's employment, the decision must be reviewed for approval by Human Resources and by Management before any such action is taken.

Exceptions

Any deviation or exception to this policy must be approved by Management.

Non-compliance

Any violation of this policy will result in disciplinary action, up to and including termination of employment.

Reference

1 R v Mohan (1976) Court of Appeal, [1976] QB 1. Available at: www.oxbridgenotes.co.uk/law_cases/mohan (Accessed: 19 September 2023).

16

ANTI-MONEY LAUNDERING

Introduction

Money laundering is one of those activities that does exactly what it says on the tin. It is all about laundering or cleaning "dirty money". It may sound simple but the activity is complex and difficult, and of course completely illegal.

Money laundering is the process of concealing the origin of money that has been obtained by illegal means. It passes through a complex series of transactions between banks and companies and individuals, with the objective to return the money after it has been cleaned to the party that started the process in the first place. This is necessary because the money launderer has a problem in accounting for the proceeds of crime. He or she needs to avoid the attention of law enforcement and so considerable time and effort go into the process to ensure safe access to and use of the money in a clean state after its return to the legitimate economy. Essentially the banking system is being used for this purpose. But other sectors of the economy may also be used and abused. For example, a house purchase or

DOI: 10.4324/9781003258995-20

the purchase of some other expensive asset such as jewellery may conceal funds obtained by illegal means. For this reason, solicitors and estate agents and some other professions have specific responsibilities to combat money laundering and establish the source of funds in any large transaction. The United Nations Office on Drugs and Crime estimates that the total amount of money laundered globally in any one year is between 2% and 5% of global Gross Domestic Product, or between $800 billion and $2 trillion in US dollars.

The definition of money laundering is often expanded by regulators such as the US Office of the Comptroller of the Currency to mean any financial transaction that generates an asset or value as the result of an illegal act such as tax evasion or false accounting. In many countries there are sophisticated financial and other systems to enable law enforcement authorities to detect suspicious transactions, and some countries have set up international arrangements to co-operate with each other. The concealment of source of funds in a particular transaction may constitute money laundering, whether intentional or not, by the use of systems or services that do not identify where the money has come from.

The terrorist attacks on the World Trade Centre in New York in September 2001 led to the introduction of the Patriot Act in the US and similar legislation worldwide. This legislation provides for the use of money laundering laws to combat terrorism financing. The Group of Seven (G7) countries, that is, the most developed economies, established the Financial Action Task Force on Money Laundering to put pressure on countries around the world to increase surveillance and monitoring of financial transactions, and to share this information. Anti-money laundering legislation has become a heavy burden for financial institutions to comply with in order to identify their clients and the source of funds used in large transactions. Before it left the European Union at the end of 2020, the UK had introduced similar legislation to that in effect in the rest of Europe prior to that time. The Proceeds of Crime Act 2002 was amended and supplemented by regulations in 2017 and 2019 pursuant to relevant EU directives.

European Union

In July 2021 the European Commission presented new proposals to strengthen the existing money laundering rules across Europe. More correctly, these are *anti-money laundering* (AML) rules. These proposals will streamline the efforts of EU member states to combat the use of the financial system for illegal purposes. They also propose the creation of a new EU authority to carry on the fight and enforce the new rules. The aim is to improve the detection of suspicious transactions and close off any loopholes used by criminals to launder the proceeds of their crimes through the financial system. In particular, the new AML rules will apply to cryptocurrencies such as bitcoin for the first time. Providers of cryptocurrency services such as exchanges and brokers will be obliged to prevent their services being used to launder money that represents the proceeds of crime.

Stages of money laundering

Typically there are three distinct stages in a money laundering process:

Stage 1: Placement
This is the first stage where the money which represents the proceeds of crime is placed into the financial system, for example lodged into a bank account. The criminal is anxious to avoid the attention of law enforcement.

Stage 2: Layering
In this stage the money is *layered* or *structured*. It is divided into small amounts or transactions that make it hard to detect. The money may also be transferred to another country or converted to another form such as stocks and shares to add another layer of complexity.

Stage 3: Integration
This is the final stage of money laundering, in which the money is now returned to the criminal 'legitimately' after it was placed in the financial system. The money is now integrated with a legitimate source of funds such as a bank account to make it look like everything is above board.

Money laundering policy

Every financial institution and every company that provides financial services of any kind must have a comprehensive and up-to-date AML policy.

This policy will provide the basis for robust procedures to ensure AML compliance.

AML procedures in most companies are based on the 'five pillars':

- policies and procedures
- designation of an AML officer
- maintain formal AML programme
- risk assessments and
- client/customer due diligence.

So an AML policy plays a central role in compliance with the requirements. This will determine the procedures and controls that are required to implement the policy. In turn these will determine the content of employee training and testing, and client due diligence (CDD).

What is CDD? This is a process of checks to help identify clients/customers and make sure they are who they say they are. The company must be in a position to identify any activity or transaction that might constitute money laundering, and this will be easier if the company knows the client and understands the reason behind the particular transaction. So CDD is required when companies that are required to have AML procedures, that is, financial services providers, enter into a business relationship with a client or a potential client, in order to assess their risk profile and verify their identity. The specific data that must be collected includes data about the client from trusted sources to determine the purpose of the client relationship and the intended nature and key beneficiaries of the relationship. If the client is deemed to be a higher risk, for example a political or public figure or someone from a high-risk country, enhanced due diligence measures are required that may involve a close monitoring of the client relationship and deeper investigation into the client's identity or business.

A robust AML policy will help to shape the company's procedures to detect and prevent money laundering. To focus resources on the areas of greatest risk, the company should adopt a risk-based approach to compliance with AML requirements. This in turn requires a company-wide risk assessment.

Every company faces different risks and will have their own approach to mitigate them. The company's policy should provide a general overview of the firm's approach to alleviate these risks and provide the basis for day-to-day AML procedures. For example, when onboarding a new client, the procedures will state what identification documents are acceptable, what is an acceptable proof of address, what forms need to be completed, what searches and checks need to be done.

As per the firm-wide risk assessment, the AML policy should be updated regularly, at least every two years. In addition to this, trigger events such as a change in legislation or guidance, identification of a new money laundering risk, or new systems and processes must prompt an update. You should document who has updated it, what has been updated and when it was updated. The policy and any changes to it must be formally approved by the company's Money Laundering Reporting Officer (MLRO).

To meet regulatory requirements, the AML policy should at a minimum cover the following matters:

- Company-wide risk assessment
- Due diligence
- Client risk assessment
- Training
- Record-keeping
- Suspicious activity reporting
- Tipping off and
- Ongoing monitoring.

Sample AML policy

Below is a sample anti-money laundering policy for use by companies that are in scope of AML obligations because they are at risk of being used for money laundering purposes.

[company name]

Money Laundering Reporting Officer

The MLRO of [company name] is [insert individual's name]. The alternative MLRO is [insert individual's name]. Their responsibilities are as follows:

- Oversight of, and be involved in, AML risk assessments;
- Take reasonable steps to access any relevant information about the business;

- Obtain and use national and international research about AML;
- Create and maintain the company's risk-based approach to money laundering;
- Support the company's focus on money laundering risks in each business function. This involves developing and implementing systems, controls, policies, and procedures that are appropriate to each function;
- Take steps to ensure the creation and maintenance of comprehensive AML documentation;
- Develop CDD procedures and processes;
- Ensure systems and controls needed to enable staff to make internal suspicious transaction reports (STRs);
- Receive internal STRs and make external STRs to the relevant authorities as required;
- Take remedial action where AML controls are ineffective;
- Take steps to establish and maintain arrangements for relevant AML awareness and training;
- Receive the findings of relevant audits and compliance reviews (both internal and external) and communicate these to the board of directors;
- Report to the board of directors at least annually, providing an assessment of the operations and effectiveness of the business' AML systems and controls. This should take the form of a written report. These written reports should be supplemented with regular ad hoc meetings or comprehensive management information to keep senior management engaged with AML compliance and up to date with relevant national and international developments in AML, including new areas of risk and regulatory practice. The board of directors should be able to demonstrate that it has considered these reports and taken appropriate action to remedy any AML deficiencies.

MLRO report

The MLRO will conduct a test and document a report testing the firm's AML systems and controls.

Company-wide risk assessment

The company will conduct a money laundering risk assessment across the organization.

Suspicious transaction reports (STRs)

The company has in place internal reporting procedures to enable relevant employees to disclose their knowledge or suspicions of money laundering. All employees must report any knowledge or suspicions to the MLRO. The MLRO will consider the internal report and will then decide whether to submit an external STR to the relevant authorities. Should the MLRO decide not to submit an external STR, they will document their reason(s).

Internal STRs

Employees must report escalate any suspicious activity to the MLRO immediately.

Consequence of failure to report

A person commits an offence if, during the course of business he develops knowledge or suspicion (or has reasonable grounds for doing so) that another person is engaged in money laundering, and he does not make the required disclosure as soon as is practicable. The UK Proceeds of Crime Act 2020 ("the Act") provides that an offence is committed regardless of whether it subsequently transpires that the money laundering cannot be proven, or that it did not occur.[1]

The required disclosure is a disclosure of the information or other matter to the MLRO or the relevant authorities.

Tipping off

Employees must not commit the offence of *tipping off*. The Act provides that an employee commits an offence if they know or suspect that a disclosure has been made, and he makes a disclosure which is likely to prejudice any investigation which might be conducted following the disclosure.[2] An employee also commits an offence if they know or suspect that an appropriate officer is conducting or about to conduct a confiscation investigation, a civil recovery investigation, a detained cash investigation or a money laundering investigation and either makes a disclosure which is likely to prejudice it or falsifies, conceals, destroys, or otherwise disposes of relevant document or causes another to do so.[3]

Training

The company provides comprehensive and mandatory AML training that includes the MLRO and employees' responsibilities. The MLRO is responsible for ensuring that all relevant employees undertake the AML training at the appropriate time. All training will be conducted internally or externally on an annual basis. The AML training covers the following matters:

- AML "red flags";
- AML laws and regulations;
- Conducting of CDD;
- Suspicious transaction reports;
- Tipping off; and
- Case studies with examples of money laundering activities.

Client risk assessment

Client risk is the overall money laundering risk posed by a client. The most important question is whether the client or its beneficial owner(s) has/have any characteristics known to be frequently used by money launderers. All clients will be risk categorised, for example hold a risk rating of high, medium, or low as follows:

1. **High-risk client**

    Any client who has one or more of the following risk factors will be considered as high-risk:

    - The business relationship is conducted in unusual circumstances;
    - The client is a resident of, or transacts business with, a geographical area of high risk;
    - Cash-intensive business, e.g. takeaway, retail shop, scrap metal dealers, car wash, nail-bar;
    - The corporate structure of the client is unusual or more complex than required by the nature of the client's business;
    - High-net-worth individual, e.g. any individual or entity with assets of over €1 million;
    - Politically exposed person;
    - High-value business, e.g. jeweller, car dealership, art dealer; or

- High-risk sector such as buying and selling property, import and export businesses, currency exchange services, cryptocurrency, visa and immigration services, investment services, precious metals.

2. **Low-risk client**

    A low-risk client is an entity that is:

    - a public body;
    - a publicly owned enterprise, i.e. a listed company; or
    - a company whose securities are listed on a regulated market.

3. **Medium-risk client**

    Any client who does not have any high or low-risk factors will be classified as medium-risk.

Due diligence policy

The company will carry out onboarding and ongoing monitoring of new and existing clients respectively. We will obtain documentation to identify them and verify their address. We will carry out independent checks in the case of clients that are incorporated entities in order to establish the legal status of the entity, its corporate structure (including beneficial ownership), the nature of the business, the relevant transaction, and the source of any funds introduced by the client.

Ongoing monitoring

[Company name] will review any client who is classified as high risk every six months. All medium and low-risk clients will be reviewed every 12 months. The review will ensure that all due diligence information is still relevant and up to date. This review will include:

- Checking that identification and address is still valid;
- Checking that the publicly available information about the client matches our records; and
- Checking that annual turnover of the client is in line with what we would expect.

> Events that would prompt an immediate review of their rating will include:
>
> - A change in the client's identity;
> - A change in beneficial ownership of the client;
> - A change in the service provided to the client; and
> - Information that is inconsistent with our knowledge of the client.

References

1 *Proceeds of Crime Act 2002, c.29*. Available at: www.legislation.gov.uk/ukpga/2002/29/section/330 (Accessed: 19 September 2023).
2 *Proceeds of Crime Act 2002, c.29*. Available at: www.legislation.gov.uk/ukpga/2002/29/section/333 (Accessed: 19 September 2023).
3 *Proceeds of Crime Act 2002, c.29*. Available at: www.legislation.gov.uk/ukpga/2002/29/section/342 (Accessed: 19 September 2023).

17

INSIDER TRADING

Introduction

Insider trading, also called insider dealing, consists of the trading of a public company's stock or other securities such as bonds or stock options based on material, non-public information about the company. For this purpose, a public company is one whose stocks or shares are listed on a public exchange such as the London Stock Exchange or the New York Stock Exchange. In many countries some kinds of trading based on insider information are illegal while others are perfectly in order. Illegal trading is regarded as unfair to investors who do not have access to the same kind of information because the investor with insider information could potentially make a large profit as a result. The rules governing insider trading are complex and vary from country to country.

Trading by 'insiders', such as company directors or managers, is often allowed as long as it does not rely on relevant information that is not available to the public. In many countries this kind of trading must be reported to the authorities so that it can be monitored. For example, in the United

DOI: 10.4324/9781003258995-21

States and some other countries trading done by certain officers of the company and key employees, and even major shareholders, must be reported. In these cases, insiders in the US must file the trade with the US Securities and Exchange Commission (SEC) when buying or selling shares of their own companies.

The US was the first country to deal with insider trading. The Securities Exchange Act of 1934 was introduced after the stock market crash of 1929. But even before that the US had taken steps to prevent illegal trading, or fraud as it was called at the time. In 1909 the US Supreme Court ruled in the case of *Strong v. Repide*[1] that a company director who bought the company's stock when he knew the stock price was about to increase on the basis of inside information had committed fraud by buying the stock but not disclosing the information in his possession. SEC regulations now require that if a company discloses material non-public information to one individual, it must also disclose that information to the public.

However, the more recent European approach constitutes a stricter regime to prevent illegal insider trading. In the European Union and the United Kingdom post-Brexit, all trading on non-public information is subject to market abuse legislation, with civil and criminal penalties. And the penalties can be substantial regardless of where the offence takes place. In the US, the Insider Trading Sanctions Act of 1984 and the Insider Trading and Securities Fraud Enforcement Act of 1988 provide for fines for illegal insider trading up to three times the amount of any profit gained from the trade. The SEC and the various stock exchanges around the world monitor all trading activity, looking for anything suspicious. After a SEC investigation, Mathew Martoma who was a hedge fund trader and was accused of making the largest insider trading profit in history at a value of $276 million. He was convicted in February 2014 and sentenced to nine years in prison.[2]

'Insiders'

In the US, Canada, Australia, and Germany, corporate insiders are defined as a company's officers, directors, and owners of more than 10% of a class of the company's shares. Trades made by these insiders in their company's own stock, based on material non-public information, are illegal because the individuals concerned are acting in breach of the *fiduciary* duty, that is, duty of care, that they owe to the company's shareholders. The corporate insider, in working for the company, has undertaken a legal obligation to put the shareholders' interests before their own in matters related to the company. For example, insider trading would occur if a director was informed prior to a public announcement that the company would be subject to a takeover by a third party, and then bought shares in the company knowing that the share price would rise.

In many countries, including the US, the definition of "insiders" extends to any individual who trades shares based on material non-public information in breach of their position of trust. This may include anyone who misappropriates material non-public information and trades on that information. In a case in 1997, *United States v. O'Hagan*,[3] the US Supreme Court applied this misappropriation theory to convict a lawyer of illegal insider trading. Mr O'Hagan was a partner in a law firm representing Grand Metropolitan while it was considering a tender offer to purchase another company, Pillsbury. He used this inside information by buying stock options on Pillsbury stock, resulting in a profit of more than $4.3 million.

Not all trading by insiders is illegal. For example, many employees of public companies have shares or share options as part of their employment contracts. These trades in the US are made public through SEC filings. Or an insider might plan to retire after a certain period of time and, as part of his or her retirement plan, he or she may have entered into a legal agreement to sell a specified amount of the company's stock every month until retirement. If the individual later comes into possession of material non-public information about the company, any trades based on the original agreement will not be regarded as illegal insider trading.

To make it even more complicated, there are insiders and insiders. In a case in 1984, *Dirks v. Securities and Exchange Commission*,[4] the US Supreme Court defined the concept of "constructive insiders", who are lawyers, investment bankers, and others who receive confidential information about a company in the course of providing professional services. Constructive insiders are also liable to prosecution for illegal insider trading if the information was provided on the basis that it would remain confidential.

In July 2023 a police officer was convicted by a federal jury in Boston, US of conspiring to trade on inside information about a company's planned acquisition of a company that manufactures semiconductor chips.[5] The police officer obtained material non-public information from his brother who was a senior executive at the semiconductor company, and used this information to make a profit in buying and selling the company's shares.

Europe and elsewhere

In the UK the relevant laws are the Criminal Justice Act 1993 and the Financial Services and Markets Act 2000 which defines the offence of "market abuse". The European Union first took action in 2014 with the Criminal Sanctions for Market Abuse Regulation.[6] The common principle is that it is illegal to trade on the basis of market-sensitive information that is not generally known. This is a much broader scope than inside information under US law. One of the key differences is that there need not be any relationship between the individual and the company that issues the shares: all that is required is that the individual engaged in trading while in the possession of inside information.

Insider trading in India is an offence under the Securities and Exchange Board of India Act, 1992. This is defined as access to non-public, price-sensitive information about the shares of the company that leads to someone who subscribes, buys, sells, or deals in, these shares, or agrees to do so or counsels another to do so. Price-sensitive information is information that materially affects the value of the shares. In Australia if an individual possesses inside information and knows, or ought reasonably to know, that the information is not generally available and is materially price-sensitive, the individual must not trade on the basis of that information.[7] He or she cannot procure another individual to trade on the same basis. Information is considered to be generally available if it consists of "readily observable matter" or it has been made known to investors.

Examples of illegal trading

Below are some examples of insider trading that would be illegal as we've discussed in this chapter:

- A company director knows that a merger is due to be announced shortly and that the company's shares will probably increase in value. He buys 1,000 shares in his mother's name so he can make a profit using his

insider information without reporting the trade and in advance without news of the trade being made public.
- A senior employee overhears a discussion in which a company director talks about how the company is about to go into liquidation as a result of severe financial problems. The employee knows that his friend owns shares in the company. He warns his friend that he needs to sell his shares immediately.
- A government employee is aware that a new regulation will significantly benefit an electricity company. The employee buys shares of the electricity company and then arranges for the regulation to come into effect as soon as possible.
- A senior manager finds out about a merger between the company and another company. Knowing that the merger will lead to the purchase of shares at a high price, the manager buys shares the day before the merger is due to be completed.

Sample insider trading policy

Below is a sample insider trading policy for reference.

[company name]

I. Purpose

Anyone who has knowledge of material non-public information may be considered an "insider" for purposes of the laws prohibiting insider trading. As a result, it is a violation of our policy and the applicable laws for any officer, director, or employee of the company to: 1. trade in securities of the company while aware of 'material non-public information' concerning the company; or 2. communicate or disclose material non-public information to outsiders so they may trade in securities of the Company based on that information. The company has adopted this policy for all of its directors, officers, and employees and their family members, as well as for others who have access to information through business relationships with the company.

Violation of this policy by any officer or employee may result in disciplinary action up to and including dismissal.

II. Scope

This policy covers all directors, officers, and employees of the Company and their respective family members and any outsiders whom the Insider Trading Compliance Officer may designate as insiders because they have access to material non-public information about the company.

The Policy applies to any and all transactions in the Company's securities.

III. Definition of "material non-public information"

"Material Information" is any information about the company that a reasonable investor would consider important in making an investment decision to buy or sell the company's securities. Information is considered 'non-public' until it has been widely disseminated to the public and there has been sufficient time for the market to digest that information.

IV. Prohibited activities

An insider may not trade in company securities while aware of material non-public information about the company.

An insider may not trade in company securities during any special trading blackout periods as designated by the Compliance Officer.

An insider may not disclose to any person the applicability of a blackout period without prior permission of the Compliance Officer.

The Compliance Officer may not trade in company securities unless the trade(s) have been approved by the Chief Financial Officer or Chief Executive Officer in accordance with the procedures set forth below.

An insider may not disclose material non-public information about the company to any outside person, including family members, unless required as part of the insider's regular duties for the company or authorized by the Compliance Officer. All inquiries from outsiders regarding material non-public information about the company must be forwarded to the Compliance Officer.

Without the prior approval of the Compliance Officer, or the Chief Executive Officer, an insider may not accept outside employment, as a consultant, independent contractor, or employee, where the insider is being compensated for their knowledge of the company.

An insider identified by the Compliance Officer as being subject to a special blackout period may not trade in company securities during such a special blackout period. The Compliance Officer may, following consultation with the Chief Financial Officer or Chief Executive Officer, declare such special blackout periods from time to time as conditions warrant. An insider, whether or not subject to a special blackout period, may not disclose to any outside third party that a special blackout period has been declared.

V. Violations

An insider who violates this policy or any applicable law or relation or knows of any such violation by any other insider must report the violation immediately to the Compliance Officer. Upon receipt of this report, the Compliance Officer will:

- Investigate the matter to determine whether a violation may have occurred;
- Report the potential violation of this Policy to the board of directors if the Compliance Officer concludes a violation may have occurred; and
- Upon determining that any such violation has occurred, determine whether the company should release any material non-public information.

If the Compliance Officer determines that a violation of the policy has occurred, the company may discipline the insider, including immediate dismissal. The company may also report the violation to relevant authorities.

VI. Compliance Officer

The company has designated [name of individual] as its Compliance Officer for purposes of this policy.

References

1. Strong v. Repide (1909) Supreme Court, 213 US 419. *Justia US Supreme Court*. Available at: http://supreme.justia.com/us/213/419/ (Accessed: 19 September 2023).
2. Yoshita Singh, "Indian-origin fund manager indicted in insider trading", 26 December 2012, www.rediff.com/money/report/indian-origin-fund-manager-indicted-in-insider-trading/20121225.htm.
3. United States v. O'Hagan (1997) Supreme Court, 521 US 642. *Justia US Supreme Court*. Available at: https://supreme.justia.com/cases/federal/us/521/642/ (Accessed: 19 September 2023).
4. Dirks v. Securities and Exchange Commission (1983) Supreme Court, 463 US 646. *Justia US Supreme Court*. Available at: https://supreme.justia.com/cases/federal/us/463/646/ (Accessed: 19 September 2023).
5. United States Attorney's Office, District of Massachusetts, "Needham Police Officer Convicted of Insider Trading Conspiracy", 20 July 2023, www.justice.gov/usao-ma/pr/needham-police-officer-convicted-insider-trading-conspiracy.
6. Regulation (EU) No 596/2014 of the European Parliament and of the Council of 16 April 2014 on market abuse (market abuse regulation) and repealing Directive 2003/6/EC of the European Parliament and of the Council and Commission Directives 2003/124/EC, 2003/125/EC and 2004/72/EC (2014) *Official Journal* L 173 1-61.
7. *Corporations Act 2001, No. 50 of 2001*. Available at: www5.austlii.edu.au/au/legis/cth/consol_act/ca2001172/s1042a.html and www5.austlii.edu.au/au/legis/cth/consol_act/ca2001172/s1043a.html (Accessed: September 2023).

18
ACCOUNTING AND AUDIT

Introduction

Knowledge is power. And knowledge or information about the company's financial affairs is key to making the right decisions at the right time. The objective of accounting or financial reporting is to provide accurate financial information about the company that is useful to existing and potential investors, lenders, and other creditors in making decisions about investing in or lending to the company. And the company has choices about how to do this. In this chapter we discuss what the company is allowed to do. These choices require judgement on the part of the person preparing the accounts, and standards are needed in order to ensure consistency in the way these judgements are made. Industry bodies such as those responsible for the Generally Accepted Accounting Principles (GAPP) in the US, and the International Financial Accounting Standards (IFRS) in many other countries including the UK and Ireland, play a central role in setting these standards. (IFRS is principles-based and can therefore reflect the economic reality of a transaction or event. GAAP, on the other hand, is a stricter

DOI: 10.4324/9781003258995-22

rules-based approach. The differences between the two standards are evident in accounting policies – some policies that are allowed under GAAP may not be allowed under IFRS.)

The regulatory authorities in different countries enforce the rules which may or may not reflect the standards set by industry. The authorities have the final say in establishing financial reporting standards or rules in their own country. For example, in order to ensure compliance, listed companies in the UK and Ireland use the UK version of GAAP, while non-listed companies (who are the vast majority of companies) use IFRS. If the company is listed on an EU stock exchange, it must follow IFRS according to EU regulations.

Accounting policies

Accounting or financial reporting policies set out the principles and procedures that are implemented by the company in order to prepare its financial statements. These statements are the written records that state the business activities and the financial performance of a company. Financial statements are often audited by government agencies, accountants, firms, and so on to ensure accuracy and for tax, financing, or investing purposes. Financial statements include:

- Balance sheet
- Income statement and
- Cash flow statement.

First, the balance sheet provides an overview of assets, liabilities, and shareholders' equity at a point in time. Second, the income statement primarily focuses on a company's revenues and expenses during a particular period. After expenses are deducted from the revenues, the statement produces a company's profit figure called net income. Finally, the cash flow statement measures how well a company generates cash to pay its debt obligations, to fund its operating expenses, and to fund investments.

The principles and procedures set out in accounting or financial reporting include any accounting methods, measurement systems, and procedures for disclosing whatever information must be disclosed. Accounting policies differ from accounting principles in that the principles are the rules of accounting and the policies describe how the company complies with these rules. We can think of accounting principles as a framework in which the company is expected to manage its financial reporting. The framework is flexible and allows the company to decide between different accounting policies that are more or less advantageous. However, as we have seen, all accounting policies are required to conform to GAAP in the US and/or IFRS in the UK, and the equivalent principles in other countries.

What are these accounting policies? They are a set of standards that govern how a company prepares its financial statements. These policies are used to deal with complex activities such as depreciation methods, recognition of goodwill for revenue purposes, preparation of research and development costs, inventory valuation, and the consolidation of financial accounts. The accounting policies of the company will indicate whether its approach to reporting financial results, including earnings, is conservative or aggressive. Investors should take this into account in assessing a key financial indicator such as the quality of earnings, that is, that the company's earnings result clearly from higher sales or lower costs, or both. The company's external auditors will also review the company's policies to ensure they conform to GAAP or IFRS, as the case may be. For example, companies are allowed to value their inventory of products using the first in first out (FIFO), or last in first out (LIFO) methods of accounting:

> Under the FIFO inventory cost method, when a company sells a product, the cost of the inventory produced or acquired first is considered to be sold. Under the LIFO method, when a product is sold, the cost of the inventory produced last is considered to be sold. In periods of rising inventory prices, a company can use these accounting policies to increase or decrease its earnings [by minimizing the costs of goods]. For example, a company in the manufacturing industry buys inventory at $10 per unit for the first half of the month and $12 per unit for the second half of the month. The company ends up purchasing a total of 10 units at $10 and 10 units at $12 and sells a total of 15 units for the entire month. If the company uses FIFO, its cost of goods sold is: (10 x $10) + (5 x $12) = $160. If it uses LIFO, its cost of goods sold is: (10 x $12) + (5 x $10) = $170.[1]

An aggressive approach to financial reporting aims to enhance the company's reported performance and financial position by inflating the amount of revenues, earnings, and/or operating cash flow reported in the period; or by decreasing expenses for the period and/or the amount of debt reported on the balance sheet. A conservative approach in financial reports will not seek to do any of these and can result from either accounting standards that specifically require a conservative treatment of a specific transaction or event, or judgements made in applying these accounting standards. Finance managers in the company may be tempted to produce low-quality financial reports in order to conceal poor performance or some other improper reason.

Financial statements

Financial statements should amount to a fair presentation of the company's financial position as a going concern. The IFRS provides that a complete set of financial statements must include:[2]

- Statement of financial position of the company's assets and liabilities, i.e. balance sheet;
- Statement of the company's income, either separate statements for net income and gross (pre-tax) income or one statement for both net and gross income;
- Statement of changes in the company's equity, i.e. share capital;
- Cash flow statement; and
- Notes including a summary of accounting policies and other information.

Financial statements that are based on recognized reporting standards will be reliable and free from manipulation but the quality of these statements can vary between companies. A high-quality set of financial statements provides information that is useful to assess the company's performance and prospects. In particular, the quality of reported results or earnings quality pertains to the earnings and cash generated by the company's operations. High-quality earnings result from operations that a company will likely be able to sustain in the future. As we have seen, these earnings result either from higher sales of the company's products or services, or lower costs, or indeed both if that is achievable.

Low-quality financial statements, on the other hand, contain inaccurate, misleading or incomplete information. And lapses in quality have caused a series of financial scandals that resulted in losses for investors and a loss of confidence in the financial system. Enron Corporation, Tyco International and WorldCom in the US are recent examples.

FRS 18

Financial Reporting Standard (FRS) 18 deals primarily with the selection, application, and disclosure of accounting policies. Its objective is to ensure that for all material items:

- an entity adopts the accounting policies most appropriate to its particular circumstances for the purpose of giving a true and fair view;
- an entity should prepare its financial statement on a going concern basis, unless:
    - the entity is being liquidated or has ceased trading, or
    - the directors either intend to liquidate the entity or to cease trading, or have no realistic alternative but to do so.
- the accounting policies adopted are reviewed regularly to ensure that they remain appropriate, and are changed when a new policy becomes more appropriate to the entity's particular circumstances; and
- sufficient information is disclosed in the financial statements to enable users to understand the accounting policies adopted and how they have been implemented.

The FRS requires accounting policies to be consistent with accounting standards, Urgent Issues Task Force (UITF) Abstracts, and companies legislation. Where this constraint allows a choice, the FRS requires an entity to select whichever of those accounting policies is judged to be most appropriate to its particular circumstances for the purpose of giving a true and fair view.

An entity should judge the appropriateness of accounting policies to its particular circumstances against the objectives of the company.

The constraints that an entity should take into account are the need to balance the different objectives, and the need to balance the cost of providing information with the likely benefit of such information to users of the entity's financial statements.

An entity's accounting policies should be reviewed regularly to ensure that they remain the most appropriate to its particular circumstances. An entity should implement a new accounting policy if it is judged more appropriate to the entity's particular circumstances than the present accounting policy.

The FRS requires specific disclosures about the accounting policies followed and changes to these policies. It also requires, in some circumstances, disclosures about the estimation techniques used in applying those policies.

FRS 102

The Financial Reporting Standard applicable in the UK and Ireland was introduced in March, 2018. This is known as FRS 102 and it applies to the preparation of financial statements in the UK and Ireland.

> The Standard aims at striking a balance between clear guidance and necessary detail. The disclosures illustrated, therefore, do not include all possible disclosures as this would clearly make any guidance too unwieldy to be of wide, practical use. For this reason they should not be used as a substitute for completing a disclosure checklist.
>
> FRS 102 is designed to apply to the general purpose financial statements and financial reporting of legal entities including those that are not constituted as companies and those that are not profit-oriented. FRS 102 is subject to a periodic review at least every five years. The last periodic review, the Triennial Review 2017, was completed in December 2017, with an effective date of 1 January 2019. The next periodic review of FRS 102 commenced in March 2021 and resulting amendments are expected to be effective no earlier than 1 January 2024.[3]

Audit

"The auditors won't like it". How often has the CEO or the head of a corporate function heard those words? These words may or may not strike fear in the heart of everyone who hears them but at the very least knowing how the company's auditors will regard a corporate action or decision will often dictate what the action or decision will be. So we need to understand what audit is concerned about and why everyone in the organization should be concerned as well.

Before we consider the elements of an audit policy, what do we mean by an "audit"? It has been defined as:

an independent examination of financial information of any entity, whether profit oriented or not, irrespective of its size or legal form when such an examination is conducted with a view to express an opinion thereon.[4]

However, as well as an examination, the audit will also try to ensure that the company's books of accounts are properly maintained as required by law.

Therefore a comprehensive audit policy will describe the rules and standards that a company applies to the conduct of an internal audit or the conduct of an external audit by an accounting firm. In addition to financial matters, the audit policy is important for maintaining information security, detecting any security incidents, and to meet relevant compliance requirements. However, the main purpose of the audit policy is to set out the framework within which the company's internal audit function provides objective and independent assurance and advice regarding the controls in place to mitigate against the risks faced by the company in doing business. These risks include financial risks such as loss of revenue which may result in loss of profit and other risks such as security risk, legal risk, and reputational risk.

A set of instructions to put in place a comprehensive audit policy is at the end of this chapter.

Financial audit

Usually an audit means a financial audit. This is conducted to arrive at an opinion whether financial statements are prepared in accordance with specific accounting standards. In arriving at this opinion, the auditor gathers evidence to determine whether the statements contain material errors or misstatements. The audit opinion is intended to provide a reasonable assurance that the financial statements are presented fairly, in all material respects, and/or give a true and fair view of the company's financial position. This reflects the purpose of an audit which is to provide an objective examination of the financial statements to ensure the confidence of readers of these statements and to reduce the risk for investors.

It is perhaps inevitable that larger companies are subject to the most rigorous standards. These may or may not be listed on a stock exchange. Small and medium-sized companies often follow more simplified standards, for example the cash method of accounting which records revenue when cash is received, and expenses when they are paid in cash. The larger companies often operate on an accrual basis which records income when it is *earned*, and expenditure when it is *incurred*. Accounting standards set out in detail what accruals must be made, how the financial statements are to be presented, and what additional disclosures are required, if any.

Sarbanes–Oxley

The Sarbanes–Oxley Act of 2002 in the US, known as SOX for short, was the first step towards an international audit requirement for large companies. A series of financial scandals that involved companies such as Enron Corporation, Tyco International, and WorldCom had shaken the confidence of investors in the truthfulness of financial statements. The Act imposed an obligation on companies that are listed on a US stock exchange to evaluate the effectiveness of their own internal controls, including financial reporting. It aims to protect investors from fraud in the reporting of financial results. Accountants, auditors, and corporate officers are now subject to strict new rules about record-keeping. (The Act is named after its two sponsors in Congress – Senator Paul Sarbanes and Representative Michael Oxley.)

The Act of 2002 obliges senior corporate officers, that is, the company's directors and senior managers, to certify that the company's financial statements "comply with [Securities Exchange Commission] disclosure requirements and fairly present in all material aspects the operations and financial condition of the issuer".[5] The company's management and auditors must establish internal controls and reporting methods to ensure the adequacy of these controls.[6] Finally, the Act lays down specific rules for record-keeping. These have to do with the retention period for storing records, and specific business records that must be stored, including electronic communications, and destruction and falsification of records.[7]

The financial statements in scope are written records of the company's business activities and financial performance. They are often audited by government agencies and internal and external accountants, to ensure accuracy and for tax, financing, or investing purposes. Financial statements consist of:

- Balance sheet – assets, liabilities and equity, i.e. share capital;
- Profit and loss account – income and expenditure; and
- Cash flow statement – cash income for operating expenses.

Internal controls

What are these internal controls that SOX is aimed at upholding? These are the mechanisms, rules, and procedures of a company to ensure the integrity of financial information, to promote accountability, and to prevent fraud. In addition to ensuring the company complies with laws and regulations and prevents employees from committing fraud or misappropriating the company's property, internal controls can help to improve operational efficiency by improving the accuracy and timeliness of financial reporting. As part of a standard audit, external auditors will test a company's internal controls and provide an opinion as to their effectiveness. This opinion will normally accompany the financial statements. Internal audits on the other hand will evaluate a company's internal controls, including its corporate governance and accounting processes. These help to ensure compliance with laws and regulations and accurate and timely financial reporting as well as helping to maintain operational efficiency by identifying problems before they are discovered in an external audit.

IFRS

As we discussed in Chapter 18, the International Financial Reporting Standards, or IFRS for short, are accounting standards issued by the IFRS Foundation, a non-profit accounting organization, and the International Accounting Standards Board, and constitute a standardised way of stating a company's financial performance. By complying with these requirements, the company's financial statements will be understandable and comparable between different countries. IFRS deal with specific aspects of auditing such as an auditor's responsibilities, audit planning, internal controls, audit evidence, and audit reports. IFRS have replaced many different national accounting standards around the world but have not replaced accounting standards in the US where the Generally Accepted Accounting Principles, or US GAAP, is applied. The UK and Ireland have adopted a version of IFRS in the form of The Financial Reporting Standard, or FRS102. However, in order to ensure compliance, listed companies in the UK use the UK version of GAAP, while non-listed companies use IFRS. If the company is listed on an EU stock exchange, it must follow IFRS, according to EU regulations.

Auditors and Brexit

The UK withdrew from the European Union on 31 January, 2020 and the transition period ended on 31 December 2020. From that date the UK became a "third country" (a third country is any country that is not a member state of the EU) and auditors in the UK were advised by the European Commission in a guidance note[8] to take appropriate action, where needed. This includes registration as a third-country auditor or third-country audit firm in the EU in order to comply with the Statutory Audit Directive,[9] in particular in relation to voting rights and members of the administrative or management body of the audit firm. This may be needed for the firms concerned to carry out statutory audits in the EU, that is, audits of EU companies as required by law.

audit policy

Below is a set of instructions and suggestions for drafting a comprehensive audit policy. As with all policy documents, it should use plain language with well-defined terms, clear and consistent terminology, and an easy-to-follow structure. However, the precise structure will necessarily reflect the nature, scale and complexity of the company.

[Company name]

Introduction

Explain the context for the policy, including the purpose, roles and responsibilities, engagement with key stakeholders, and policy review and updates.

Risks and uncertainties

Set out the company's approach to audit and assurance and how it relates to the company's most important business risks. How does the board determine the nature and extent of the key business risks the company is willing to take in order to achieve its long-term strategic objectives? How does the board ensure that appropriate assurance is received in respect of all the relevant risks and uncertainties?

The UK Corporate Governance Code extends the board's responsibility to present a fair, balanced, and understandable assessment to interim and other price-sensitive public records and reports to regulators, as well as to information required to be presented by statutory instruments. Therefore the audit policy should address the board's approach to assurance over interim reports; gender and ethnicity pay gap disclosures; the modern slavery statement; and analyst presentations and market announcements.

Provision 28 of the UK Corporate Governance Code recommends that the board carry out a robust assessment of the company's emerging and principal risks; and confirm that it has completed this assessment, including a description of its principal risks, what procedures are in place to identify emerging risks, and an explanation of how these are being managed or mitigated.

How do the 'three lines of defence' for risk management operate within the company, that is, management, compliance, and internal audit?

Assurance sources

Consider the different sources of assurance and the degree of assurance provided. What role do the three lines of defence play, that is, business, compliance, and internal audit? Do assurance activities provide high, moderate, or limited assurance? When was the assurance received? What is the role of external assurance providers versus internal assurance providers? The company should have appropriate assurance over all the areas of interest to key stakeholders.

Consultation

How will the company engage with key internal and external stakeholders? The board of directors should take steps to ensure this is not a tick-box exercise. How can the board encourage active engagement with stakeholders in order to get meaningful input?

Internal controls

Describe the board's approach to assurance in relation to the system of internal controls. This should cover all material controls including financial, operational, and compliance controls, including the role of internal audit. Provision 29 of the UK Corporate Governance Code recommends that the board should monitor the company's internal control systems and, at least annually, carry out a review of its effectiveness and report on that review.

How are the internal controls defined? What processes are in place for the board's on-going monitoring of the design and operating effectiveness of material internal controls? How are significant failings or weaknesses defined? What process are in place to review the effectiveness of internal controls?

Resilience statement

The new requirement of a "Resilience Statement" by the directors was proposed by the UK government in May 2022. The statement obliges the directors to disclose how the company is addressing risks or resilience issues, including threats to business continuity, supply chain, and cyber security, including the internal review approach and the extent to which the auditors have been engaged. How does the board assure itself about the accuracy of the Resilience Statement? What, if any, external forms of assurance are provided?

Statutory audit

The policy should set out the approach adopted by the company to the appointment or reappointment of the external auditor, including audit tenders. How is the scope of the audit determined, for example geography, risk profile, and so on. Does the audit committee arrange for any additional work to be undertaken? How does the audit committee assess the effectiveness of the audit, including the role played by management?

Information in the Annual Report

Explain the board's approach to determining whether the Annual Report is fair and balanced and provides the information necessary for shareholders to assess the company's position, performance, business model, and strategy.

Set out the external auditor's responsibilities in relation to the other information presented with the financial statements; and the role of internal audit.

Explain the board's approach in determining any specific assurance received in respect of the other information included within the Annual Report.

Assurance over other aspects of corporate reporting

The UK Corporate Governance Code extends the board's responsibility to present a fair, balanced and understandable assessment to interim and other price-sensitive public records and reports to regulators, as well as information required to be presented by statutory instruments. Therefore the policy should address the board's approach to assurance over interim reports; gender and ethnicity pay gap disclosures; the modern slavery statement; and analyst presentations and market announcements.

Responsibility

The board of directors is responsible for the audit policy while delegating the implementation of it to the audit committee of the board and the internal board function. In developing the policy, the audit committee will work closely with the senior management team and consult with any other relevant committee and internal body as appropriate.

Review and update

The company will put processes in place to keep the policy up to date.

References

1. Alicia Tuovila, "What Are Accounting Policies and How Are They Used?", 28 September 2022, https://www.investopedia.com/terms/a/accounting-policies.asp.
2. CFA Institute, Financial Reporting Standards, www.cfainstitute.org/membership/professional-development/refresher-readings/financial-reporting-standards, 2023.
3. Association of Chartered Certified Accountants, "UK Accounting Standards", January 2013, www.accaglobal.com/uk/en/technical-activities/technical-resources-search/2013/january/uk-accounting-standards.html#Financial-Reporting-Standards.

4 Kamal Gupta, *Contemporary Auditing* (New Delhi: Tata McGraw Hill, 2005), 1095.
5 *Section 302, Sarbanes–Oxley Act of 2002, 15 USC 7201*. Available at: www.govinfo.gov/content/pkg/PLAW-107publ204/html/PLAW-107publ204.htm (Accessed: 20 September 2023).
6 *Section 404, Sarbanes–Oxley Act of 2002, 15 USC 7201*. Available at: www.govinfo.gov/content/pkg/PLAW-107publ204/html/PLAW-107publ204.htm (Accessed: 20 September 2023).
7 *Section 802, Sarbanes–Oxley Act of 2002, 15 USC 7201*. Available at: www.govinfo.gov/content/pkg/PLAW-107publ204/html/PLAW-107publ204.htm (Accessed: 20 September 2023).
8 European Commission, "Notice to Stakeholders – Withdrawal of the United Kingdom and EU Rules in the Field of Statutory Audit", *REV/1*.
9 Directive 2006/43/EC of the European Parliament and of the Council of 17 May 2006 on statutory audits of annual accounts and consolidated accounts, amending Council Directives 78/ 660/EEC and 83/349/EEC and repealing Council Directive 84/253/EEC (2006) *Official Journal* L 157, 87-106.

SOURCES OF ADDITIONAL INFORMATION

The Chartered Governance Institute UK & Ireland

Saffron House
6–10 Kirby Street
London EC1N 8TS
United Kingdom
www.cgi.org.uk
info@cgi.org.uk
Tel. +44 (0)20 7580 4741

Corporate Governance Institute (Ireland)

2059 Castle Drive
Citywest Business Campus
Dublin D24 YD8
Ireland
www.thecorporategovernanceinstitute.com
info@thecorporategovernanceinstitute.com
Tel. +353 1 4370602

Institute of Directors

116 Pall Mall
London SW1Y 5ED

United Kingdom
www.iod.com
businessinfo@iod.com
Tel. +44 2083 554313

Institute of Directors in Ireland

Europa House
Harcourt Street
Dublin D02 WR20
Ireland
www.iodireland.ie
info@iodireland.ie
Tel. +353 1 4110010

Data Protection Commission (Ireland)

21 Fitzwilliam Square South
Dublin D02 RD28
Ireland
www.dataprotection.ie
info@dataprotection.ie
Tel. +353 57 8684800

Information Commissioner's Office

Wycliffe House
Water Lane
Wilmslow
Cheshire SK9 5AF
www.ico.org.uk
icocasework@ico.org.uk
Tel. +44 3031 231113

Companies House

Crown Way
Cardiff CF14 3UZ
United Kingdom
www.companieshouse.gov.uk
enquiries@companieshouse.gov.uk
Tel. +44 303 1234500

Companies Registration Office (Ireland)

Bloom House
Gloucester Place Lower
Dublin D01 C8P4
Ireland
www.cro.ie
cro.info@enterprise.gov.ie
Tel. +353 1 8045200

The European Business Centre for Corporate Sustainability and Responsibility

Rue Victor Oudart 7
1030 Brussels
Belgium
www.csreurope.org
sc@csreurope.org
Tel. +32 2541 1610

European Commission – Directorate-General for Climate Action

1049 Brussels
Belgium
https://commission.europa.eu/about-european-commission/departments-and-executive-agencies/climate-action_en
Tel. +32 2 299 11 11

Health and Safety Authority (Ireland)

The Metropolitan Building
James Joyce Street
Dublin D01 KOY8
Ireland
www.hsa.ie
wcu@hsa.ie
Tel. +353 1 6147000

Health and Safety Executive

Redgrave Court
Merton Road
Bootle
Merseyside L20 7HS
United Kingdom
www.hse.gov.uk
Tel. +44 300 790 6787

European Agency for Safety and Health at Work

12 Santiago de Compostela
Edificio Miribilla
5th Floor
E-48003 Bilbao
Spain
www.osha.europa.eu
information@osha.europa.eu
Tel. +32 2401 6859

European Data Protection Board

Rue Wiertz 60
B-1047
Brussels
Belgium
www.edpb.europa.eu

US Environmental Protection Agency

1200 Pennsylvania Avenue
NW Washington DC 20460
USA
www.epa.gov
Tel. +1 800 4248802

Environment Agency

National Customer Contact Centre
PO Box 544
Rotherham S60 1BY
United Kingdom
www.gov.uk/ea
enquiries@environment-agency.gov.uk
Tel. +44 3708 506506

Confederation of British Industry

Cannon Place
78 Cannon Street
London EC4N 6HN
United Kingdom
www.cbi.org.uk
enquiries@cbi.org.uk
Tel. +44 207379 7400

Ibec (Irish Business and Employers Confederation)

84/86 Lower Baggot Street
Dublin D02 H720
Ireland
www.ibec.ie
info@ibec.ie
Tel. +353 1 6051500

Central Bank of Ireland

PO Box 559
Dublin 1
www.centralbank.ie
enquiries@centralbank.ie
Tel. +353 1 2245800

Financial Conduct Authority

12 Endeavour Square
London E20 1JN
United Kingdom

www.fca.org.uk
frm@qeries@fca.org.uk
Tel. +44 2070661000

Fraud Advisory Panel

Chartered Accountants' Hall
Moorgate Place
London EC2R 6EA
United Kingdom
www.fraudadvisorypanel.org
info@fraudadvisory.panel.org
Tel. +44 2079 208637

Transparency International

Alt-Moabit 96
10559 Berlin
Germany
www.transparency.org
ti@transparency.org
Tel. +49 303438200

Garda National Economic Crime Bureau (Ireland)

Harcourt Square
Harcourt Street
Dublin D02 DH43
Ireland
www.garda.ie
Tel. +353 1 6663776

Serious Fraud Office

2-4 Cockspur Street
London SW1Y 5BS
United Kingdom
www.sfo.gov.uk
information.officer@sfo.gov.uk
Tel. +41 2072 397272

Financial Reporting Council

8th Floor
125 London Wall
London EC2Y 5AS
United Kingdom
www.frc.org.uk
enquiries@frc.org.uk
Tel. +44 20794 22300

International Compliance Association UK

Fort Dunlop
6th Floor
Fort Parkway
Birmingham B24 9FD
United Kingdom
www.int-comp.org
icainfo@int-comp.org
Tel. +44 121 3627534

International Compliance Association UAE

Dubai International Financial Centre
Centre of Excellence
Building 2, Level 3
Dubai
United Arab Emirates
www.int-comp.org
mariak@int-comp.org
Tel. +971 4401 9310

International Compliance Association Singapore

77 Robinson Road
#07-01
Singapore 068896
www.int-comp.org
enquiries@int-comp.org
Tel. +65 6500 0010

International Compliance Association Hong Kong

Office Unit 503-504
5th Floor Haleson Building
I Jubilee Street Central
Hong Kong
www.int-comp.org
enquirieshk@int-comp.com

Association of Compliance Officers of Ireland

5 Fitzwilliam Square East
Grand Canal Dock
Dublin D02 R744
Ireland
www.acoi.ie
info@acoi.ie
Tel. +353 1 7790200

American Institute of Healthcare Compliance

5000 Gateway Drive
Suite 202
Menina
OH 44256
USA
www.aihc-assn.org
Tel. +1 330241 5635

Governance Professionals of Canada

21 St. Clair Avenue East
Suite 802
Toronto ON M4T 1L9
Canada
www.gpccanada.org
info@gpccanada.org
Tel. +416 9215449

Australian Competition and Consumer Commission

GPO Box 3131
Canberra ACT 2601
Australia
www.accc.gov.au
Tel. +61 262431305

Environment and Climate Change Canada

Fontaine Building
12th Floor
200 Sacre-Coeur Blvd.
Gatineau QC KIA OH3
Canada
www.ec.gc.ca
environment@ec.gc.ca
Tel. +1 819 9383338

US Securities and Exchange Commission

100 F Street
NE Washington DC 20549
USA
www.sec.gov

US Food and Drugs Administration

10903 New Hampshire Avenue
Silver Spring
MD 20993-0002
USA
www.fda.gov
Tel. +1 888 4636332

APPENDICES

APPENDICES

APPENDIX 1

UNITED NATIONS GUIDING PRINCIPLES ON BUSINESS AND HUMAN RIGHTS 2011

A. Foundational principles

Business enterprises should respect human rights. This means that they should avoid infringing on the human rights of others and should address adverse human rights impacts with which they are involved. The responsibility to respect human rights is a global standard of expected conduct for all business enterprises wherever they operate. It exists independently of States' abilities and/or willingness to fulfil their own human rights obligations, and does not diminish those obligations. And it exists over and above compliance with national laws and regulations protecting human rights. Addressing adverse human rights impacts requires taking adequate measures for their prevention, mitigation, and where appropriate, remediation. Business enterprises may undertake other commitments or activities to support and promote human rights, which may contribute to the enjoyment of rights. But this does not offset a failure to respect human rights throughout their operations. Business enterprises should not undermine States' abilities to meet their own human rights obligations, including by actions that might weaken the integrity of judicial processes.

The responsibility of business enterprises to respect human rights refers to internationally recognized human rights – understood, at a minimum, as those expressed in the International Bill of Human Rights and the principles concerning fundamental rights set out in the International Labour Organization's Declaration on Fundamental Principles and Rights at Work.

The responsibility to respect human rights requires that business enterprises:

(a) Avoid causing or contributing to adverse human rights impacts through their own activities, and address such impacts when they occur;
(b) Seek to prevent or mitigate adverse human rights impacts that are directly linked to their operations, products, or services by their business relationships, even if they have not contributed to those impacts.

The responsibility of business enterprises to respect human rights applies to all enterprises regardless of their size, sector, operational context, ownership, and structure. Nevertheless, the scale and complexity of the means through which enterprises meet that responsibility may vary according to these factors and with the severity of the enterprise's adverse human rights impacts.

In order to meet their responsibility to respect human rights, business enterprises should have in place policies and processes appropriate to their size and circumstances, including:

(a) A policy commitment to meet their responsibility to respect human rights;
(b) A human rights due diligence process to identify, prevent, mitigate, and account for how they address their impacts on human rights;
(c) Processes to enable the remediation of any adverse human rights impacts they cause or to which they contribute.

As the basis for embedding their responsibility to respect human rights, business enterprises should express their commitment to meet this responsibility through a statement of policy that: (a) Is approved at the most senior level of the business enterprise; (b) Is informed by relevant internal and/or external expertise; (c) Stipulates the enterprise's human rights expectations of personnel, business partners and other parties directly linked to its operations, products or services; (d) Is publicly available and communicated internally and externally to all personnel, business partners and other relevant parties; (e) Is reflected in operational policies and procedures necessary to embed it throughout the business enterprise.

In order to identify, prevent, mitigate, and account for how they address their adverse human rights impacts, business enterprises should carry out human rights due diligence. The process should include assessing actual and potential human rights impacts, integrating and acting upon the findings, tracking responses, and communicating how impacts are addressed. Human rights due diligence:

(a) Should cover adverse human rights impacts that the business enterprise may cause or contribute to through its own activities, or which may be directly linked to its operations, products, or services by its business relationships;
(b) Will vary in complexity with the size of the business enterprise, the risk of severe human rights impacts, and the nature and context of its operations;
(c) Should be ongoing, recognizing that the human rights risks may change over time as the business enterprise's operations and operating context evolve.

In order to gauge human rights risks, business enterprises should identify and assess any actual or potential adverse human rights impacts with which they may be involved either through their own activities or as a result of their business relationships. This process should: (a) Draw on internal and/or independent external human rights expertise; (b) Involve meaningful consultation with potentially affected groups and other relevant stakeholders, as appropriate to the size of the business enterprise and the nature and context of the operation.

In order to prevent and mitigate adverse human rights impacts, business enterprises should integrate the findings from their impact assessments across relevant internal functions and processes, and take appropriate action.

(a) Effective integration requires that: (i) Responsibility for addressing such impacts is assigned to the appropriate level and function within the business enterprise; 21 (ii) Internal decision-making, budget allocations, and oversight processes enable effective responses to such impacts.

(b) Appropriate action will vary according to: (i) Whether the business enterprise causes or contributes to an adverse impact, or whether it is involved solely because the impact is directly linked to its operations, products, or services by a business relationship; (ii) The extent of its leverage in addressing the adverse impact.

In order to verify whether adverse human rights impacts are being addressed, business enterprises should track the effectiveness of their response. Tracking should: (a) Be based on appropriate qualitative and quantitative indicators; (b) Draw on feedback from both internal and external sources, including affected stakeholders.

In order to account for how they address their human rights impacts, business enterprises should be prepared to communicate this externally, particularly when concerns are raised by or on behalf of affected stakeholders. Business enterprises whose operations or operating contexts pose risks of severe human rights impacts should report formally on how they address them. In all instances, communications should: (a) Be of a form and frequency that reflect an enterprise's human rights impacts and that are accessible to its intended audiences; (b) Provide information that is sufficient to evaluate the adequacy of an enterprise's response to the particular human rights impact involved; (c) In turn not pose risks to affected stakeholders, personnel or to legitimate requirements of commercial confidentiality.

In all contexts, business enterprises should:

(a) Comply with all applicable laws and respect internationally recognized human rights, wherever they operate;
(b) Seek ways to honour the principles of internationally recognized human rights when faced with conflicting requirements;
(c) Treat the risk of causing or contributing to gross human rights abuses as a legal compliance issue wherever they operate.

Where it is necessary to prioritize actions to address actual and potential adverse human rights impacts, business enterprises should first seek to prevent and mitigate those that are most severe or where delayed response would make them irremediable. [www.ohchr.org/documents/publications/guidingprinciplesbusinesshr_en.pdf]

APPENDIX 2

COP 27 AT SHARM EL-SHEIKH IMPLEMENTATION PLAN 2022

The Conference of the Parties:

Being guided by science and principles,

Reaffirming the outcomes of all previous sessions of the Conferences of the Parties,

Also reaffirming the critical role of multilateralism based on United Nations values and principles, including in the context of the implementation of the Convention and the Paris Agreement, and the importance of international cooperation for addressing global issues, including climate change, in the context of sustainable development and efforts to eradicate poverty,

Noting the importance of transitioning to sustainable lifestyles and sustainable patterns of consumption and production in efforts to address climate change,

Also noting the importance of pursuing an approach to education that promotes a shift in lifestyles while fostering patterns of development and sustainability based on care, community and cooperation,

Acknowledging that climate change is a common concern of humankind and that Parties should, when taking action to address climate change, respect, promote and consider their respective obligations on human rights, the right to a clean, healthy and sustainable environment, the right to health, the rights of indigenous peoples, local communities, migrants, children, persons with disabilities and people in vulnerable situations and the right to development, as well as gender equality, empowerment of women and intergenerational equity,

Noting the importance of ensuring the integrity of all ecosystems, including in forests, the ocean and the cryosphere, and the protection of biodiversity, recognized by some cultures as Mother Earth, and also noting the importance of "climate justice", when taking action to address climate change,

Emphasizing that enhanced effective climate action should be implemented in a manner that is just and inclusive while minimizing negative social or economic impacts that may arise from climate action, Recognizing the fundamental priority of safeguarding food security and ending hunger, and the particular vulnerabilities of food production systems to the adverse impacts of climate change,

Also recognizing the critical role of protecting, conserving, and restoring water systems and water-related ecosystems in delivering climate adaptation benefits and co-benefits, while ensuring social and environmental safeguards,

1 Underlines the urgent need to address, in a comprehensive and synergetic manner, the interlinked global crises of climate change and biodiversity loss in the broader context of achieving the Sustainable Development Goals, as well as the vital importance of protecting, conserving, restoring, and sustainably using nature and ecosystems for effective and sustainable climate action;

2 Acknowledges that the impacts of climate change exacerbate the global energy and food crises, and vice versa, particularly in developing countries;

3 Stresses that the increasingly complex and challenging global geopolitical situation and its impact on the energy, food, and economic situations, as well as the additional challenges associated with the socioeconomic recovery from the coronavirus disease 2019 pandemic, should not be used as a pretext for backtracking, backsliding or deprioritizing climate action;

I. Science and urgency

4 Recognizes the importance of the best available science for effective climate action and policymaking;

5 Takes note of the 2022 adaptation gap and emissions gap reports of the United Nations Environment Programme, and recent global and regional reports of the World Meteorological Organization on the state of the climate;
6 Reiterates that the impacts of climate change will be much lower at the temperature increase of 1.5 °C compared with 2 °C and resolves to pursue further efforts to limit the temperature increase to 1.5 °C;
7 Recognizes the impacts of climate change on the cryosphere and the need for further understanding of these impacts, including of tipping points;

II. Enhancing ambition and implementation

8 Resolves to implement ambitious, just, equitable, and inclusive transitions to low emission and climate-resilient development in line with the principles and objectives of the Convention, the Kyoto Protocol, and the Paris Agreement, taking into account this decision, the Glasgow Climate Pact and other relevant decisions of the Conference of the Parties;

III. Energy

9 Emphasizes the urgent need for immediate, deep, rapid, and sustained reductions in global greenhouse gas emissions by Parties across all applicable sectors, including through increasing the use of low-emission and renewable energy, just energy transition partnerships, and other cooperative actions;
10 Recognizes that the unprecedented global energy crisis underlines the urgency to rapidly transform energy systems to be more secure, reliable, and resilient, including by accelerating clean and just transitions to renewable energy during this critical decade of action;
11 Stresses the importance of enhancing a clean energy mix, including low-emission and renewable energy, at all levels as part of diversifying energy mixes and systems, in line with national circumstances and recognizing the need for support towards just transitions;

IV. Mitigation

12 Recognizes that limiting global warming to 1.5 °C requires rapid, deep, and sustained reductions in global greenhouse gas emissions of 43 per cent by 2030 relative to the 2019 level;

13 Also recognizes that this requires accelerated action in this critical decade, on the basis of equity and the best available scientific knowledge, reflecting common but differentiated responsibilities and respective capabilities, in the light of different national circumstances and in the context of sustainable development and efforts to eradicate poverty;

14 Calls upon Parties to accelerate the development, deployment, and dissemination of technologies, and the adoption of policies, to transition towards low-emission energy systems, including by rapidly scaling up the deployment of clean power generation and energy efficiency measures, including accelerating efforts towards the phasedown of unabated coal power and phase-out of inefficient fossil fuel subsidies, while providing targeted support to the poorest and most vulnerable in line with national circumstances and recognizing the need for support towards a just transition;

15 Reiterates its invitation to Parties to consider further actions to reduce by 2030 non-carbon dioxide greenhouse gas emissions, including methane;

16 Emphasizes the importance of protecting, conserving, and restoring nature and ecosystems to achieve the Paris Agreement temperature goal, including through forests and other terrestrial and marine ecosystems acting as sinks and reservoirs of greenhouse gases and by protecting biodiversity, while ensuring social and environmental safeguards;

17 Recognizes the importance of maximizing the positive and minimizing the negative economic and social impacts of the implementation of response measures;

V. Adaptation

18 Notes with serious concern the existing gap between current levels of adaptation and levels needed to respond to the adverse effects of climate change in line with findings from the contribution of Working Group II to the Sixth Assessment Report of the Intergovernmental Panel on Climate Change;

19 Urges Parties to adopt a transformational approach to enhancing adaptive capacity, strengthening resilience, and reducing vulnerability to climate change;

20 Also urges developed country Parties to urgently and significantly scale up their provision of climate finance, technology transfer and

capacity-building for adaptation so as to respond to the needs of developing country Parties as part of a global effort, including for the formulation and implementation of national adaptation plans and adaptation communications;

21 Highlights the role of the Least Developed Countries Fund and the Special Climate Change Fund in supporting actions by developing countries to address climate change, and welcomes the pledges made to the two Funds and invites developed countries to further contribute to the two Funds;

22 Emphasizes the importance of protecting, conserving, and restoring water and water-related ecosystems, including river basins, aquifers, and lakes, and urges Parties to further integrate water into adaptation efforts;

VI. Loss and damage

23 Notes with grave concern, according to information in the contributions of Working Groups II and III to the Sixth Assessment Report of the Intergovernmental Panel on Climate Change, the growing gravity, scope, and frequency in all regions of loss and damage associated with the adverse effects of climate change, resulting in devastating economic and non-economic losses, including forced displacement and impacts on cultural heritage, human mobility, and the lives and livelihoods of local communities, and underlines the importance of an adequate and effective response to loss and damage;

24 Expresses deep concern regarding the significant financial costs associated with loss and damage for developing countries, resulting in a growing debt burden and impairing the realization of the Sustainable Development Goals;

25 Welcomes the consideration, for the first time, of matters relating to funding arrangements responding to loss and damage associated with the adverse effects of climate change, including a focus on addressing loss and damage, under the Conference of the Parties;

26 Further welcomes the adoption of decisions establishing the institutional arrangements of the Santiago network for averting, minimizing, and addressing loss and damage associated with the adverse effects of climate change to enable its full operationalization, including supporting its mandated role in catalysing technical assistance for the

implementation of the relevant approaches at the local, national, and regional level in developing countries that are particularly vulnerable to the adverse effects of climate change;

VII. Early warning and systematic observation

27 Emphasizes the need to address existing gaps in the Global Climate Observing System, particularly in developing countries, and recognizes that one-third of the world, including 60 percent of Africa, does not have access to early warning and climate information services, as well as the need to enhance coordination of activities by the systematic observation community and the ability to provide useful and actionable climate information for mitigation, adaptation, and early warning systems, as well as information to enable understanding of adaptation limits and of attribution of extreme events;

28 Welcomes and reiterates the United Nations Secretary-General's call made on World Meteorological Day on 23 March 2022 to protect everyone on Earth through universal coverage of early warning systems against extreme weather and climate change within the next five years and invites development partners, international financial institutions, and the operating entities of the Financial Mechanism to provide support for the implementation of the Early Warnings for All initiative;

VIII. Implementation – pathways to just transition

29 Affirms that sustainable and just solutions to the climate crisis must be founded on meaningful and effective social dialogue and participation of all stakeholders and notes that the global transition to low emissions provides opportunities and challenges for sustainable economic development and poverty eradication;

30 Emphasizes that just and equitable transition encompasses pathways that include energy, socioeconomic, workforce, and other dimensions, all of which must be based on nationally defined development priorities and include social protection so as to mitigate potential impacts associated with the transition, and highlights the important role of the instruments related to social solidarity and protection in mitigating the impacts of applied measures;

IX. Finance

31 Highlights that about USD 4 trillion per year needs to be invested in clean energy technologies by 2030 to be able to reach net zero emissions by 2050, and that, furthermore, a global transformation to a low-carbon economy is expected to require an investment of at least USD 4–6 trillion per year;

32 Also highlights that delivering such funding will require a transformation of the financial system and its structures and processes, engaging governments, central banks, commercial banks, institutional investors, and other financial actors;

33 Notes with concern the growing gap between the needs of developing country Parties, in particular those due to the increasing impacts of climate change and their increased indebtedness, and the support provided and mobilized for their efforts to implement their nationally determined contributions, highlighting that such needs are currently estimated at USD 5.8–5.9 trillion10 for the pre-2030 period;

34 Expresses serious concern that the goal of developed country Parties to mobilize jointly USD 100 billion per year by 2020 in the context of meaningful mitigation action and transparency on implementation has not yet been met and urges developed country Parties to meet the goal;

35 Emphasizes that accelerated financial support for developing countries from developed countries and other sources is critical to enhancing mitigation action and addressing inequities in access to finance, including its costs, terms and conditions, and economic vulnerability to climate change for developing countries, and that scaled-up public grants for mitigation and adaptation for vulnerable regions, in particular sub-Saharan Africa, would be cost-effective and have high social returns in terms of access to basic energy;

36 Notes that global climate finance flows are small relative to the overall needs of developing countries, with such flows in 2019–2020 estimated to be USD 803 billion,13 which is 31–32 per cent of the annual investment needed to keep the global temperature rise well below 2 °C or at 1.5 °C, and also below what would be expected in the light of the investment opportunities identified and the cost of failure to meet climate stabilization targets;

37 Urges developed country Parties to provide enhanced support, including through financial resources, technology transfer, and capacity-building, to assist developing country Parties with respect to both mitigation and adaptation, in continuation of their existing obligations under the Convention, and encourages other Parties to provide or continue to provide such support voluntarily;

38 Calls on the shareholders of multilateral development banks and international financial institutions to reform multilateral development bank practices and priorities, align and scale up funding, ensure simplified access, and mobilize climate finance from various sources and encourages multilateral development banks to define a new vision and commensurate operational model, channels and instruments that are fit for the purpose of adequately addressing the global climate emergency, including deploying a full suite of instruments, from grants to guarantees and non-debt instruments, taking into account debt burdens, and to address risk appetite, with a view to substantially increasing climate finance;

39 Calls on multilateral development banks to contribute to significantly increasing climate ambition using the breadth of their policy and financial instruments for greater results, including on private capital mobilization, and to ensure higher financial efficiency and maximize the use of existing concessional and risk capital vehicles to drive innovation and accelerate impact;

40 Emphasizes the ongoing challenges faced by many developing country Parties in accessing climate finance and encourages further efforts, including by the operating entities of the Financial Mechanism, to simplify access to such finance;

41 Takes note of the report on the determination of the needs of developing country Parties related to implementing the Convention and the Paris Agreement and in this context urges developed country Parties to provide resources for the second replenishment of the Green Climate Fund while demonstrating progression from the previous replenishment and in line with the programming capacity of the Fund;

X. Technology transfer and deployment

42 Welcomes with appreciation the first joint work programme of the Technology Executive Committee and the Climate Technology Centre

and Network for 2023–2027, which will facilitate the transformational change needed to achieve the goals of the Convention and the Paris Agreement, invites Parties and stakeholders to cooperate and engage with the Technology Executive Committee and the Climate Technology Centre and Network to support the implementation of the joint work programme activities, including on technology needs assessments, action plans, and road maps, acknowledges the findings in the final report on the first periodic assessment of the effectiveness and adequacy of the support provided to the Technology Mechanism in supporting the implementation of the Paris Agreement and decides that the main challenges identified therein should be considered under the global stocktake;

43 Highlights the importance of cooperation on technology development and transfer and innovation in implementing the joint work programme activities;

44 Welcomes the forward-looking conclusions of the Subsidiary Body for Implementation to continue consideration of the Poznan strategic programme on technology with the aim of supporting the implementation of relevant activities, such as those identified and prioritized in developing countries' nationally determined contributions, national adaptation plans, technology needs assessments and technology action plans, and long-term strategies;

XI. Capacity-building

45. Notes that capacity gaps and needs still exist in developing countries and calls on developed country Parties to increase support for long-term country-driven capacity-building interventions to enhance the effectiveness, success, and sustainability of those interventions;

XII. Taking stock

46. Notes the importance of the periodic review of the long-term global goal under the Convention and welcomes the adoption of a decision on the second periodic review of the long-term global goal under the Convention and of overall progress towards achieving it;

XIII. Ocean

47 Welcomes the outcomes of and key messages from the ocean and climate change dialogue in 2022 and decides that future dialogues will, from 2023, be facilitated by two co-facilitators, selected by Parties biennially, who will be responsible for deciding the topics for and conducting the dialogue;

48 Encourages Parties to consider, as appropriate, ocean-based action in their national climate goals and in the implementation of these goals, including but not limited to nationally determined contributions, long-term strategies, and adaptation communications;

XIV. Forest

49 Recalls that, in the context of the provision of adequate and predictable support to developing country Parties, Parties should collectively aim to slow, halt, and reverse forest cover and carbon loss, in accordance with national circumstances;

50 Encourages Parties to consider, as appropriate, nature-based solutions or ecosystem-based approaches, taking into consideration United Nations Environment Assembly resolution 5/5,21 for their mitigation and adaptation action while ensuring relevant social and environmental safeguards.

APPENDIX 3

EU WHISTLEBLOWING DIRECTIVE

DIRECTIVE (EU) 2019/1937 OF THE EUROPEAN PARLIAMENT AND OF THE COUNCIL of 23 October 2019 on the protection of persons who report breaches of Union law

Article 1 Purpose

The purpose of this Directive is to enhance the enforcement of Union law and policies in specific areas by laying down common minimum standards providing for a high level of protection of persons reporting breaches of Union law.

Article 2 Material scope

1   This Directive lays down common minimum standards for the protection of persons reporting the following breaches of Union law:

(a) breaches falling within the scope of the Union acts set out in the Annex that concern the following areas: (i) public procurement; (ii) financial services, products and markets, and prevention of money laundering and terrorist financing; (iii) product safety and compliance; (iv) transport safety; (v) protection of the environment; (vi) radiation protection and nuclear safety; (vii) food and feed safety, animal health and welfare; (viii) public health; (ix) consumer protection; (x) protection of privacy and personal data, and security of network and information systems;

(b) breaches affecting the financial interests of the Union as referred to in Article 325 TF and as further specified in relevant Union measures;

(c) breaches relating to the internal market, as referred to in Article 26(2) TFEU, including breaches of Union competition and State aid rules, as well as breaches relating to the internal market in relation to acts which breach the rules of corporate tax or to arrangements the purpose of which is to obtain a tax advantage that defeats the object or purpose of the applicable corporate tax law.

2 This Directive is without prejudice to the power of Member States to extend protection under national law as regards areas or acts not covered by paragraph 1.

Article 3 Relationship with other Union acts and national provisions

1 Where specific rules on the reporting of breaches are provided for in sector-specific Union acts those rules shall apply. The provisions of this Directive shall be applicable to the extent that a matter is not mandatorily regulated in these sector-specific Union acts.

2 This Directive shall not affect the responsibility of Member States to ensure national security or their power to protect their essential security interests.

3 This Directive shall not affect the application of Union or national law relating to any of the following: (a) the protection of classified information; (b) the protection of legal and medical professional privilege; (c) the secrecy of judicial deliberations; (d) rules on criminal procedure.

4 This Directive shall not affect national rules on the exercise by workers of their rights to consult their representatives or trade unions, and on protection against any unjustified detrimental measure prompted by such consultations as well as on the autonomy of the social partners and their right to enter into collective agreements.

Article 4 Personal scope

1 This Directive shall apply to reporting persons working in the private or public sector who acquired information on breaches in a work-related context including, at least, the following: (a) persons having the status of worker, including civil servants; (b) persons having self-employed status; (c) shareholders and persons belonging to the administrative, management, or supervisory body of an undertaking, including non-executive members, as well as volunteers and paid or unpaid trainees; (d) any persons working under the supervision and direction of contractors, subcontractors and suppliers.
2 This Directive shall also apply to reporting persons where they report or publicly disclose information on breaches acquired in a work-based relationship that has since ended.
3 This Directive shall also apply to reporting persons whose work-based relationship is yet to begin in cases where information on breaches has been acquired during the recruitment process or other pre-contractual negotiations.
4 The measures for the protection of reporting persons set out in Chapter VI shall also apply, where relevant, to: (a) facilitators; (b) third persons who are connected with the reporting persons and who could suffer retaliation in a work-related context, such as colleagues or relatives of the reporting persons; and (c) legal entities that the reporting persons own, work for or are otherwise connected with in a work-related context.

Article 5 Definitions

For the purposes of this Directive, the following definitions apply:

(1) "breaches" means acts or omissions that: (i) are unlawful and relate to the Union acts and areas falling within the material scope referred to in Article 2; or (ii) defeat the object or the purpose of the rules in the Union acts and areas falling within the material scope referred to in Article 2;
(2) "information on breaches" means information, including reasonable suspicions, about actual or potential breaches, which occurred or are

very likely to occur in the organisation in which the reporting person works or has worked or in another organisation with which the reporting person is or was in contact through his or her work, and about attempts to conceal such breaches;

(3) "report" or "to report" means, the oral or written communication of information on breaches;

(4) "internal reporting" means the oral or written communication of information on breaches within a legal entity in the private or public sector;

(5) "external reporting" means the oral or written communication of information on breaches to the competent authorities;

(6) "public disclosure" or "to publicly disclose" means the making of information on breaches available in the public domain;

(7) "reporting person" means a natural person who reports or publicly discloses information on breaches acquired in the context of his or her work-related activities;

(8) "facilitator" means a natural person who assists a reporting person in the reporting process in a work-related context, and whose assistance should be confidential;

(9) "work-related context" means current or past work activities in the public or private sector through which, irrespective of the nature of those activities, persons acquire information on breaches and within which those persons could suffer retaliation if they reported such information;

(10) "person concerned" means a natural or legal person who is referred to in the report or public disclosure as a person to whom the breach is attributed or with whom that person is associated;

(11) "retaliation" means any direct or indirect act or omission which occurs in a work-related context, is prompted by internal or external reporting or by public disclosure, and which causes or may cause unjustified detriment to the reporting person;

(12) "follow-up" means any action taken by the recipient of a report or any competent authority, to assess the accuracy of the allegations made in the report and, where relevant, to address the breach reported, including through actions such as an internal enquiry, an investigation, prosecution, an action for recovery of funds, or the closure of the procedure;

(13) "feedback" means the provision to the reporting person of information on the action envisaged or taken as follow-up and on the grounds for such follow-up;
(14) "competent authority" means any national authority designated to receive reports in accordance with Chapter III and give feedback to the reporting person, and/or designated to carry out the duties provided for in this Directive, in particular as regards follow-up.

Article 6 Conditions for protection of reporting persons

1 Reporting persons shall qualify for protection under this Directive provided that: (a) they had reasonable grounds to believe that the information on breaches reported was true at the time of reporting and that such information fell within the scope of this Directive; and (b) they reported either internally or externally or made a public disclosure.
2 Without prejudice to existing obligations to provide for anonymous reporting by virtue of Union law, this Directive does not affect the power of Member States to decide whether legal entities in the private or public sector and competent authorities are required to accept and follow up on anonymous reports of breaches.
3 Persons who reported or publicly disclosed information on breaches anonymously, but who are subsequently identified and suffer retaliation, shall nonetheless qualify for protection, provided that they meet the conditions laid down in paragraph 1.
4 Persons reporting to relevant institutions, bodies, offices or agencies of the Union breaches falling within the scope of this Directive shall qualify for protection as laid down in this Directive under the same conditions as persons who report externally.

Article 7 Reporting through internal reporting channels

1 As a general principle and without prejudice to Articles 10 and 15, information on breaches may be reported through the internal reporting channels and procedures provided for.

Article 8 Obligation to establish internal reporting channels

1. Member States shall ensure that legal entities in the private and public sector establish channels and procedures for internal reporting and for follow-up, following consultation and in agreement with the social partners where provided for by national law.
2. The channels and procedures referred to in paragraph 1 of this Article shall enable the entity's workers to report information on breaches. They may enable other persons who are in contact with the entity in the context of their work-related activities to also report information on breaches.
3. Paragraph 1 shall apply to legal entities in the private sector with 50 or more workers.
4. The threshold laid down in paragraph 3 shall not apply to entities falling within the scope of Union acts referred to.
5. Reporting channels may be operated internally by a person or department designated for that purpose or provided externally by a third party. The safeguards and requirements referred to in Article 9(1) shall also apply to entrusted third parties operating the reporting channel for a legal entity in the private sector.
6. Legal entities in the private sector with 50 to 249 workers may share resources as regards the receipt of reports and any investigation to be carried out. This shall be without prejudice to the obligations imposed upon such entities by this Directive to maintain confidentiality, to give feedback, and to address the reported breach.
7. Following an appropriate risk assessment taking into account the nature of the activities of the entities and the ensuing level of risk for, in particular, the environment and public health, Member States may require legal entities in the private sector with fewer than 50 workers to establish internal reporting channels and procedures.

Article 9 Procedures for internal reporting and follow-up

1. The procedures for internal reporting and for follow-up as referred to in Article 8 shall include the following:

    (a) channels for receiving the reports which are designed, established, and operated in a secure manner that ensures that the confidentiality of the identity of the reporting person and any third party mentioned in the report is protected, and prevents access thereto by non-authorised staff members;

(b) acknowledgment of receipt of the report to the reporting person within seven days of that receipt;

(c) the designation of an impartial person or department competent for following-up on the reports which may be the same person or department as the one that receives the reports and which will maintain communication with the reporting person and, where necessary, ask for further information from and provide feedback to that reporting person;

(d) diligent follow-up by the designated person or department referred to in point (c);

(e) diligent follow-up, where provided for in national law, as regards anonymous reporting;

(f) a reasonable timeframe to provide feedback, not exceeding three months from the acknowledgment of receipt or, if no acknowledgement was sent to the reporting person, three months from the expiry of the seven-day period after the report was made;

(g) provision of clear and easily accessible information regarding the procedures for reporting externally to competent authorities pursuant to Article 10 and, where relevant, to institutions, bodies, offices, or agencies of the Union.

2   The channels provided for in point (a) of paragraph 1 shall enable reporting in writing or orally, or both. Oral reporting shall be possible by telephone or through other voice messaging systems, and, upon request by the reporting person, by means of a physical meeting within a reasonable timeframe.

Article 10 Reporting through external reporting channels

Reporting persons shall report information on breaches using the channels and procedures referred to in Articles 11 and 12, after having first reported through internal reporting channels, or by directly reporting through external reporting channels.

Article 11 Obligation to establish external reporting channels and to follow up on reports

1. Member States shall designate the authorities competent to receive, give feedback and follow up on reports, and shall provide them with adequate resources.
2. Member States shall ensure that the competent authorities:

    (a) establish independent and autonomous external reporting channels, for receiving and handling information on breaches;
    (b) promptly, and in any event within seven days of receipt of the report, acknowledge that receipt unless the reporting person explicitly requested otherwise or the competent authority reasonably believes that acknowledging receipt of the report would jeopardise the protection of the reporting person's identity;
    (c) diligently follow up on the reports;
    (d) provide feedback to the reporting person within a reasonable timeframe not exceeding three months, or six months in duly justified cases;
    (e) communicate to the reporting person the final outcome of investigations triggered by the report, in accordance with procedures provided for under national law;
    (f) transmit in due time the information contained in the report to competent institutions, bodies, offices, or agencies of the Union, as appropriate, for further investigation, where provided for under Union or national law.

3. Member States may provide that competent authorities, after having duly assessed the matter, can decide that a reported breach is clearly minor and does not require further follow-up pursuant to this Directive, other than closure of the procedure. This shall not affect other obligations or other applicable procedures to address the reported breach, or the protection granted by this Directive in relation to internal or external reporting. In such a case, the competent authorities shall notify the reporting person of their decision and the reasons therefor.
4. Member States may provide that competent authorities can decide to close procedures regarding repetitive reports which do not contain any

meaningful new information on breaches compared to a past report in respect of which the relevant procedures were concluded, unless new legal or factual circumstances justify a different follow-up. In such a case, the competent authorities shall notify the reporting person of their decision and the reasons therefor.

5 Member States may provide that, in the event of high inflows of reports, competent authorities may deal with reports of serious breaches or breaches of essential provisions falling within the scope of this Directive as a matter of priority.

6 Member States shall ensure that any authority which has received a report but does not have the competence to address the breach reported transmits it to the competent authority, within a reasonable time, in a secure manner, and that the reporting person is informed, without delay, of such a transmission.

Article 12 Design of external reporting channels

1 External reporting channels shall be considered independent and autonomous, if they meet all of the following criteria: (a) they are designed, established, and operated in a manner that ensures the completeness, integrity and confidentiality of the information and prevents access thereto by non-authorised staff members of the competent authority; (b) they enable the durable storage of information to allow further investigations to be carried out.

2 The external reporting channels shall enable reporting in writing and orally. Oral reporting shall be possible by telephone or through other voice messaging systems and, upon request by the reporting person, by means of a physical meeting within a reasonable timeframe.

3 Competent authorities shall ensure that, where a report is received through channels other than the reporting channels referred to in paragraphs 1 and 2 or by staff members other than those responsible for handling reports, the staff members who receive it are prohibited from disclosing any information that might identify the reporting person or the person concerned, and that they promptly forward the report without modification to the staff members responsible for handling reports.

Article 13 Information regarding the receipt of reports and their follow-up

Member States shall ensure that competent authorities publish on their websites in a separate, easily identifiable, and accessible section at least the following information:

(a) the conditions for qualifying for protection under this Directive;
(b) the contact details for the external reporting channels as provided for under Article 12, in particular the electronic and postal addresses, and the phone numbers for such channels, indicating whether the phone conversations are recorded;
(c) the procedures applicable to the reporting of breaches, including the manner in which the competent authority may request the reporting person to clarify the information reported or to provide additional information, the timeframe for providing feedback, and the type and content of such feedback;
(d) the confidentiality regime applicable to reports;
(e) the nature of the follow-up to be given to reports;
(f) the remedies and procedures for protection against retaliation and the availability of confidential advice for persons contemplating reporting;
(g) a statement clearly explaining the conditions under which persons reporting to the competent authority are protected from incurring liability for a breach of confidentiality; and
(h) contact details of the information centre or of the single independent administrative authority.

Article 14 Review of the procedures by competent authorities

Member States shall ensure that competent authorities review their procedures for receiving reports, and their follow-up, regularly, and at least once every three years. In reviewing such procedures, competent authorities shall take account of their experience as well as that of other competent authorities and adapt their procedures accordingly.

Article 15 Public disclosures

1. A person who makes a public disclosure shall qualify for protection under this Directive if any of the following conditions is fulfilled: (a) the person first reported internally and externally but no appropriate action was taken in response to the report within the timeframe referred to or (b) the person has reasonable grounds to believe that: (i) the breach may constitute an imminent or manifest danger to the public interest, or (ii) in the case of external reporting, there is a risk of retaliation or there is a low prospect of the breach being effectively addressed, due to the particular circumstances of the case.
2. This Article shall not apply to cases where a person directly discloses information to the press pursuant to specific national provisions establishing a system of protection relating to freedom of expression and information.

Article 16 Duty of confidentiality

1. Member States shall ensure that the identity of the reporting person is not disclosed to anyone beyond the authorised staff members competent to receive or follow up on reports, without the explicit consent of that person. This shall also apply to any other information from which the identity of the reporting person may be directly or indirectly deduced.
2. By way of derogation from paragraph 1, the identity of the reporting person and any other information referred to in paragraph 1 may be disclosed only where this is a necessary and proportionate obligation imposed by Union or national law in the context of investigations by national authorities or judicial proceedings, including with a view to safeguarding the rights of defence of the person concerned. Disclosures made pursuant to the derogation provided for in paragraph 2 shall be subject to appropriate safeguards under the applicable Union and national rules. In particular, reporting persons shall be informed before their identity is disclosed, unless such information would jeopardise the related investigations or judicial proceedings. When informing the reporting persons, the competent authority shall send them an

explanation in writing of the reasons for the disclosure of the confidential data concerned.

3 Member States shall ensure that competent authorities that receive information on breaches that includes trade secrets do not use or disclose those trade secrets for purposes going beyond what is necessary for proper follow-up.

Article 17 Processing of personal data

Any processing of personal data carried out pursuant to this Directive, including the exchange or transmission of personal data by the competent authorities, shall be carried out in accordance with Regulation (EU) 2016/679 and Directive (EU) 2016/680. Personal data which are manifestly not relevant for the handling of a specific report shall not be collected or, if accidentally collected, shall be deleted without undue delay.

Article 18 Record keeping of the reports

1 Member States shall ensure that legal entities in the private and public sector and competent authorities keep records of every report received, in compliance with the confidentiality requirements provided for in Article 16. Reports shall be stored for no longer than it is necessary and proportionate in order to comply with the requirements imposed by this Directive, or other requirements imposed by Union or national law.

2 Where a recorded telephone line or another recorded voice messaging system is used for reporting, subject to the consent of the reporting person, legal entities in the private and public sector and competent authorities shall have the right to document the oral reporting in one of the following ways: (a) by making a recording of the conversation in a durable and retrievable form; or (b) through a complete and accurate transcript of the conversation prepared by the staff members responsible for handling the report. Legal entities in the private and public sector and competent authorities shall offer the reporting person the opportunity to check, rectify, and agree the transcript of the call by signing it.

3   Where an unrecorded telephone line or another unrecorded voice messaging system is used for reporting, legal entities in the private and public sector and competent authorities shall have the right to document the oral reporting in the form of accurate minutes of the conversation written by the staff member responsible for handling the report. Legal entities in the private and public sector and competent authorities shall offer the reporting person the opportunity to check, rectify, and agree the minutes of the conversation by signing them.
4   Where a person requests a meeting with the staff members of legal entities in the private and public sector or of competent authorities for reporting purposes, legal entities in the private and public sector and competent authorities shall ensure, subject to the consent of the reporting person, that complete and accurate records of the meeting are kept in a durable and retrievable form. Legal entities in the private and public sector and competent authorities shall offer the reporting person the opportunity to check, rectify and agree the minutes of the meeting by signing them.

Article 19 Prohibition of retaliation

Member States shall take the necessary measures to prohibit any form of retaliation against persons referred to in Article 4, including threats of retaliation and attempts of retaliation including in particular in the form of:

(a) suspension, lay-off, dismissal or equivalent measures;
(b) demotion or withholding of promotion;
(c) transfer of duties, change of location of place of work, reduction in wages, change in working hours;
(d) withholding of training;
(e) a negative performance assessment or employment reference;
(f) imposition or administering of any disciplinary measure, reprimand, or other penalty, including a financial penalty;
(g) coercion, intimidation, harassment, or ostracism;
(h) discrimination, disadvantageous, or unfair treatment;
(i) failure to convert a temporary employment contract into a permanent one, where the worker had legitimate expectations that he or she would be offered permanent employment;

(j) failure to renew, or early termination of, a temporary employment contract;
(k) harm, including to the person's reputation, particularly in social media, or financial loss, including loss of business and loss of income;
(l) blacklisting on the basis of a sector or industry-wide informal or formal agreement, which may entail that the person will not, in the future, find employment in the sector or industry;
(m) early termination or cancellation of a contract for goods or services;
(n) cancellation of a licence or permit;
(o) psychiatric or medical referrals.

Article 20 Measures of support

1 Member States shall ensure that persons referred to in Article 4 have access, as appropriate, to support measures, in particular the following: (a) comprehensive and independent information and advice, which is easily accessible to the public and free of charge, on procedures and remedies available, on protection against retaliation, and on the rights of the person concerned; (b) effective assistance from competent authorities before any relevant authority involved in their protection against retaliation, including, where provided for under national law, certification of the fact that they qualify for protection under this Directive; and (c) legal aid in criminal and in cross-border civil proceedings.
2 Member States may provide for financial assistance and support measures, including psychological support, for reporting persons in the framework of legal proceedings.

Article 21 Measures for protection against retaliation

1 Member States shall take the necessary measures to ensure that persons referred to in Article 4 are protected against retaliation.
2 Without prejudice to Article 3(2) and (3), where persons report information on breaches or make a public disclosure in accordance with this Directive they shall not be considered to have breached any restriction on disclosure of information and shall not incur liability of any kind in respect of such a report or public disclosure provided that they had reasonable grounds to believe that the reporting or public disclosure of

such information was necessary for revealing a breach pursuant to this Directive.

3 Reporting persons shall not incur liability in respect of the acquisition of or access to the information which is reported or publicly disclosed, provided that such acquisition or access did not constitute a self-standing criminal offence. In the event of the acquisition or access constituting a self-standing criminal offence, criminal liability shall continue to be governed by applicable national law.

4 Any other possible liability of reporting persons arising from acts or omissions which are unrelated to the reporting or public disclosure or which are not necessary for revealing a breach pursuant to this Directive shall continue to be governed by applicable Union or national law.

5 In proceedings before a court or other authority relating to a detriment suffered by the reporting person, and subject to that person establishing that he or she reported or made a public disclosure and suffered a detriment, it shall be presumed that the detriment was made in retaliation for the report or the public disclosure. In such cases, it shall be for the person who has taken the detrimental measure to prove that that measure was based on duly justified grounds.

6 Persons referred to in Article 4 shall have access to remedial measures against retaliation as appropriate, including interim relief pending the resolution of legal proceedings, in accordance with national law.

7 In legal proceedings, including for defamation, breach of copyright, breach of secrecy, breach of data protection rules, disclosure of trade secrets, or for compensation claims based on private, public, or on collective labour law, persons referred to in Article 4 shall not incur liability of any kind as a result of reports or public disclosures under this Directive. Those persons shall have the right to rely on that reporting or public disclosure to seek dismissal of the case, provided that they had reasonable grounds to believe that the reporting or public disclosure was necessary for revealing a breach, pursuant to this Directive. Where a person reports or publicly discloses information on breaches falling within the scope of this Directive, and that information includes trade secrets, and where that person meets the conditions of this Directive, such reporting or public disclosure shall be considered lawful.

8   Member States shall take the necessary measures to ensure that remedies and full compensation are provided for damage suffered by persons referred to in Article 4 in accordance with national law.

Article 22 Measures for the protection of persons concerned

1   Member States shall ensure, in accordance with the Charter, that persons concerned fully enjoy the right to an effective remedy and to a fair trial, as well as the presumption of innocence and the rights of defence, including the right to be heard and the right to access their file.
2   Competent authorities shall ensure, in accordance with national law, that the identity of persons concerned is protected for as long as investigations triggered by the report or the public disclosure are ongoing.

Article 23 Penalties

1   Member States shall provide for effective, proportionate, and dissuasive penalties applicable to natural or legal persons that:

   (a) hinder or attempt to hinder reporting;
   (b) retaliate against persons referred to in Article 4;
   (c) bring vexatious proceedings against persons referred to in Article 4;
   (d) breach the duty of maintaining the confidentiality of the identity of reporting persons.

2   Member States shall provide for effective, proportionate, and dissuasive penalties applicable in respect of reporting persons where it is established that they knowingly reported or publicly disclosed false information. Member States shall also provide for measures for compensating damage resulting from such reporting or public disclosures in accordance with national law.

Article 24 No waiver of rights and remedies

No waiver of rights and remedies Member States shall ensure that the rights and remedies provided for under this Directive cannot be waived or limited by any agreement, policy, form, or condition of employment.

Article 25 More favourable treatment and non-regression clause

1. Member States may introduce or retain provisions more favourable to the rights of reporting persons than those set out in this Directive.
2. The implementation of this Directive shall under no circumstances constitute grounds for a reduction in the level of protection already afforded by Member States in the areas covered by this Directive.

Article 26 Transposition and transitional period

1. Member States shall bring into force the laws, regulations and administrative provisions necessary to comply with this Directive by 17 December 2021.
2. By way of derogation from paragraph 1, as regards legal entities in the private sector with 50 to 249 workers, Member States shall by 17 December 2023 bring into force the laws, regulations, and administrative provisions necessary to comply with the obligation to establish internal reporting channels under Article 8(3).

[https://eur-lex.europa.eu/legal-content/EN/TXT/PDF/?uri=CELEX:32019L1937&from=en]

APPENDIX 4

COVID-19: BACK TO THE WORKPLACE – ADAPTING WORKPLACES AND PROTECTING WORKERS

EU guidance for a safe return to the workplace

Contents

Background and scope of guidelines

These non-binding guidelines aim to help employers and workers to stay safe and healthy in a working environment that has changed significantly because of the COVID-19 pandemic. They give advice on:

Risk assessment and appropriate measures

- minimising exposure to COVID-19
- resuming work after a period of closure
- coping with a high rate of absence
- managing workers working from home

The guidelines include examples of general measures, which depending on the particular work situation, can help employers achieve an appropriate safe and healthy work environment when undertaking or resuming activities.

This document provides links to relevant information from EU-OSHA and includes a list of resources from various providers that target different industries and jobs. Please note that the information in this guidance does not cover the healthcare setting, for which specific advice is available (e.g. from ECDC, WHO, CDC).

For any specific questions or worries not addressed in this document, refer to information from the local authorities, such as the health service or the labour inspectorate.

Introduction

Following the novel coronavirus disease 2019 (COVID-2019) pandemic, the Member States of the European Union (EU) have put in place a number of measures, including those affecting workplaces, to fight the spread of the disease. The world of work is severely affected during this crisis, therefore, all sections of society – including businesses, employers, and social partners – must play a role in order to protect workers, their families, and society at large.

The nature and extent of the measures range from restrictions on movement and suspension of non-essential activities, to limits on the number of persons occupying a space, banning of certain activities, and obligation to follow individual hygiene measures. Their application may differ according to the evolution of the pandemic, the sector, occupation, or a health-related characteristic of the individual. As a result of these measures, workers may be required to work from home, or if their work cannot be performed at a distance, to stay at home.

Once the measures achieve a sufficient reduction in COVID-19 transmission rates, the resumption of work activities is authorised. Often, this is done stepwise, with work that is considered essential for health protection and the economy authorised first.

While vaccination will in time lead to the relaxation of measures, it is not clear to what extent, or when, 'normal' work activities will resume. It is highly likely that certain measures will remain in place for some time or be reintroduced at some point to avoid future increase in infection rates.

The COVID-19 crisis is putting pressure on employers and workers as a result of having to implement new procedures and practices in a very short time, or having to suspend their work and business activities. In this context occupational safety and health offers practical support for resuming or maintaining work, and contributes to suppressing transmission of COVID-19.

Update your risk assessment and take appropriate measures

Just as under normal working conditions, the identification and assessment of risks in both physical and psychosocial working environments is the starting point for managing occupational safety and health (OSH) under COVID-19 measures. Employers are obliged to revise their risk assessment when there is a change to the work process and to consider all risks, including those affecting mental health. When revising the risk assessment, attention should be given to any anomalies or situations that cause problems and to how these can help the organisation become more resilient in the long term. Remember the importance of involving workers and their representatives in the risk assessment revision and call on your risk prevention or occupational health provider if you have one. As input to your assessment, obtain up-to-date information from the public authorities on the COVID-19 situation in your area. Once the risk assessment is updated, the next step is to make an action plan with appropriate measures. Below are some examples of pandemic-related issues to consider when drawing up such an action plan.

Minimising exposure to COVID-19 at work

The implementation of safe work practices to limit exposure to COVID-19 at work requires first assessing the risks, and then implementing the hierarchy of controls. This means putting in place control measures to first eliminate the risk and if this is not possible, minimise worker exposure. Start first with collective measures and if necessary supplement them with individual measures, such as personal protective equipment (PPE). Below are some examples of control measures, however, not all of them will be applicable to all workplaces or jobs due to their nature.

- Carry out only essential work for the time being; it may be possible to postpone some work to when the risk is lower. If possible, deliver services remotely (phone or video) instead of in person. Ensure that only workers who are essential to the job are present at the workplace and minimise the presence of third parties.
- Reduce, as far as possible, physical contact between workers (e.g. during meetings or during breaks). Isolate workers who can carry out their tasks alone safely and who do not require specialised equipment or

machinery that cannot be moved. For example, whenever possible, arrange for them to work alone in a spare office, staff room, canteen, or meeting room. If possible, ask vulnerable workers to work from home older people and those with chronic conditions (including hypertension, lung or heart problems, diabetes, or who are undergoing cancer treatment or some other immunosuppression) and pregnant workers. Workers with close family members who are at high risk may also need to telework.

- Eliminate, and if not possible limit, physical interaction with and between customers. For example, through online or phone orders, contactless delivery or managed entry (while also avoiding crowding outside), and physical distancing both inside and outside the premises.
- When delivering goods, do so through pick-up or delivery outside the premises. Advise drivers on good hygiene in the cab and provide them with appropriate sanitation gel and wipes. Delivery workers must be allowed to use facilities such as toilets, cafeterias, changing rooms and showers, albeit with the appropriate precautions (such as allowing only one user at a time and regular cleaning).
- Place an impervious barrier between workers, especially if they are not able to keep a two-metre distance from each other. Barriers can be purpose-made or improvised using items such as plastic sheeting, partitions, mobile drawers, or storage units. Things that are not solid or that have gaps, like pot plants or trolleys, or that create a new risk, such as from tripping or falling objects are to be avoided. If a barrier cannot be used, additional space between workers should be created by, for example, ensuring they have at least two empty desks either side of them.
- If close contact is unavoidable, keep it to less than 15 minutes. Reduce contact between different parts of your business at the start and end of shifts. Arrange the timing of meal breaks to reduce the number of people sharing a cafeteria, staff room, or kitchen. Ensure there is only one worker at a time in bathrooms and changing rooms. Place a sign on the main door indicating when one of the toilets is in use to ensure that only one person at a time enters. Organise shifts to take account of cleaning and sanitation tasks.
- Supply soap and water or appropriate hand sanitiser at convenient places and advise workers to wash their hands frequently. Clean your

- premises frequently, especially counters, door handles, tools, and other surfaces that people use.
- Where possible, ensure good ventilation, opening windows and doors so as to allow the flow of fresh air from outdoors.
- According to the provisions in place in your area, the use of surgical or 'hygienic' facemasks may be considered in the workplace and in all enclosed, shared spaces, such as cars, vans, and public transport. These facemasks are designed as a hygiene measure, preventing the spread of the coronavirus through droplets expelled by coughing or sneezing that fall on surfaces touched by others and through aerosol that is exhaled, staying suspended in the air until inhaled by others.
- If you have identified a risk of infection despite having applied all feasible safety measures, then provide all necessary PPE. It is important to train workers in correct use of PPE, ensuring that they follow the regulations and guidance available on use of facemasks and gloves.
- Place posters that encourage staying home when sick, cough, and sneeze etiquette, and hand hygiene at the entrance to the workplace and in other areas where they will be seen.
- Facilitate workers' use of individual rather than collective transport, for example by making available car parking or a place for storing bicycles securely, and encouraging workers to walk to work, if possible.
- Put in place policies on flexible leave and remote working to limit presence at the workplace, when needed.
- Avoid excessive workload on cleaning staff by taking appropriate measures, such as assigning additional staff to the tasks and asking workers to leave their workspace tidy. Provide workers with tissues and waste bins lined with a plastic bag so that they can be emptied without contacting the contents.

Refer to COVID-19: guidance for the workplace for further information on preparing your workplace for COVID-19, including what to do if someone infected with COVID-19 has been in the workplace and advice on travel and meetings. Information is available for 'frontier and posted workers' (persons who work in one country and return regularly to the country where they reside).

Resuming work after a period of closure

If your workplace has been closed for a period for reasons related to COVID-19, make a plan for when work resumes that takes account of health and safety. You should consider the following in your plan:

- Update your risk assessment as described above and refer to COVID-19: guidance for the workplace.
- Carry out adaptations to the layout of the workplace and the organisation of work that will reduce COVID-19 transmission before resuming work fully and before all workers return to the workplace. Consider resuming work in stages to allow adaptations to be carried out. Be sure to inform workers about the changes and provide them with new procedures and training, if necessary, before they resume work.
- Contact your occupational health service and health and safety advisor if you have access to one and discuss your plan with them.
- Pay special attention to workers who are at high risk and be prepared to protect the most vulnerable, including older people and those with chronic conditions (including hypertension, lung or heart problems, diabetes, or who are undergoing cancer treatment or some other immunosuppression) and pregnant workers. Pay attention also to workers with close family members who are at high risk.
- Consider putting in place support for workers who may be suffering from anxiety or stress. This could range from managers asking workers more often how they are, facilitating exchanges or buddying between colleagues, changes in work organisation and work tasks, to an employee assistance programme or coaching service, as well as offering contact with an occupational health service. Be aware that workers may have gone through traumatic events such as the serious illness or death of a relative or friend, or be experiencing financial difficulties or problems with their personal relationships.
- Workers who are returning to the workplace after a period of isolation, whether as an individual measure or as part of a collective isolation, are likely to have worries, particularly about the risk of infection. These worries – especially if there have been changes to the job – may well result in stress and mental health problems. When physical distancing measures are in place, these problems are not only more likely, but the

usual coping mechanisms, such as personal space, or sharing problems with others, are not available (see Return to work after sick leave due to mental health problems). Provide workers with information on publicly available sources of support and advice. Mental Health Europe has information on how to look after your mental health and cope with the COVID-19 threat.

- Workers might be worried about an increased chance of infection at the workplace and may not want to return. It is important to understand their concerns, provide information about the measures taken and the support available to them.

Coping with a high rate of absence

Depending on the infection rates in your local area and the protocols in effect, many of your workers may be absent because of COVID-19. If a worker is in isolation at home as a precaution, they may be able to continue their work remotely (see below), or if this is not the case, the worker will not be able to work for a period.

Workers who are confirmed as having COVID-19 may be absent and unable to work for significantly longer and those who become seriously ill may require a further period of rehabilitation once cured of the infection. In addition, some workers may be absent because they have to take care of a relative.

- The absence of a substantial number of workers, even if only temporary, may cause a strain on continuing activities. While the available workers should be flexible, it is important that they do not find themselves in a situation that will endanger their health or safety. Keep any additional workload as low as possible and ensure that it does not last too long. Line managers have an important role in monitoring the situation and ensuring that individual workers are not overburdened. Respect the rules and agreements on working hours and rest periods and allow the workers the right to disconnect when off work.
- When adapting work to cope with a reduced workforce, for example by putting in place new methods and procedures and changing roles and responsibilities, consider whether staff need additional training

and support, and make sure that all workers are competent to carry out the task they are required to perform.
- Cross-train workers to perform essential functions so the workplace can operate even if key workers are absent.
- If relying on interim staff, it is important to inform them about workplace risks and provide them with training if necessary.

Managing workers working from home

As part of the physical distancing measures taken in most Member States, workers are encouraged or obliged to work from home if the nature of their job allows it. For many of these workers, it may be their first time as 'teleworkers' and their working environment is likely to be deficient in many respects compared to their workplace. The extent to which the home environment can be adapted will vary according to the situation of the worker and the time and resources available for adaptations.

Advice on staying safe and healthy while working from home is available but is largely directed at those who telework regularly or long-term. Below are some suggestions to minimise the risks to workers who have not been able to prepare their home workplace properly.

- Carry out a risk assessment involving workers who telework and their representatives.
- Allow workers to take equipment from their workplace to their work home on a temporary basis (if they cannot fetch it themselves, consider arranging its delivery). This could include items such as computer, monitor, keyboard, mouse, printer, chair, footrest, or lamp. Keep a record of who takes what items to avoid confusion when normal work resumes.
- Provide teleworkers with guidance on setting up a workstation at home that applies good ergonomics, such as good posture and frequent movement, as far as possible.
- Encourage workers to take regular breaks (around every 30 minutes) to stand up, move, and stretch.
- Give teleworkers support in the use of IT equipment and software. Tele and video conferencing tools may become essential for work, but may be problematic for workers not used to them.

- Ensure that there is good communication at all levels that includes those working from home. This ranges from the strategic information provided by top-level management to line managers' duties, without forgetting the importance of routine social interaction among colleagues. While the former can be addressed in scheduled online meetings, the latter can be encouraged through online chats or 'virtual coffee' meetings.
- Do not underestimate the risk of workers feeling isolated and under pressure, which in the absence of support can lead to mental health problems. Effective communication and support from the manager and colleagues and being able to maintain informal contact with colleagues is important. Consider having regular staff or team meetings held online or rotate which employees can be present at the workplace, if a gradual return to work has been initiated.
- Be aware that your employee may have a partner who is also teleworking or children who may need care as they are not at school, or who need to connect remotely to continue their schoolwork. Others may need to care for elderly or chronically ill people and those that are in confinement. In these circumstances, managers will need to be flexible in terms of working hours and productivity of their staff and will need to make the workers aware of their understanding and flexibility.
- Assist workers in setting healthy boundaries between work and free time by communicating clearly when they are expected to be working and available.

Involve workers

The participation of workers and their representatives in OSH management is a key to success and a legal obligation. This applies also to measures undertaken at workplaces in relation to COVID-19; a time when events develop quickly, with a high level of uncertainty and anxiety among workers and the population at large.

It is important that you consult your workers and/or their representatives and the health and safety representatives early on about planned changes and how temporary processes will work in practice. Engaging with your workers in assessing risks and developing responses is an important part of good health and safety practice. Health and safety representatives and health and safety committees are in a unique position to help design preventive measures and to ensure that they are implemented successfully.

Consider also how to ensure that agency workers and contractors have access to the same information as direct employees.

Take care of workers who have been ill

According to the World Health Organization, the most common symptoms of COVID-19 are fever, tiredness, and dry cough. Some people become infected but do not develop any symptoms and do not feel unwell. Most people (about 80%) recover from the disease without needing special treatment. A small proportion of those who get COVID-19 become seriously ill and develop difficulty breathing. Older people, and those with underlying medical problems like high blood pressure, heart problems or diabetes, are more likely to develop a serious illness.

Persons who have become seriously ill may require special consideration even after being declared fit for work. There are some indications that coronavirus patients may suffer from reduced lung capacity following a bout of the disease. Workers in this situation may need their work to be adapted and may need time off to undergo physiotherapy. Workers who have had to spend time in intensive care (IC) may face specific challenges. The worker's doctor and the occupational health service, if available, should advise on the manner and timing of their return to work:

- **Muscle weakness**. This is more serious the longer someone has been in IC. The reduced muscle capacity also manifests itself, for example, in respiratory complaints. Another common but less frequently recognised phenomenon is Post Intensive Care Syndrome (PICS). This happens to an estimated 30 to 50% of people admitted to IC and is comparable to a post-traumatic stress disorder.
- **Problems with memory and concentration**. These complaints often only develop over time. Once someone has started working, this is not always recognised. The symptoms visible at work are memory and concentration problems, difficulty performing the tasks satisfactorily and poorer problem-solving skills. It is therefore important to be alert to this if you know that someone has been in IC. Good guidance is very important, because it is difficult for some workers to return to their previous level of performance.

- **Long time for resuming work.** Data show that a quarter to a third of those who are in IC can develop problems, independent of their age. Approximately half of patients need a year to resume work and up to a third may never return.

Occupational physicians and health services are best placed to advise on how to take care of workers who have been ill and on any adaptations that may need to be made in their work. If you do not have an occupational health service, it is important to address these issues with sensitivity and to respect workers' privacy and confidentiality.

Be aware of the risk that workers who have been ill with COVID-19 may suffer stigma and discrimination.

Plan and learn for the future

Even though vaccination against COVID-19 will in time bring the current pandemic to an end, it is important to draw up or update crisis contingency plans for shutdown and start-up events in the future, as described in COVID-19: guidance for the workplace. Even small businesses can make a checklist that will help prepare them should any such events occur in the future.

Enterprises that have used teleworking for the first time may consider adopting it as a modern, long-term working practice. The experience gained during the COVID-19 pandemic may feed into developing a teleworking policy and procedures or revising existing ones.

Stay well informed

The amount of information related to COVID-19 can be overwhelming and it can be difficult to differentiate the reliable and accurate from the vague and misleading. Always check that the original source of the information is an established and qualified provider. Official sources of information on COVID-19 include:

- World Health Organization
- European Centre for Disease Prevention and Control
- European Commission

- European Agency for Safety and Health at Work

As the pandemic crisis subsides thanks to vaccination and COVID-19 counter measures start to be relaxed, information may be issued that is specific to particular industries, communities, or groups, and it may be updated frequently. In your country, the ministries for health and for labour will have relevant information and may provide links to more specialized sources.

Sectors and occupations

People with jobs that put them in physical contact with many others are at the greatest risk of contracting COVID-19. Apart from workers in the healthcare, residential and home care, essential workers at increased risk include, for example, those involved in food supply and retail, waste collection, utilities, police and security, and public transport.

In the same way that some countries restricted work in some sectors before others – usually suspending education, leisure and entertainment first, and industry and construction last – the return to work following relaxation of the measures may well be similarly staggered, but in reverse order. Sector-specific guidance related to COVID-19 is available from several countries and a selection is listed below.

Check the websites of EU-OSHA or your national OSH authority or institute for further examples.

[https://oshwiki.eu/wiki/COVID-19:_Back_to_the_workplace_-_Adapting_workplaces_and_protecting_workers]

INDEX

ABMS (anti-bribery management system) 119, 153–4
accountability 21, 24; and CSR 70–1; in data security 50; and sustainability 67–8
accounting policies 35, 205–9
accounting principles 205–6
accounting standards 204–5, 207–8, 210–12
accrual accounting 211
accuracy, and data protection 44, 55
additional information, sources of 218–26
AI (artificial intelligence) 52–3
Amazon 4–5, 12–13
AML (anti-money laundering) 188–91, 193
Annual Report 69, 85–6, 215–16
anti-bribery *see* bribery, legislation on
anti-fraud culture 181; *see also* fraud
"anything of value" 122
Apple 14
applicability 18
archiving 51, 54, 56

assurance 24–5, 210, 213–14, 216
audience building 137–8
audit 10, 209–10; financial 210–11; for fraud 181; for money laundering 191; statutory 213, 215
audit committees 28, 215–16
audit policy 210, 213–14, 216
audit trails 34
Australia, corporate failures in 27

B2B (business-to-business) 46, 136, 139
B2C (business-to-consumer) 14, 136
balance sheet 102, 112, 205, 207, 211
bank fraud 178
benefits fraud 179
biodiversity 97, 104, 234, 236
Biological Agents Directive 78, 145
blacklisting 168, 256
blackout period, special 202
blogs 136–7, 140
board of directors 4, 26; adopting policies 7, 17; and audit 214, 216; and corporate governance 22, 24; and fraud 181, 183; and

insider trading 202; meetings 5–6, 26; and modern slavery 91–2; and money laundering 191; and sustainability 67
Boothby, Lord 26
Brexit 43, 105, 213
bribery 115–16; as fraud 179; legislation on 117–18, 121–2; in NFRD 100; policy against 9, 119–24; whistleblowing on 164
bullying 130, 154
burden of proof 162
business advantage, improper 120–2
business environment, analysing 15
business ethics 23; and CSR 66–7, 72
business relationships: and fraud 182; and human rights 230–2; and insider trading 200; and money laundering 189, 193
business risks, important 213
business strategy 7, 13–14, 16, 67

Cadbury Code 27–8
California, data protection in 42, 45–6
capacity-building 237, 240–1
cash flow statement 205, 207, 211
cash method of accounting 211
CCPA (California Consumer Privacy Act) 10, 42, 45–6
CDD (client due diligence) 189, 191, 193
CEO (Chief Executive Officer) 4, 6, 20, 27–8, 201–2, 209
certification bodies, independent 49
charity 23, 65–7, 122
ChatGPT 52–3
Chief Financial Officer 160, 201–2
circular economy 97, 104
cleaning 146
CLERP (Corporate Law Economic Reform Program) 27

client relationship 189
climate action 99, 234
climate change 25, 97, 99, 104, 233–9, 242
Coca-Cola Inc 68
code of conduct/ethics 8–9, 20, 125–7; and corporate governance 27–8; employee 129–32; and fraud 180
collaboration, and CSR 71
commitments 18
community investment 74
community-based networks 135–6
company objectives 7, 13, 24, 26, 32
company policies 4; classification of 7–10; content of 17–18; and corporate governance 23–4; formulation and implementation 30–7; framework of 18–19; strategy and 5–7, 12–13, 16–17; template for 32–4; use of term 7, 17; writing 31–2
compensation fraud 179
competent authorities, and whistleblowing 160, 162–3, 247
competition 14–15
compliance: accountability for 34–5; and CSR 72; requirements for 32; training and awareness in 35–6; *see also* culture of compliance
compliance officer, and whistleblowing 160
confidential data 50, 57, 254
confidential information 50; and ChatGPT 53; in code of conduct 131–2; and insider trading 198; security policy on 57–8, 60; and social media 139, 141
confidentiality, and whistleblowing 154, 163, 166, 169–71, 253–4
confidentiality audits 59
conflicts of interest 8–9, 127–9; and corporate governance 19, 24; policy on 125, 129–32

consultation 170, 214, 231, 244
consumer protection 42, 166, 244
cookies 46–8
COP27 conference 95–6; *see also* Sharm el-Sheikh Implementation Plan
core values 16, 19
corporate citizenship, good 20
corporate conduct 9
corporate governance 21–2; auditing 212; and company policy 31; definition of 23–4; G20/OECD principles of 28–9; good 3–5, 7, 16–17, 19, 27; models of 27; pillars of 24–5; and sustainability 98
corporate scandals 27
corruption 9, 116–17; legislation on 117–18; policy against 119–24
COVID-19 23, 234; and CSR 66; and the environment 95; EU guidance on 260–71; health and safety material on 77; and remote working 143–7
CPI (Corruption Perceptions Index) 158
credit cards 49–50
CRM (customer relationship marketing) 137
cross-cutting standards 103
crowdsourcing 136
cryptocurrencies 188, 194
CSR (Corporate Social Responsibility) 9, 18, 23, 65–6; and environment policy 110; international standards for 69–70; sample policy 71–4
CSRD (Corporate Sustainability Reporting Directive) 69, 101–6
culture of compliance 3–4, 16, 19–20, 30, 119, 126–7
customer sentiment analysis 136
cyber security 51, 215
cyberattacks 50–1

data breach 50, 53, 56–7, 61
data controller 43–5
data minimisation 44, 55
data privacy *see* data protection
data processing 43–6, 48
data protection 4, 42–4, 51; and AI 52; cookies and marketing 46–7; policy for 8–9, 13, 18, 35; rights and principles 44–6; sample policy 53–6; and whistleblowing 159, 169
data security 8–9, 17, 41, 49; sample policy 56–62; and social media 138
data security audits 57, 59, 62
data storage, on whistleblowing 160
data subjects 43–5, 54
data theft 179
debit card payments 49–50
decision-making 12, 17, 68–9, 93, 231
demotion 84, 167, 255
digital access to data 57–60, 62
directors, non-executive 25–7, 162
discrimination: unlawful 84, 89; for whistleblowing 159, 165, 167
disloyalty 126, 154
dismissal: challenges to 36; reasonable notice of 84; summary 129
diversity 73; in employment policy 85–6
donations 73
double materiality 102
double-jobbing 129
due diligence: and bribery and corruption 119, 123; human rights 230; and modern slavery 91, 93; for money laundering 194; *see also* CDD
duty of care 127–8, 149, 197–8
duty to inform 160

early warning 238
ecological units 96

economic activities, sustainable 104–5
economies of scale 14
EFRAG (European Financial Reporting Advisory Group) 101, 103
employee fraud 179
employees 7–10; communication with 12, 14; in corporate governance 19, 23–4, 26, 28; fair treatment of 17; and sustainability 68
employment contract, temporary 167–8, 255–6
employment law 83–4
employment references 168, 255
EMS (environmental management system) 106, 108–9
energy: renewable 66, 97, 99, 235; sustainable 12, 99
enforcement 18, 126, 142
Enron Corporation 27, 208, 211
enterprise social networking 137
environment 9, 95–6; whistleblowing on damage to 154–5, 157
environment policy 99, 107–11
environmental impact 68, 96, 106, 109–10
environmental movement 97
environmental protection 18, 23, 72–3, 159
ePrivacy regulations 46–8
Equality Act 2010 84
ESA (European Supervisory Authorities) 69
escalation 18
ESG (environment, social and governance) 25–6, 67, 69, 97–8
ESRS (European Sustainability Reporting Standards) 103
ethical standards, high 23, 66
ethics 22–3, 126; see also business ethics; codes of conduct/ethics
EU (European Union) 28; audit in 213; and COVID-19 145–6, 260–71; data protection in 42–4, 46–8 (see also GDPR); data security in 51; environment and sustainability in 99–101 (see also CSRD); health and safety requirements 77–8; insider trading in 197, 199; legislation on bribery and corruption 118; and money laundering 187–8; and sustainability 69; Taxonomy Regulation 103–5; Whistleblowing Directive 159–63, 169, 243–59
euro-crime 118
European Agency for Safety and Health at Work 77, 221
European Data Act 48
European Green Deal 100, 104
executive committees 7, 17, 160
external reporting channels 249–52

Facebook 133, 135, 140; and privacy regulations 46; remote working at 145
failure to report 192
fair employment 9, 83; policy 84–5, 87–9
fair treatment 17, 92
fairness 24–5; and AI 52
faithless servant doctrine 126
false representation 178, 183
falsification of documents 182, 211
FCPA (US Foreign Corrupt Practices Act) 117–22
fiduciary duty see duty of care
FIFO (first in first out) 206
finance policies 175
financial accounts 8, 206
financial information 204, 210; and data security 49–50; integrity of 212
financial penalties 168, 255
financial products, pre-contractual disclosure 69

financial reporting 28, 206–7, 212
Financial Reporting Council 28
financial reporting policies *see* accounting policies
financial statements 28, 205–12, 215
fire risks 77
flexible working 148–9
FMPs (financial market participants) 69
Ford Motor Company 68
foreign officials 117, 121–2
forests 97, 234, 236, 242
forgery 178, 182
fraud 10, 177–8; civil and criminal 178–80; corruption as 116; measures against 180–1; reporting 184; whistleblowing on 154–5, 164, 167
fraud policy 181–5
fraud prevention, training in 180
FRS (Financial Reporting Standards): FRS18 208–9; FRS102 209, 212

G7 187
G20 28
GAPP (Generally Accepted Accounting Principles) 204–6, 212
Gates, Bill 28
GDPR (General Data Protection Regulation) 10, 42–6, 50, 53, 57
gender balance 17
gender equality 98, 234
General Electric Corp 68
Germany: corporate governance in 26, 28; data protection in 48
gifts: bribery with 116, 120, 122; inappropriate 129
gilets jaunes 134
global warming 97
Google 13, 46, 66, 126
greenhouse gas emissions 68, 97, 100, 111, 235–6
greenwashing 104
grievances 167

habitat 96
harassment 84, 89–90; and whistleblowing 164, 168
hashtags 135
hazards 76–7
health and safety 9, 75; and COVID-19 262; employer's duties 76–7; international standard for 78–9; and whistleblowing 155, 157
health and safety committees 76, 269
health and safety management system 79
health and safety policy 79–80; sample 80–1
health and safety representatives 76, 268
health and safety risk assessments 77, 80–1, 145, 149–50
Heineken 68
hiring procedures 180
homeworking *see* remote working
hotline 153, 160, 170, 180
HR (human resources) 8; and fair employment 88–90; and remote working 147; and whistleblowing 160
human environment 96
human rights 25; and climate change 233; and CSR 70–1, 73; UN guiding principles on 229–32
human trafficking 67, 86, 90–2, 94

IEC (International Electrotechnical Commission) 49
IFRS (International Financial Accounting Standards) 204–7, 212
improper behaviour 116, 153–4
inclusion 73, 85–6, 97
income statement 205
independent contractors 88, 92, 156, 202
India, insider trading in 199

individual conduct 9, 113
Information Commissioner's Office 51, 54, 56, 61–2, 219
information management 51–2
information security 49, 148
innovation 14; and CSR 71
insider trading 10, 126, 196–8; examples of 199–200; sample policy 200–2
insiders, use of term 197–200
Instagram 135
insurance: and AI 52; for employees 76; and remote working 150; whistleblowing on 155
insurance companies 43, 100, 102, 105
insurance fraud 178
integrity 16; and CSR 71
integrity and confidentiality, of data 44, 49, 57, 61, 251
intellectual properties 49–50, 179, 182
interests, use of term 128
Intergovernmental Panel on Climate Change 236–7
internal audit 210, 212, 214–15
internal controls 180, 211–12, 214–15
internal reporting channels 247–9, 259
International Covenant on Civil and Political Rights 67
International Covenant on Economic, Social and Cultural Rights 67
International Labour Organization 78, 230
internet, in code of conduct 132
Internet of Things 47
invoices, false 123, 179
Ireland: data protection in 45; financial reporting standards 209; whistleblowing legislation in 154, 156–7, 161
irregularities 183
ISMS (information security management system) 49

ISO (International Standards Organization) 23; and data security 49
ISO 14001 106–8
ISO 26000 23, 66, 70
ISO 37001 118–19, 153–4
ISO 45001 78
ISO/IEC 27000 49

Johnson & Johnson 67
just transition 235–6, 238

key words, defining 18
kickbacks 116, 120, 179
KPIs (key performance indicators) 79

labour, forced 73, 86
lawful purposes 43, 55
leadership: and corporate governance 22, 24–5; and strategic management 15; and sustainability 67
Lehman Brothers 27
liability, and AI 52
LIFO (last in first out) 206
LinkedIn 12, 133, 135, 139–40
Lloyd's Bank 12
long-term objectives 14, 25, 213, 241

Madoff, Bernie 177
marketing 8, 22; and data protection 46–7; and social media 136–7
market-sensitive information 199
marriages, forced 86
Martoma, Mathew 197
material non-public information 198, 200–1
Maxwell, Robert 27
measurement 16, 108, 126
media-sharing networks 135
medical referrals 168, 256
mens rea 177
mental health 77, 262, 266

micro companies 102, 112n7
Microsoft Teams 137
minimum standards 77, 161
misappropriations 118, 179, 182–3
miscarriage of justice 155, 157
mission statements 4–5, 11–12, 18, 20, 31
MLRO (Money Laundering Reporting Officer) 190–3
modern slavery 70, 86–7; statement 90–4, 214, 216
money laundering 10, 186–8; stages of 188; whistleblowing on 159, 162, 167, 243; *see also* AML
money laundering policy 188–90; sample 190–5
Morgan Stanley v. Skowran 126
multilateral development banks 240

Nadir, Asil 27
natural environment 72, 96–7
natural resources 96–7, 99, 108
NDA (non-disclosure agreement) 156
nepotism 129
NFRD (Non-Financial Reporting Directive) 100–3
Nike 5, 68
NIS2 (Network and Information Security Directive) 51
non-compliance, consequences of 18, 28
nonprofit organizations 74, 136, 158, 212
norms of behaviour, international 70

objectives 17
objectives decisions 17
occupational requirements 84
ocean 97, 234, 242
OECD (Organisation for Economic Co-operation and Development) 28–9
online sales 8, 47

operational controls 79, 107
operational efficiency 212
opportunities 14
organisational culture 164

Paris Climate Accords 99, 233, 235–6, 240–1
Parmalat scandal 27
pay gap disclosures 214, 216
payroll fraud 179
PCI DSS (Payment Card Industry Data Security Standard) 49–50
PepsiCo 68
performance assessment, negative 168, 255
personal data 8, 41; breach 61–2; processing 254; protection of 42–5, 54–5, 244; security of 51, 56
physical access to data 57, 60
Pinterest 134–5
policy management system 34–7
Polly Peck 27
Porter, Michael 13
position of trust, abuse of 178
PPE (personal protective equipment) 262, 264
price-sensitive information 199
proactiveness 72–3
procedures 32
product safety 97, 159, 243
productivity: and AI 52; and social media 138
profit and loss account 211
promotion, loss of opportunity for 167, 255
protected disclosures 156–7, 162, 166–9
psychiatric referrals 168, 256
public disclosures 246–7, 253, 256–8
public health 159, 166, 244, 248
public procurement 159, 166, 243
public relations, positive 23, 66

public sector: and CSR 66, 69; and data protection 48
pump and dump 129
punitive damages 178
purpose limitation 44
purposes 17

recruiting, on social media 137
recycling 73, 97, 104, 110
red flags 122–3, 193
Reddit 135
redundancy payments 84
regulatory agencies 154, 183
regulatory obligations 4, 17, 35, 84–5
remote working 9, 78, 143–4; and COVID-19 263, 267–8; policy on 146–51
remuneration 28, 68
reporting persons 246; protecting 169, 247
reputational harm 120, 167
re-sharing 134–5
resilience statement 215
resource allocation plan 16
retaliation, prohibition of 154–5, 159, 167–8, 255–8
review 10; of environment policy 109; schedule for 37; and update 14, 31–2, 94, 216
review board networks 136
reward and risk 24
risk and reward
risk assessments: for bribery and corruption 119; for COVID-19 261–2; for health and safety 77, 80–1, 145, 149; for modern slavery 93; for money laundering 189–91, 193–4
risk management 22, 24, 98, 106; three lines of defence in 214
risks, and hazards 76–7
risks and failures 14

roles and responsibilities: in corporate governance 26–7; in policy 18
RTS (regulatory technical standards) 69
rule of law 70, 117

Sarbanes-Oxley Act 27–8, 211–12
scope 18
SEC (Securities and Exchange Commission) 28, 197–8, 211, 226
self-dealing 128
SEO (search engine optimization) 137
sexual harassment 89
SFDR (Sustainable Finance Disclosure Regulation) 69
shareholders: and board of directors 26; and corporate governance 19, 22, 24; duty of care to 198
Sharm el-Sheikh Implementation Plan 96, 233–42
Slack 137
slavery *see* modern slavery
smartphones 47, 50
SMEs (small and medium-sized enterprises) 102, 112n6
SMM (social media marketing) 137
SMO (social media optimization) 137
smoke-free legislation 77
social media 9, 23, 133–4; benefits of 137–8; for business 136–7; challenges of 138; in code of conduct 131; forms of 135–6; reputational harm on 167
social media analytics 136
social media policy 60, 138–42
social media strategy 138–9
social networks 134–7, 140–1
South Africa 50
SOX *see* Sarbanes-Oxley Act
speak up 9, 164–5
spyware 50
staff turnover 79, 144
stakeholder management 24–5

stakeholders 14, 19, 23–4; respect for interests of 70; and sustainability 68
standards of conduct 130
Starbucks 4–5, 68
stock exchanges 117, 197, 205, 210–12
storage limitation 44
strategic management 15
strategy 4–7, 11; and corporate governance 22; definition of 12–13; developing 13–15; formulation and implementation of 15; ownership of 24
Strong v Repide 197
STRs (suspicious transaction reports) 191–3
subjective decisions 17
supply chains 51; and modern slavery 87, 90–3; and sustainability 68; threats to 215
suspicious activities 190, 192
suspicious transactions 187–8 *see also* STRs
sustainability 25, 98–9; and CSR 67–8; disclosure 69
sustainability policy 110–11
sustainability reporting 101–3
sustainable development 70, 98–9, 110, 233, 236
Sustainable Development Goals (SDGs) 98, 110, 116–17, 234, 237
SWOT analysis 16

tactics 16
tax evasion 87, 187
tax fraud 159
TBL (triple bottom line) 66, 69
TCFD (Task Force on Climate-Related Financial Disclosures) 105–6
technology transfer 236, 240–1
TED 12
telephone marketing 47
telework *see* remote working
termination, early 167–8, 256

terrorist financing 162, 167, 187, 243
Tesco 12, 14
Tesla 12
theft 177–9
TikTok 135
time to market 14
tipping off 190, 192–3
topical standards 103
torts 178
trade secrets 161, 254, 257
trade unions 76, 244
transfer of duties 167, 255
transparency 21, 24–5; and AI 52; and CSR 70; and data protection 44; and sustainability 68, 103
Transparency International 158, 223
Twitch 135
Twitter *see* X
Tyco International 208, 211

UITF (Urgent Issues Task Force) 208
UK (United Kingdom): audit in 213; Corporate Governance Code 27, 85–6, 214–16; corporate governance in 26–8; data protection in 42–3, 45; data security in 50–1; employment law in 83–4; financial reporting standards 209; health and safety in 75–6; insider trading in 197, 199; modern slavery in 87; and money laundering 187; sustainability reporting in 105–6; Whistleblowing Code of Practice 163–5; whistleblowing legislation 155–6, 161; *see also* Brexit
UKBA (UK Bribery Act 2010) 117, 119, 121
UK-EU Trade and Co-operation Agreement 161
undue influence 128
unfair treatment 83, 93, 167–8, 255

INDEX   281

United Nations: Convention Against Corruption 118; Global Compact 74; Guiding Principles on Business and Human Rights 70, 229–32; and TBL 66, 69
United States v. O'Hagan 198
Universal Declaration of Human Rights 67, 70
US (United States): audit requirements in 211; corporate governance in 27–8; criminal fraud in 178; insider trading in 196–7

value proposition, predetermined 24
ventilation 77, 145, 264
victimization 84
viral content 134
viral marketing 136
vision 11, 16
volunteering 73
VPN (Virtual Private Network) 147

water, sustainable use and protection of 104
WhatsApp 45

whistleblowing 9, 153–4, 165; global perspective on 158–9; legal protection for 155–7
whistleblowing policy 155, 159, 163–5; sample 165–72
whistleblowing reporting system 169–70
Wikipedia 136
workers, definition of 162
working environment, healthy and safe 76–7
working hours: reduction in 167, 255; and remote work 147
work-life balance 17, 144
work-related injuries 76
World Health Organization 23, 66, 76, 269–70
WorldCom 27, 208, 211

X (formerly Twitter) 133–6, 139–40, 142, 240

Yammer 137
Yelp 136
YouTube 135, 140